Russian Writers
and Soviet Society
1917-1978

Russian Writers and Soviet Society 1917-1978

Ronald Hingley

Random House New York

First American Edition
Copyright © 1979 by Ronald Hingley
All rights reserved under International and Pan-American Copyright
Conventions. Published in the United States by Random House, Inc.,
New York. Originally published in Great Britain by Weidenfeld & Nicol-
son Ltd.

Library of Congress Cataloging in Publication Data
Hingley, Ronald.
Russian writers and Soviet society, 1917-1978.
Bibliography: p.
Includes index.
1. Russian literature—20th century—History and criticism. I. Title.
PO3022.H5   891.7′09′0042   78-21814
ISBN 0-394-42732-7

Manufactured in the United States of America

9 8 7 6 5 4 3 2

Век мой, зверь мой, кто сумеет
Заглянуть в твои зрачки
И своею кровью склеит
Двух столетий позвонки?

Contents

Introduction

The interplay of modern Russian social and literary forces makes an exhilarating study, many of its aspects being unprecedented in the world's pre-1917 cultural history. Yet by no means all established traditions have been cast aside in the new epoch. For example, belles-lettres still fulfil, in Soviet Russian as formerly in Imperial Russian society, a significant function somewhat differing from that which they have in any Western country. Imaginative literature – whether published in Russia, secretly circulated there, or brought out abroad – is traditionally a major vehicle for such political controversy as Tsarist and post-Tsarist conditions have permitted. It is – again by tradition – a source from which readers expect not merely to derive entertainment, but also to learn how life should be lived. It is, further, the window through which we can catch glimpses, true and distorted, of Russia; and how often it happens, paradoxically, that the very distortions provide the truest insights.

Imaginative writings of the Soviet period can provide clues, such as nothing else will furnish, to a newly evolved civilization fascinating to outsiders. Thus the study of the literature transcends the literary element that it comprehends, being indispensable to the historian, sociologist and student of current affairs. Modern Russian belles-lettres would therefore be well worth examining even if they lacked literary merit; as indeed certain of the most socially significant writings arguably do. But it does not follow that the literature as a whole is ill equipped to hold its ground purely as literature. On the contrary, it exhibits enormous variety and originality, together with a formidable capacity to shock, tantalize, surprise and delight.

That these facts are generally recognized is suggested by the large array of modern Russian literary works – including novels, short stories, poetry and memoirs – published in English and other languages over the years, and especially in the last two decades. We also have some admirable literary histories, beginning with the two by Gleb Struve, and including those of Deming Brown and Edward J. Brown, to mention only a few among the valuable aids to study that are included in the Bibliography. But what we do not have is a single work adequately and compendiously treating the literature of the whole period in its social context, not chronologically but topic by topic. That is what is offered here, as an adjunct to such differently conceived studies as those mentioned above and not with the remotest suggestion of superseding either them or another contribution which, among the many surveys of modern Russian literature, is probably the least remote from the present volume in scope and intention. This is Boris Thomson's useful *The Permanent Revolution*, which – like the studies indicated above and others too numerous to mention – has had some influence on the pages that follow. However, closely concerned though Professor Thomson is with the Soviet socio-literary context, his book differs radically from mine in its approach and structural pattern, besides covering a much shorter time span (1917–46, treated chronologically in two sections separated by the year 1928).

The preparation of the present study has re-involved me in twentieth-century Russian studies, which I had temporarily abandoned with the completion of my biography of Stalin in late 1972. That investigation has provided valuable insights into the background of the present work, for so intimate has been the interpenetration of politics and letters in the Soviet era that it was a master politician who chiefly determined the course of literary history, not any combination of writers. The subject falls, as we shall see, into three clearly differentiated periods: before Stalin, during Stalin and after Stalin.

The most significant twentieth-century literary works are likely to be less familiar to potential users of this study than are those of the Russian nineteenth century. Even the best-known of modern Russian writers – including Sholokhov, Pasternak and Solzhenitsyn – cannot simply be paraded as a sequence of known factors. Still less may the assumption of familiarity be made about the many relatively obscure authors, works and historical episodes that clamour for inclusion. The present study accordingly contains (in Chapters 2–4): a chronological review of the main historical events; an analysis of interacting Russian and foreign influences at home and abroad; a general review of the various literary genres. The incorporation of these passages was dictated by the material itself, for my book has insisted on being constructed on the 'zooming' principle, to express the matter in cinematic terms: it begins with long-distance shots and moves from panorama to close-up, except that the zoom is here designed to be leisurely and deliberate rather than a sudden swoop. Part One accordingly frames the subject in its widest historical and literary dimensions, beginning with a discussion of the ordeals and upheavals that outside observers must take especial pains to include in their sympathies. Part Two examines the literary implications of the country's social and political composition – its peoples, its power structure, its class system and its patterns of domestic life – through a medium-angle lens that enables us to take in more detail without forgetting the wider perspectives. Finally, in Part Three we focus on the literary profession in such detail as space permits: the movements and theories; the control mechanisms; the psychology of writers who accept or reject official pressures in varying degrees; the technical processes whereby a literary work progresses from pen to print.

In preparing this volume I have been able to exploit the preferential access enjoyed by Western scholars to much information about Russian society that is sedulously concealed from its rank and file. Soviet-domiciled Russians do of course feel the texture and vibrations of their milieu with greater sensitivity than that to which foreigners can aspire. On the other hand, foreigners can obtain Russian literary material and can probe its conditioning factors far more easily. Even Soviet-published works can often be bought, borrowed, consulted or even (I suppose) stolen with less difficulty in London, Paris or New York – and perhaps in Hoboken, Le Touquet or Minchinhampton – than is possible in Moscow or Leningrad, not to mention the host of officially disapproved works that are easily obtainable in the West but can only be consulted with difficulty and risk in the USSR itself. To this we must add that some Soviet-published literary material is unrepresentative, not least in the case of deceased authors whose work is issued selectively, ideologically sensitive items tending to be omitted.

A special responsibility is accordingly placed upon the foreign specialist in modern Russian literature. Not only can he obtain the source material with comparative ease, but he is also free to judge the issues unhampered by extraneous political pressure. The result is that, far from supplying information such as Russian writers might reasonably assume their readers to possess, this new study furnishes much

information which writers of the Soviet period might well assume
their readers not to have the remotest chance of possessing; which
even the writers themselves may not possess; and which many of them
would probably be glad to have.

One feature of a study such as this is that its compiler need not
obtrude aesthetic evaluations, especially as certain authors have a
place in the book independent of the quality of their writings. For
example, whatever we may think of Nikolay Ostrovsky's *How the Steel
was Tempered* (1932–4) or of Vladimir Dudintsev's *Not by Bread
Alone* (1956) as works of art, their social significance dictates that they
must be mentioned here. Moreover, as is illustrated by the fortunes
of these particular novels – the former still an honoured Soviet classic,
the latter now forgotten or disgraced – we must beware of correlating
a work's literary quality with the degree of its acceptability to Soviet
authority. The same is true on a more exalted level. Broadly speaking,
Mayakovsky, Sholokhov and Leonov have been politically respectable,
whereas Solzhenitsyn and Pasternak (especially Pasternak the prose
writer) have not. As these names indicate, there is no monopoly of
literary excellence, any more than there is of literary incompetence, on
either side of the barrier formed by ideological acceptability; nor, as
will be seen below, is that barrier itself permanently fixed, for it has
been shifted again and again owing to fluctuations in the official 'line'.

An attempt has been made to enliven the text with illustrations taken
from literary works. That these should be somewhat impressionistic
is inevitable since there could be no question of supplying a systematic
description of the literary themes as a whole. Had this been attempted
it would have been necessary to compile an entire library rather than
a single book. When, therefore, observations on (say) Siberia are
illustrated from belles-lettres, there has been no intention of supplying
an exhaustive account of the Siberian theme in literature.

Though 'Soviet society' appears in the book's title, and though refer-
ence is repeatedly made in the text to such concepts as Soviet Russia,
Soviet literary authority, Soviet citizens and the like, attentive readers
may already have noticed that such expressions as Soviet literature,
Soviet fiction and Soviet writers are scrupulously avoided except in
quotations from other authorities. Preferring to speak of modern
Russian writers resident in the USSR, or of Russian literature in the
Soviet period, I not only depart from usage in the country of origin,

where authors are regularly designated as Soviet writers, but also diverge from Western authorities on the subject, who tend to employ such terms while sometimes making it clear that they deplore them. In his study, *Soviet Russian Literature Since Stalin* (1978), Deming Brown flies one of these expressions at his mast-head, and I think no worse of his valuable book for that; but I have not followed his practice.

The inconvenience of 'Soviet literature' and the like derives from the ambiguity, especially in the literary context, of the word Soviet. It possesses two distinct connotations, the one territorial and the other ideological, while lending itself all too easily to employment in a vague sense – part territorial, part ideological – which blurs the distinction and is often downright misleading.

Used in the territorial sense, 'Soviet author' designates a citizen of the USSR, resident in that country and writing in one of its languages – by no means necessarily in Russian. The Russian language is, after all, only the chief tongue among several score that are spoken in the Soviet Union, and in which literary works have been written. Unconcerned here with Chukchi, Lithuanian, Ukrainian or Uzbek, or with any of the other non-Russian Soviet literatures of the USSR from Abkhazian to Yakut, I might have accepted the term 'Soviet *Russian* literature' were it not that this would seem to exclude from consideration modern Russian literature written in emigration. Such self-limitation seemed undesirable, not only because émigré Russian literature has included many notable contributions, but also because so many émigré writers have remained conscious of their ties with the motherland, and have not grown new skins at the moment of quitting Soviet territory. Ivan Bunin, one of the most eminent modern Russian writers and the first (in 1933) of his country's four literary Nobel Prize winners, continued to follow literary developments in his homeland from French emigration. Moreover, though Bunin's writings lay for many years under the ban of silence imposed at home on the work of émigrés, much of his *œuvre* did eventually come to be published in the USSR after his death.[1] Another well-known literary expatriate, Vladimir Nabokov, founded his career by publishing – in Western Europe, in the 1920s and 1930s and in obscurity so far as the world at large was then concerned – six novels, and also poems and short stories, in his native tongue, using the pseudonym 'Vladimir Sirin'. He too will be kept in mind, though he naturally tends to vanish from our spectrum when, in 1940, he begins writing and publishing directly in English: his best-selling novel *Lolita* (1955) is more a work of American than of Russian literature.

Though émigré literature will only be considered incidentally it could not have been left entirely out of account since emigration need not be, as it was for Bunin and Nabokov, a permanent condition. Not a few important writers were temporary émigrés only, and for varying periods, as designated. They include Maksim Gorky (1921–31), Aleksandr Kuprin (1919–37), Aleksey Tolstoy (1918–23) and Marina Tsvetayeva (1922–39). Another leading figure, Ilya Ehrenburg, was largely resident in Western Europe in the 1920s and 1930s while he continued to revisit Soviet Russia, hovering between expatriate status and that of a Soviet citizen temporarily residing abroad.

A further difficulty is this: that, besides implying residence in and citizenship of the USSR, 'Soviet' can also denote something not necessarily correlated with territorial associations: acceptance of the country's official ideology. Many are those writers who, though indisputably Soviet by citizenship and residence, have yet been denounced in their native press as anti-Soviet, or who have even been accorded the status of what foreign observers sometimes call 'unpersons': that is, their names have ceased to appear in print, disappearing from reference works and from the indexes to the literary journals in which their writings have appeared.

The most celebrated of such 'unpersons' is now Aleksandr Solzhenitsyn, who is bound to figure prominently in any study such as this, and who has repeatedly indicated that he considers himself a Russian and not a Soviet writer. Yet even Solzhenitsyn was published for a few years in the Soviet press, thus enjoying a measure of temporary official acceptance that would entitle him to be termed, on any mechanical interpretation of the word, a Soviet author in part, if only in minuscule part. Other authors – the novelist Vladimir Maksimov, for example – have published, in their native land, work that we infer to have been officially acceptable (and therefore 'Soviet') from the mere fact of its appearance in a Soviet publication, but have emigrated in the end and brought out further writings issued under foreign imprint and therefore by implication non-Soviet, un-Soviet or anti-Soviet. Then again, Andrey Sinyavsky was publishing certain writings under his own name in the Soviet Union while other works of his were appearing simultaneously in the West under the pseudonym 'Abram Tertz'.

To these complexities it must be added that ideological disgrace need not, in the USSR, necessarily prove any more permanent a condition than foreign residence: witness the numerous writers first consigned to oblivion – and also, in many instances, to physical extinction – only to be rehabilitated and republished later in keeping with fluctuations in official literary policy: Babel, Pilnyak, Mandelstam and many others. Such writers are, from the official point of view, now Soviet, now unmentionable or anti-Soviet.

Even if the term Soviet were less fluid than it is, we could no longer continue to divide Russian writings of the modern period into two categories, Soviet and émigré, as was once the custom. Gleb Struve has spoken of the two streams in the modern literature – currents which, though they might conceivably become reunited in the future, he has treated separately in two important books. However, as mention of Pasternak, Sinyavsky and Solzhenitsyn reminds us, a third major stream has formed in modern Russian literature since the terminal dates of Struve's works (the mid-1950s) and has rendered the boundary line between Soviet and émigré literature still more difficult to draw. The new stream consists of literary works which, though written by Soviet citizens and on Soviet soil, have proved, or have seemed qualified to prove, unacceptable for publication in their country of origin, but which have found their way to foreign countries, there to be published, both in Russian and in translation, often after privately circulating at home in typescript or manuscript copies. To this category belong most of Solzhenitsyn's longer works – published abroad, but not in the Soviet Union. We may also instance *A Precocious Autobiography* (1963) by the poet Yevgeny Yevtushenko, which he published abroad without so far as is known clearing this with the Soviet authorities. Of such writings Pasternak's novel *Doctor Zhivago* (1957) was the earliest notable example in the post-Stalin period. Russians themselves term these works *samizdat* ('self-publications') when they circulate clandestinely.

To the many examples of *samizdat* belles-lettres that reach a foreign readership we shall allude, for want of a better term, as 'Export Only' literature. The term must not, however, be taken as implying that a given author was necessarily responsible for sending his work abroad in the first place; or even that he was aware of its being sent abroad. Still less should 'Export Only' be taken as suggesting that he sought or derived any financial benefit from the transaction.

What with one and the same authors now emigrating and now repatriating themselves; publishing now officially, now unofficially, now at home, now abroad; re-editing or restoring on foreign soil the text of their own Soviet-published or *samizdat*-circulated works; and what with the fluctuating political line whereby individual authors are liable to sudden disgrace, but also to eventual gradual rehabilitation, so that they are now acceptable and now unacceptable to the authorities, and that in varying degree – the term Soviet, as applied to works of literature, and even more as applied to their creators, seems to offer nothing but pitfalls. Mercifully few are the literary loyalists, however extreme, who have never betrayed any tendency to deviate from hundred-per-cent political orthodoxy, just as there are few Russian defectors, dissidents and oppositionists who consider their motherland and its way of arranging its affairs to be unrelievedly black as the pit from pole to pole. Rather, then, than attempt to assess the degree of Soviet and non-Soviet components in every individual's residential and ideological dossier, I boldly call these writers and their literature Russian; and with all the more confidence since this is not a history of modern Russian literature, but considers its subjects in relation to the society from which, whatever their place of residence and ideological leanings, they all sprang and have drawn their cultural sustenance. It is therefore a pleasure to welcome Wolfgang Kasack's recent *Lexikon der russischen Literatur ab 1917* ('Lexicon of Post-1917 Russian Literature') as a major reference work straddling Soviet-published, Export Only and émigré literature without discriminating for or against any of them.

How many currents are there, then, in modern Russian literature? By contrast with Struve's two streams others have asserted that there is only one stream.[2] For myself, as one who tends to stress the individual rather than the collective element in artistic creation, I incline to equate their total with the total of authors. In place of one or two channels I discern a very watery labyrinth or delta of interlinking rivers, torrents, trickles and backwaters; not to mention dried up wadis, sewers, soakaways and septic tanks. Many of these will be charted or at least sighted on the pages that follow.

The transliteration of Russian names is as laid down in *The Oxford Chekhov* (London, 1964–80), edited by myself: see vol. 3, pages xi–xii. Christian names have not been anglicized, so that we have

'Mikhail', for example, rather than 'Michael'; the feminine endings (where they exist) of surnames are also preserved, so that we have 'Anna Akhmatova', and not the obviously inadmissible 'Anna Akhmatov'; with the name Mandelstam I have been guided by the preference of those who bear or bore it, and with Ehrenburg, Khrushchev and certain other names I defer to common practice rather than to transliterational consistency, which would have dictated 'Erenburg' and 'Khrushchov'.

Translations into English contained in the text are my own, except where otherwise indicated. For the period preceding 1 February 1918 dates are given in the Old Style as followed in Russia before then; for the twentieth century the equivalent of these dates, in the calendar used by the rest of the civilized world, is obtained by adding thirteen days. Thus 2 March (Old Style) equals 15 March (New Style).

Over the designation of Russian works quoted in the text difficulties have arisen rendering it impracticable and indeed impossible to use, in every case, the titles employed in published translations into English. In the first place some of the works concerned have never been translated at all, though it is difficult in the case of shorter items to be certain of this in every instance. And, secondly, not a few works have been translated more than once, and under different titles. To consider a specific instance, Sholokhov's two-part novel of 1932–59, *Podnyataya tselina*, has appeared in English as *Virgin Soil Upturned* (a correct literal translation) in the version of R. Daglish (Moscow, 1956–60). The same title had also been used by an earlier translator, 'Stephen Garry' (H. C. Stevens), for his London-published version of the first part of the novel (1935); but this same text was simultaneously brought out in the USA as *Seeds of Tomorrow*. Part Two of the same novel appeared as *Harvest on the Don* in H. C. Stevens's translation (1961).

One can become dizzy contemplating these and greater complexities, and I have accordingly adopted the following procedure. Wherever a published translation of a longer work uses a title closely approximating to a literal translation of the Russian title, I have adopted that title in my text: in the instance under review, *Virgin Soil Upturned*. But where a published title diverges markedly, I retain a more literal translation, if necessary one of my own. Thus, Pavel Nilin's *Zhestokost* (1956) appears in my text as *Cruelty*, and not as *Comrade Venka* (the title of J. Barnes's translation).

These details will seem insufficient to those who would have preferred a fuller account of English translations, giving translators' names, places, dates of publication and so on. Had this been implemented, however, the resultant bibliographical material would have swamped the book, and self-denial has been practised the more willingly in view of the fact that many of the items concerned are now out of print. Anyone seeking further information under this head can find some of it in earlier bibliographies: those contained in the studies, as cited in my own Bibliography, of Vera Alexandrova, and of Edward J. Brown (1963), Marc Slonim (1964), George Gibian (1967) and Gleb Struve (1972).

When quoting the titles of Russian imaginative works in English I italicize universally, thus infringing the convention whereby the titles of short stories and short poems are given in Roman type.

I am most grateful to Messrs Weidenfeld and Nicolson, London, for kindly permitting me to incorporate, in modified form, some brief material (page 18 ff.) on geographical and climatic features from my *Russian Writers and Society in the Nineteenth Century* (2nd edition, pages 32–35). For assistance in preparing the text I am, as repeatedly in the past, greatly indebted to my wife and to Dr Jeremy Newton. I am also deeply grateful to Dr Jennifer Baines for help with material and for our discussions of Mandelstam and other poets; to Dr Geoffrey Hosking of the University of Essex for loan of the typescript of his book *Beyond Socialist Realism*, an outstandingly useful study of recent literary trends; to Dr Gregory Walker of the Bodleian Library, Oxford, for lending the typescript of unpublished material by himself on Soviet publishing conditions (see also Bibliography); also for advice on the technicalities of the same, and for the loan of material, to Mr Richard Newnham of the Pergamon Press, Oxford; to my colleague Archie Brown for the loan of material and useful advice; to my colleagues Max Hayward and Harry Willetts from whose insights into the USSR and its literary complexities I have benefited for over twenty years. I am also grateful to members of the Soviet Literature Study Group for insights gained at their annual conferences, and not least during the lively discussion following the paper which I presented to them in Oxford on 19 September 1978, and which was devoted to the aims and scope of the present – then unpublished – book.

Finally, I most particularly thank Dr Michael Nicholson of the University of Lancaster for sending me, over the years, much rich and varied material, and also for his kindness in subjecting my typescript to rigorous scrutiny at a late stage in its evolution. From his criticism and scholarship, as deployed during a marathon 26-hour editorial reading of the text in my house, the finished article has greatly benefited.

Frilford,   Ronald Hingley
ABINGDON   1979

Part One
THE HISTORICAL AND LITERARY SETTING

1 General Perspectives

To citizens of non-Communist countries the literary and social background of the Soviet Union can seem even more unfamiliar and mysterious than that of the long-defunct Russian Empire. Soviet Russian experience differs markedly from that of the Western world in three respects. Western – especially English-speaking – populations have not on the whole undergone comparably sweeping social upheavals; they have suffered less or for less prolonged periods from foreign invasion, from famine and from penal procedures imposed by their own rulers; and they have not experienced the pressure of politics on everyday life to the same extent.

We shall begin by considering these topics in turn (under the headings Revolution, Ordeals and The Political Dimension) before ending the chapter with a general survey of the USSR, its geography, demography and economy.

Revolution

Since the Russian Revolution is often conceived as a single episode it is important to remember that a complex sequence of separate events is involved. In the Russia of 1917 two successive upheavals, divided by an interval of eight months, each created a change of government by violence: in February and October. Nor were these the country's only revolutions, having been preceded by an unsuccessful attempt to overthrow the Russian monarchy in 1905; but we are not here directly concerned with the 1905 Revolution, which falls outside our period, except to note that it is often called 'the dress rehearsal for 1917'.

By contrast with the bloody but ineffectual assault of 1905, both 1917 revolutions were conspicuously successful in the sense that an existing form of government was in each case irretrievably overthrown in a matter of days. In February 1917 the ancient dynasty of the Romanovs fell from power, 304 years after the first Romanov Tsar had ascended the throne, and nearly two hundred years after the foundation of the Russian Empire with the proclamation of Peter the Great as its first Tsar-Emperor in 1721. After being overthrown by the February Revolution, the Russian Imperial Government was succeeded by a so-called Provisional Government. Then, after eight months of uncertainty and semi-anarchy, that government was in turn overthrown by the Bolshevik October Revolution, and was superseded by the form of government that continues to this day.

The February Revolution was more a collapse than a takeover. By early 1917 the cumbrous, autocratically misruled Empire had become widely discredited with its own citizens. It had lost the confidence of most sections of Russian society, it had been undermined by two and a half years of world war against the Central Powers led by Germany, and it had been eroded by decades of revolutionary propaganda. But when the last Tsar-Emperor, Nicholas II, abdicated on 2 March in response to a few days of rioting in his capital city, the fall of the monarchy surprised Russia and the world. As for Russia's Bolsheviks (or Communists, as they were soon to call themselves), February 1917 found them as a small party of some 24,000 members, many of its leaders being dispersed in exile and emigration. Neither the Bolshevik nor any other revolutionary party played a notable direct part in overthrowing the Imperial state.

By October 1917 the Bolsheviks had grown in power and confidence, and in numbers about tenfold, spurred on by their militant leader Lenin. They were particularly strong in the capital, Petrograd (now Leningrad), and especially among factory workers and troops garrisoned there. They were accordingly able to mount a victorious *coup d'état* against the Provisional Government in the city on the night of 24–25 October. After a week's fighting in Moscow (then the Empire's second city) and certain sporadic engagements elsewhere they made themselves masters of large parts of the country without much opposition.

Soviet Russia had been born. It was termed Soviet because the Bolsheviks proclaimed their new government at the opening session of the Second All-Russian Congress of Soviets, a body representing workers and soldiers. The word *sovet*, meaning 'council, counsel or advice', had first acquired revolutionary significance during the abortive

1905 Revolution, when numerous Soviets consisting of workers' and peasants' delegates had briefly come into being. Owing little or nothing of their genesis to activity by any revolutionary party, they are generally regarded as a spontaneous creation of the masses, being frequently described in popular histories as having 'sprung up everywhere'. Though they temporarily disappeared after the 1905 Revolution they left a much-prized tradition behind them, for which reason it was natural for workers', soldiers' and peasants' Soviets to emerge in 1917 and to play a significant role in the upheavals of that year.

As for the Second All-Russian Congress of Soviets and its first, momentous session on 25 October 1917 – though the Bolsheviks had recently acquired a majority on it, other left-wing parties were also substantially represented. The Bolshevik decision to rule in the name of the Soviets therefore had the effect of suggesting that their government was more broadly based than was actually the case. In order to strengthen and justify their position further the Bolsheviks also ruled for a few months (from December 1917 to March 1918) in direct coalition with another party, that of the Left Socialist Revolutionaries.

For the Russian revolutions of 1917, as for many other major events in history, official descriptive formulas have been evolved in the USSR. The earlier upset has been defined as the 'February Bourgeois-Democratic Revolution, which overthrew Tsarism and established a diarchy in Russia: the bourgeois Provisional Government and the Soviets of Workers' and Peasants' Deputies'.[1] The second upheaval is naturally regarded as the more significant of the two. According to the official formula it was:

'the Great October Socialist Revolution of 1917, accomplished by the working class of Russia in alliance with the poorest peasantry under the leadership of the Communist Party headed by V. I. Lenin. It overthrew the supremacy of the bourgeoisie and landowners, established the Dictatorship of the Proletariat, and created a new type of state – the Soviet Socialist state; it created conditions for the building of Communist society and laid the foundations of that structure.'[2]

Not only were the two revolutions of 1917 both small-scale operations effecting the transfer of power from one regime to another quickly and with few casualties, but they also had this in common: that the second upheaval surprised Russia and the world no less than the first, and that it too led to the establishment of a new form of government widely presumed vulnerable and temporary. Indeed, for several years the infant Soviet state seemed no less precarious than the avowedly provisional regime that it had swept aside in October. Many of the very Bolsheviks believed, at least into the early 1920s, that the maintenance of their political system could only be ensured if a sympathetic revolution should break out in other countries and come to their rescue.

Swift, unexpected, easily accomplished and relatively casualty-free though the transfer of power had been, both in February and in October, these events eventually provoked a sequel resulting in the death of many millions: the Civil War between the Reds (Bolsheviks) and Whites (anti-Bolsheviks). Since this represented a concerted, though ill-coordinated, attempt by Lenin's opponents to overthrow his government, it was in effect a revolutionary struggle, and for this reason the elastic term Russian Revolution is sometimes extended to cover not only the changes of power in February and October but the entire sequence of events of 1917 and the next three or four years. 'Revolution' may even be loosely extended in usage beyond that, as when for example the years 1917 to 1937 are described as the first two decades of the Revolution. We shall avoid this last use here, but shall not shrink from the phrase 'after the Revolution', meaning in effect after the two 1917 revolutions and the events that they set in motion.

Though the Civil War was the direct outcome of the events of 1917 it was separated by the better part of a year from the Bolshevik seizure of power, for not until the summer of 1918 did hostilities gather momentum. They ended, apart from certain isolated and relatively unimportant actions, two years later with the defeat of the Whites in 1920.

So much for the immediate sequel to 1917. But it must not be forgotten that the momentous upsets of that year took place during the First World War and in the wake of bloody battles fought by Russia on the Eastern Front against Germany and the other Central Powers since August 1914. Nor must we forget, though it is easy to do so, that the war continued throughout both the February and October Revolutions. But the fighting was less fierce from early 1917 onwards, for the Germans and their allies were fully extended in the West and no longer needed to commit their fullest efforts to prosecuting hostilities against an eastern enemy who already seemed to be defeating himself through internal strife. In order to weaken Russia still further the Kaiser's government had already begun to give secret financial subsidies to Russian revolutionaries opposed to the war. The Germans also made it possible for Lenin to leave Switzerland, where he was living in exile in early 1917, and to travel across Germany by train, reaching Petrograd on 3 April.

The events of 1917 caught Russia's writing fraternity as much by surprise as the rest of the community, but to politically alert Russians as a whole the surprise was tactical rather than strategic. Unable to foresee that Tsarism would be replaced at precisely this time and in precisely this way, Russian intellectuals had long discussed and predicted revolution in general terms. Many of them had anticipated it as a relief from the stuffiness and oppressiveness of the Imperial state, which had made little distinction between its most violent internal enemies and those who merely sought peaceful reform. Lumping terrorist assassins and liberal reformists together as equally pernicious, the Tsar's government had persecuted them with such insulting inefficiency that, while their contempt for the system had increased, their freedom to conspire against it had been little impaired.

Though writers' reactions to revolutionary events were far from uniform, there was a widespread tendency to welcome 1917 enthusiastically. This reaction was shared by many who later came to deplore, and to suffer from, the oppressions of the new state. 'There wasn't a man alive who didn't experience periods of hope in the revolution', according to the critic and memoirist Viktor Shklovsky.[3] Pasternak regarded revolution as a liberating experience, and the words which he puts into the mouth of his hero Yury Zhivago may be taken to express his own sentiments: 'Revolution erupted forcibly like a breath held too long. Everyone revived, became transformed, transfigured, changed. Everyone seemed to experience two such upheavals, his own personal revolution and a second one common to all.'[4]

Among writers most closely in sympathy with revolutionary aims was the poet Vladimir Mayakovsky, who was to be posthumously appointed the Soviet Union's poet laureate on Stalin's orders in the mid-1930s. In his poem *At the Top of My Voice* (1930) Mayakovsky described himself as 'a sewage disposal operative ... mobilized and drafted' by revolution. He even added that he had 'deserted that moody bitch Poetry' in order to 'go off to the front' – which was untrue in any military sense. Mayakovsky also expressed himself as willing 'to do anything' for the Revolution, a promise that he was to keep most loyally in his own idiosyncratic manner.[5] Even among Bolshevik sympathizers, however, early reactions to October were not uniformly favourable. Though Maksim Gorky was literature's most famous recruit to the Leninist cause, he strenuously opposed the Bolshevik takeover; he also denounced the new government's authoritarian assumptions in a series of articles, *Untimely Thoughts*, published in his journal *Novaya zhizn* ('New Life') until Lenin suppressed it on 16 July 1918.[6]

Whatever specific form revolutionary events might take, the abstract concept of revolution continued to fascinate, almost to hypnotize, Russian writers. So acutely sensitized to the more dangerous hidden vibrations of his era was the poet Osip Mandelstam that he is said to have fainted away, long before any Russian revolution and at the ripe age of five, on hearing the unfamiliar word 'progress'; yet even Mandelstam had moods when he feared to remain 'outside the Revolution, and miss through near-sightedness the grandiose events shaping before our eyes'. Recording this, his widow adds that the key role in the curbing of Russia's intellectuals by the Soviet state was not played by fear or bribery, prevalent though both were, but by the word *revolution*, which no one was willing to give up. 'Whole cities – nay, nations of many millions – were subdued by that word. Such potency did it possess that I really don't know why our masters needed prisons and executions as well.'[7]

The concept of revolution as a self-justifying activity long outlived Mandelstam. We find it for example in the autobiography of Yevtushenko, a poet of the post-Stalin generation. The mystique of revolution as an activity noble and praiseworthy by definition, without regard to any consequences that it may provoke, still remains embedded in Soviet ideology. This has been made possible by the practice of labelling as counter-revolutionary any attempts throughout the world to overthrow a government congenial to the Kremlin.

Ordeals

In twentieth-century Russia human life has been, over a period of four decades, a much cheaper commodity than can readily be conceived by members of societies less accident-prone. This precariousness derives from the succession of major calamities that have afflicted Russia, beginning with the First World War in August 1914. Yet the huge Russian casualties in that conflict were not out of proportion to those of other countries, for the figure of about 1·7 million Russian military deaths is smaller in proportion to the population than are the comparable statistics – then unprecedented in military history – for Germany, France and Britain.[1] This is not because warfare was less bloody on the eastern front, for it was not, but because it was considerably shorter; it tapered off in 1917 and ended entirely in early 1918. It is from then onwards that we must contemplate a prolonged sequence of catastrophes peculiar, at least in their consolidated impact, to Russia among European or semi-European countries: disasters, both natural and man-made, both self-inflicted and caused by foreign enemies, that span the decades with a brief interlude of comparative safety in 1922–9 until the Russian experience of massive accelerated mortality sharply declines from 1953 onwards.

The casualty scale defies computation. All we can say with confidence is that the victims are to be numbered in their scores of millions, for there is a divergence in the figures offered by various authorities. Of the period 1914–21 as a whole one specialist writes that Russia 'must have lost about thirteen million men' during the seven years of World and Civil War.[2] Not necessarily conflicting is another estimate, for the Civil War alone. Pointing out that there were no casualty lists, and that more perished through famine, disease and reprisals than as a direct consequence of military action, a historian of the period assesses the total number of deaths at a possible twenty-five million. Some of these are to be ascribed to the famine of 1921–2, which may have caused three to five million fatalities.[3]

Still more awesome, still more elusive is the second period of casualties and ordeals, that coinciding with Stalin's fully developed dictatorship of 1929–53. Here four major waves are to be distinguished: the forcible collectivization of the peasantry and ensuing famine (1929–33); the later and more general phase of oppression which is associated with the Moscow show trials and reached its peak in 1937; the war of 1941–5 against Hitler; the continuing post-war Stalinist terror. Once again the victims flash past in their millions and tens of millions, so that the totals of fifty or (on another page) sixty million casualties offered in Solzhenitsyn's literary memoirs may seem high, but are by no means incredible.[4] Stalin himself (in conversation with

Winston Churchill) once put the number of peasant victims, of collectivization alone, at ten million; he held up both hands to demonstrate it, at a tariff of a million lives a finger.[5]

The above statistics are invoked in an attempt to indicate the dimensions of Russia's ordeal, and without any attempt to arbitrate between conflicting estimates. To some of the unhappy circumstances we shall be forced to return, for the plain fact is that modern Russia's sufferings have been appalling and that they have been fully shared by her imaginative writers. It has been claimed that over six hundred authors were consigned to Stalin's prisons and concentration camps,[6] from which (owing to the conditions maintained in those establishments) only a minority returned.

Though Stalin's successors have never thoroughly dissociated themselves from his rule, they have unavowedly abandoned the policy of exterminating the Soviet citizenry *en masse*. They have thus created a less harsh regimen under which writers have continued to suffer severe official discipline and restrictions, including instances of imprisonment, but without feeling their lives and liberty constantly imperilled.

To what extent does post-1917 Russian literature reflect the sufferings and tragedies of the period? On this more will be said below when the incidence of censorship, and also the literature of war and the concentration camp, are considered in some detail. For the moment only general guidelines can be given. The experiences of the First World War, revolution and the Civil War are vividly described in literature published in the Soviet Union of the 1920s. But later writings are less frank in treating the second wave of casualties. This is especially true of the Stalin period, when the very mention of concentration camps became taboo for reasons of state, the mere fact of their existence being considered damaging to national prestige. Experiences of the Second World War were far from taboo, however, and are commemorated in many works; but here too the obligation to present conventional heroism on officially prescribed lines made it difficult to convey the national experience in individual and convincing terms, especially during Stalin's lifetime. Nor, even with the relaxations permitted from 1954 onwards, could these topics be treated without constraint in Soviet-published works. For the fuller picture of Russia's second major wave of casualties we are therefore heavily dependent on Export Only literature: that written in the USSR but, not being acceptable for Soviet publication, published in the West in Russian and/or in translation.

The Political Dimension

The acquisition, maintenance and extension of political power has always been a matter of overriding concern to the Soviet authorities, leading them to establish particularly close control over all media of communication. For this reason the system is commonly described (by those who do not accept its premises) as totalitarian, a feature of totalitarianism being the severe limitations placed on spoken and written expression, combined with the drive to harness all public statements to political purposes. Consequently 'No piece of literature produced in the Soviet Union can escape involvement with politics.'[1] And yet the Soviet authorities have not, even in the most rigorous periods, ever achieved total thought control. They have achieved and perhaps aimed at only partial success.

To say this is not to deny that controls have been formidable, even in the mildest phases, or that these controls have embraced areas far outside politics in the narrowest sense. Rarely since the 1920s has the Soviet-published writer been at liberty to explore, unrestricted, the nature of any aspect of reality. What is truth? Outside the totalitarian orbit the writer need not even claim to know the answer to this question. Or he may offer his own answer, however eccentric and however different from the answers of others. In the USSR, by contrast, 'There is only one reality, the truth, one correct way of seeing it, if one is sane, educated and enlightened – this is what most of Soviet literature seems to be saying. . . . Only diseased . . . minds can fail to be persuaded of the validity of the one correct explanation of reality.'[2]

Such philosophical self-confidence is by no means confined to the Soviet period, for the Russian propagation of revealed certainties goes back to long before the Revolution. In Imperial times, however, competing certainties were allowed to coexist: for instance, the religio-political revelations of a Tolstoy and a Dostoyevsky alongside the literary and political teachings of those radical critics – notably Chernyshevsky, Dobrolyubov and Pisarev – who are now acclaimed in the Soviet Union as the inspirers of present-day orthodoxies. Nor, in more modern times, has Russian political dogmatism been confined to the bounds of the USSR. Russian writers have been known to evolve comparable taboos even when operating outside the Kremlin's orbit, as when certain émigré authors combined, in 1930, to abuse Mayakovsky in the aftermath of his suicide as 'never a great Russian poet but merely a versifier attached to the Communist Party and Government of the USSR'. But this represented only one current of émigré opinion, and a more tolerant tradition was espoused by Marina Tsvetayeva; herself opposed to Mayakovsky's politics, she yet wrote a cycle of seven poems in homage to his memory, and 'vented her contempt for both the Soviet and émigré press for viewing the death of a great Russian poet solely from the political and propagandistic angle'.[3]

On Soviet soil stringent political controls have been imposed on ideological opponents from the outset. An early example is Yevgeny Zamyatin, whose novel *We* – written in 1920, depicting the horrors of an imaginary future Communist state and a forerunner of George Orwell's *1984* – was one of the first works to be banned by the censorship body, Glavlit, established in 1922. More recently, to take another example, an outstandingly anti-Soviet work such as Solzhenitsyn's *The Gulag Archipelago* (1973–5), in which he analyses the worst oppressions of the Stalin era, could not possibly be considered for publication in the author's native land under present dispensations. Such are two opponents, one early and one more recent, of Soviet methods of rule. But the authorities have also been concerned, at least since 1929, to suppress not merely political opponents such as Zamyatin and Solzhenitsyn, but also opponents of politics as such – those writers who imply that politics (no matter whether Soviet or anti-Soviet) need not be a concern of literature at all. This issue arose in 1929 when Boris Pilnyak came under fire, not for political opposition but for *apolitichnost* ('apoliticalness', or lack of concern with politics). From that time onwards it has not been sufficient, during much of the period, for a writer to abstain from criticism of the regime. His active support, not merely his neutrality, has been demanded. When, in the late 1950s, Pasternak's novel *Doctor Zhivago* failed to secure Soviet publication, this was probably due in part to the presence of individual passages critical of the Soviet dispensation. These could, however, easily have been omitted or toned down, and the real stumbling-block was surely the all-pervading *apolitichnost* of the work, with its praise of the satisfactions of domesticity and private life. Here was no frontal attack on Soviet procedures, but a more insidious and perhaps still more subversive suggestion: that politics, any politics, are not the proper stuff of decent human existence at all.

The methods for controlling literature have a strong tendency to be expressed bureaucratically, not only through the creation of official bodies to guide literature from outside, but also through the bureaucratization of the writers themselves. Elaborate measures have been taken by Soviet authority to enlist and richly reward the co-operation of those authors who possess a special vocation for manipulating their colleagues. Whether members of the Communist Party or not, these 'custodians', as we shall call them, play a vital role in directing the Soviet literary world, acting as the Party's listeners, enforcers, watchdogs and implementers. But the literary community is not unique in enjoying these amenities, for it is a basic feature of Communist policy in general to work principally through activists and custodians within each social or professional group. 'The essence of a totalitarian regime, as opposed to a simple dictatorship, is that [it] forces the majority of the population to assist in running the machine.'[4]

Since 1934 the prime instrument for inducing authors to monitor each other has been the Union of Writers of the USSR with its several thousand members, male and female, using several score languages of the Soviet Union, and with its Board of several hundred members, which in turn elects a Secretariat of several dozen members, a President and a First Secretary. From this Secretariat in turn an inner core of about a dozen, the Bureau, has been evolved to deal with current business owing to the impracticability of summoning the Secretariat, and still more the Board, at frequent intervals. Membership of the Union of Writers, of which further details are given below, is a crucial but not absolutely indispensable condition for the pursuit of literature as a profession. It obliges authors to avoid 'political irresponsibility' and actions prejudicial to the honour and dignity of their profession, on pain of carefully graded sanctions such as are more familiar (in non-Soviet societies) to military and police organizations: 'public censure', 'warning', 'severe warning', 'animadversion', 'reprimand', 'severe reprimand', with or without mandatory endorsement of the culprit's dossier, together with various combinations of these sanctions up to the supreme measure of expulsion.[5] One early study of Soviet-period literature, published in the year of the Union of Writers' First Congress, embodied the spirit of that organization in its title: *Artists*

in Uniform: a Study of Literature and Bureaucratism (by Max Eastman, 1934). Such regimentation is comically at variance with the
literary profession, or at least with the popular idea of that profession,
outside the Soviet Union; at variance, too, with the 'Bohemian' tradition of the creative arts in general. Has there been any scope in
modern Russia for the great eccentrics, debtors, drunkards, deviants,
sex-maniacs and neurotics – the Maupassants, Verlaines, Gauguins,
Chattertons, Van Goghs, Dylan Thomases and others, whose political
and general human 'unreliability' would have been enough to keep
the entire disciplinary apparatus of the Soviet Writers' or Artists'
Union in permanent day-and-night session had they come under its
jurisdiction? Such irregularities, far from being unknown in Soviet
literary annals, have been more prevalent than a contemplation of the
literary bureaucracy might suggest. One notable early Bohemian poet
was Sergey Yesenin, whose suicide (in 1925) preceded the formation
of the Writers' Union by nine years and followed a long period of
dedicated hooliganism: bouts of wild drunkenness culminating in
successful poetry recitals; mirror-smashing; 'streaking' naked through
hotel foyers; sexual promiscuity and possibly drug addiction.

Nor did the early bias of Soviet literature towards self-bureaucratiza-
tion go unnoticed and unpublished in print. 'True literature can only
exist where it is created, not by painstaking and reliable clerks, but
by madmen, hermits, heretics, dreamers, rebels and sceptics.'[6] Thus
Zamyatin wrote in 1921, himself a former Bolshevik but also one of
nature's heretics, who was later to incur official persecution. Nor have
such representations as Zamyatin's been confined to the early 1920s.
At a plenum of the Board of the Union of Writers, held at Minsk
in February 1936, Pasternak claimed that 'Unexpectedness is the
greatest gift that life can delight us with.' He added that there should
be more of it in contemporary writing, and thereby emphasized the
quality in literature to which many readers attach supreme importance:
its capacity to surprise.[7] But it was not from literature that the poet's
audience was to receive its greatest surprises, for he spoke only a few
months before the onset of Stalin's severest oppressions.

Writers obliged, on pain of official reprimand and worse, to show
political reliability and loyalty to a system of imposed ideas, might
seem bereft of the capacity to cause surprise of any kind. It is therefore with satisfaction that we record the modern literature as having
never, even in its most regimented phases, been wholly robbed of its

potentiality for astonishing those who study it. The shocks that it springs tend to differ from those contributed by other literatures, but the unexpected can, happily, never be discarded as *a priori* impossible. For all the discipline to which authors have been subjected, and have been induced to subject each other, literature has always remained a source of contrary, anarchic, Bohemian, anti-regimentation principles. As this may remind us, the Russians have, throughout their history, tended to embrace one or other of these contrary principles, excess of anarchy and excess of order, with a degree of fervour distinguishing them from many another people. It has not only been in the twentieth century that they have had 'to choose between two unthinkable alternatives: anarchy and a rule of iron requiring the renunciation of all values, material and spiritual, of personal freedom and of basic legal principles'.[8] Hence what has been well termed 'the odd sense of tension which Soviet literature derives from its non-literary context'.[9] Its thrills may be compared with that of watching an escapologist free himself, against all probability, from a maze of padlocked chains, or with that of observing a motor-cycling acrobat leap fourteen double-decker buses; for such are the hazards and difficulties besetting the craft of letters in the Soviet context.

The degree of liberty which writers may be thought to enjoy in the USSR – another fluctuating factor – is open to widely varying interpretations. A recent statement of the official view was made at the Sixth Congress of the Union of Writers of the USSR by Georgy Markov – the organization's First Secretary, and thus the country's senior literary functionary. Dismissing bourgeois (i.e. Western) claims to enjoy freedom of the press and creative independence as so much poppycock (*brekhnya*), he adds: 'Only in the Soviet Union and in other Socialist countries does the concept of the freedom of the press and talent have a genuine foundation.'[10]

Without entering deeply into the merits of this statement we may yet venture to suggest that it by no means represents the diametrical opposite of the truth. Lacking freedom in any 'bourgeois' sense of the word, the profession of letters at least constitutes an area of lesser rather than greater regimentation in Soviet affairs. On the economic level alone it presents exceptional features owing to the personal nature of an activity that has never been effectively pursued by any collective, despite early attempts, long abandoned, to organize writers in 'brigades' during the First Five Year Plan (1928–32). Where else but in the creative arts can we find thousands of individual producers, each making his own individual contract with an organ controlled by the State (a periodical or publishing house) and working at times of his own choosing on material which, though he may feel hampered in his choice of it, is nowadays rarely directly chosen for him by official mandate? But some approximate economic parallels do exist, including the work done by collective farmers on their private plots and sold at market prices, as will be further discussed below (pages 162 and 205).

In sum, the profession of letters has lent itself less to institutionalization than any other, except perhaps the oldest of all. And it remains one of the least restricted Soviet professions, owing to the latitude traditionally extended in Russia to belles-lettres but largely withheld from other areas. 'Literature is the only field of Soviet cultural or social activity in which overt differences of an ideological nature are allowed to manifest themselves.'[11] It is partly for this reason that foreign specialists outside the literary field, seeking information on such topics as Soviet agricultural conditions or the status of women, sometimes quarry the country's imaginative literature – and not only for illustrations, but even, in the absence of other reliable information, for evidence.

Hence the special role of officially approved literature as a barometer by which atmospheric pressures in the Soviet Union may be gauged. Nor has one traditional role of nineteenth-century Russian literature, that of championing oppressed individuals against the State, become obsolete even in Soviet-published works, though unofficial literature (privately circulated works, often published in the West) has naturally played the paramount role.

We now turn to two common misconceptions that tend to recur in discussions of Soviet literary controls by Western non-Marxists. To imply, as is not uncommon, that regimentation is imposed on belles-lettres as a matter of principle can be misleading. The philosophy is not uncompromising hostility to all artistic merit, but rather cautious benevolence. Nor is this inconsistent with the assignment of absolute priority to political considerations, for literature of high quality is a potential political asset, not a debit; just as are high-quality hydro-electric stations and combine harvesters. There is, then, no objection whatever to literary merit as such. The difficulty is, rather, that so many literary works of high potency tend to exert a disquieting and unpredictable influence on their readers. Such a work may not necessarily be subversive in content, but it always has a potentiality for stimulating independent thought and speculation. It is presumably this tendency that most arouses the authorities' apprehensions, for their official doctrines already cover most aspects of human behaviour, purveying clear analyses and uncompromising recommendations designed for uncritical acceptance by the populace. The doctrine most emphatically does not leave scope for any perpetual running reappraisal of human values under the influence of cultural and aesthetic shocks caused by exposure to original works of art.

Such are the factors, rather than any *a priori* dislike of artistic excellence, that tend to provoke the imposition of restrictive cultural policies. But we should perhaps differentiate between the supreme political policy-makers – indifferent or even benevolent towards artistic excellence, provided always that it is not ideologically dangerous – and those senior literary functionaries who are themselves failed or mediocre writers, and who may genuinely fear and distrust the superior talents over whom they exercise a measure of control. This consideration apart, we must most emphatically not assume that official hostility to artistic excellence is an absolute or a matter of political principle. Still less should we assume that the many persecutions of writers, together with the banning of many works, have always been instituted for persecution's sake. One effect of the present study will, it is hoped, be to reveal a greater degree of latitude in Soviet cultural policies than has sometimes been allowed by critics – and also a greater degree of skill, flexibility and ingenuity in the cause of eluding regimentation, and this by no means always without the connivance of authority.

We must also avoid suggesting that all writers of the Soviet period have necessarily felt intolerably frustrated by the restrictions to which they have been subjected. Admittedly some of the most original talents have suffered unbearable psychological tension and severe cultural asphyxia. However, many others have positively thrived in literature's hot-house atmosphere, as it has been well called,[12] without being unduly exposed to successive freezes and thaws to which reference will be made on later pages. Writers as a whole undoubtedly appreciate the many perquisites and privileges available to political conformists.

The Soviet Panorama

Geography
In area the USSR is the largest sovereign state in the world, covering 8,650,000 square miles and thus being more than twice as big as Canada, which is the next largest country. But the USSR stands only third in terms of population, having reached the 250-million mark, according to official calculations, on 9 August 1973.

The USSR's frontiers largely coincide with those of the Russian Empire in its last years, the most notable variations being in the west. Here certain comparatively small areas, not having been part of the later Russian Empire, were ceded to or annexed by the USSR just before or after the Second World War: Galicia, Northern Bukovina and Transcarpathia. A part of East Prussia including Kaliningrad (formerly Königsberg) has also belonged to the USSR since 1945. The Baltic States that are now republics of the USSR and were formerly part of the Russian Empire (Estonia, Latvia and Lithuania) enjoyed independence between the Revolution and 1939, but were then annexed by the USSR. Later in the same year they were followed by the eastern part of Poland as it had been in its inter-war boundaries: this was incorporated in the Soviet Union when Poland as a whole was partitioned between Germany and the USSR after being defeated at the beginning of the Second World War. Previously much of Poland, as it is in its present boundaries, had belonged to the late Russian Empire; the country enjoyed independence in 1918–39, and suffered German occupation during the Second World War; in 1945 it recovered its nominal independence, but became a 'satellite' state within the Soviet bloc.

The largest long-term territorial loss suffered by the USSR, when compared with Imperial Russia, has been Finland. It was part of the Russian Empire for over a century before declaring its independence in 1917, and has come to pursue a foreign policy calculated to avoid antagonizing the Soviet Union while evading the *de facto* impairment of sovereignty imposed by satellite status.

The USSR has an Arctic climate in the extreme north, a subtropical climate on parts of the Black Sea coast, of Transcaucasia and of Central Asia, and a monsoon-type climate on the Pacific coast of the far east.

The rest of the country has a continental climate with long, cold winters and short, fairly hot summers. From west to east the range of temperature, between the cold of winter and the heat of summer, becomes ever wider until the coastal zone is reached. Eastern Siberia has an extreme continental climate. It can have heatwaves in summer, with attendant mosquitoes, but its winters are phenomenally severe. Though the Russian winter can be monotonous it is also awesome and picturesque, being rendered more tolerable by a tendency for the coldest days to be windless, at least in the north and centre. In the south blizzards are more prevalent, and southern winters too can be severe. In keeping with the tendency for Russian seasons to be more dramatic in their impact than those of milder climes, the advent of spring is spectacular, as winter's bleak, silent monochrome rapidly yields to colours, scents and bird song, while the breaking ice of the rivers thunders like an artillery barrage. But the Russian spring is also remarkable for flooding, and for creating seas of mud such as occur in autumn too and sometimes isolate rural communities from the outside world for weeks on end. To these conditions Russians apply the term *bezdorozhye*, 'roadlessness', and they are described for example in Vladimir Tendryakov's story *Pot-Holes* (1961). The small town of Gustoy Bor that forms the scene of the action is thirty miles from the nearest railway, and prolonged rain always condemns it to various inconveniences: no salt or paraffin in the shops, no new films and a delay in the delivery of mail and newspapers.

Turning from the seasons to physical relief, we find the European USSR and much of Siberia together forming a huge plain flanked by mountains to east and south and extending from the western frontier through sixty degrees of longitude to the River Yenisey in central Siberia. The Ural Mountains (highest point 6,210 feet) are the boundary between Russia in Europe and Russia in Asia, forming a natural barrier, but one easily traversed. It is on the southern and eastern marches that major natural barriers are found. They begin in the south-west with the Carpathian Mountains and Crimean Upland, continuing in grander style with the Caucasian chain and – beyond the Caspian – the Pamir, Tien Shan, Altay and Sayan ranges. The USSR's southern border is, accordingly, almost entirely marked off by mountains or seas, while eastern Siberia is crossed by mountain chains, the Yablonovy, Stanovoy and others.

The USSR's vegetation is deployed in uneven, broad zones running in roughly horizontal bands across European Russia and Siberia. In the extreme north are arctic wastes and tundra. South of those are, first the forest and then, to the south of that, the steppe – the word denotes a large treeless plain or prairie covered with herbaceous vegetation and having a dry climate. Most of the forest zone is coniferous and is sometimes called, especially with reference to Siberia, the taiga. But in European Russia a wedge of mixed forest, coniferous and deciduous, stretches south of the coniferous belt from the western frontier and tapers off near Kazan on the Volga. As has happened in other countries, the USSR's timber resources have been extensively exploited industrially. We may observe the process in Leonid Leonov's novel *Sot* (1931), set in the forests of northern European Russia; that this exploitation has threatened to go too far, menacing the country's timber resources as a whole despite replanting programmes, is eloquently argued at great length in the same author's later novel *The Russian Forest* (1953).

To travel southwards in Russia is not to be struck by any abrupt change from forest to steppe. First comes a transitional area, part woods and part steppe, sometimes termed the wooded steppe or meadow-grass steppe, south of which is the steppe proper, also called feather-grass steppe; that in turn blends into arid (also called saline or wormwood) steppe, merging further to the south-east with the sand or stone deserts of Central Asia. The steppe proper and the wooded steppe are fertile crop-raising country, coinciding partly with the black earth (*chernozyom*) belt that stretches from the western frontier to the Altay foothills and reaches its greatest breadth of just under two hundred miles in European Russia. This has been famous as one of the world's granaries, but its crop-bearing potential is limited by inadequate rainfall and by a northerly mean latitude that imposes a short growing season.

The USSR possesses the two largest lakes in the world, so large that they are termed seas: the Caspian and the Aral. It also contains the largest lakes in Asia (Baikal and Balkhash) and in Europe (Ladoga and Onega). The country is well stocked with rivers, having the longest in Europe, the Volga (2,300 miles in length), and three Siberian rivers that dwarf even the Volga: the Ob (3,500 miles from the source of its chief tributary, the Irtysh), the Yenisey (3,700 miles from the source of the Selenga) and the Lena (2,670 miles). Navigable rivers, among which the Volga is particularly important, amount to over three hundred thousand miles.

Many important rivers of European Russia rise in a small area of the western midlands formed by the Valday and Central Russian Uplands. They include the Volga and its tributary the Oka, and also the Western Dvina, Dnieper and Don. Being close to each other and easily linked by portages in early times – and later by canal – the rivers provide a valuable communication network, especially as most are slow-flowing and navigable far upstream. But many become icebound in winter, flood heavily in spring and form shallows in summer. Another disadvantage is that the rivers do not seem to lead anywhere, but pour into landlocked or partly landlocked seas: the Caspian, the Sea of Azov, the Black Sea, the Gulf of Riga, the Gulf of Finland and the White Sea. Others, including the three longest Siberian rivers, drain into the inhospitable Arctic Ocean. Many ports too become icebound for long periods, a factor further restricting access to the world's sea routes.

Owing to the immense distances to be traversed, and to the impossibility of even attempting to provide a network of adequate paved motorways linking important centres by land, water transport plays a vital role in the USSR's communications, and has been extensively developed since the Revolution. The Northern Sea Route, traversing Arctic waters between the Barents Sea in the west and the Bering Straits in the east, has been expanded as an important transport facility by the use of sophisticated ice-breaking techniques. The canal system had already been more than doubled in length by the late 1950s (from about forty thousand miles in 1913 to about eighty-five thousand miles in 1959). An especially important part has also been played in the development of the economy, and not least in the publicizing of that development, by huge dams and accompanying hydroelectric stations, of which that of Dneproges at Zaporozhye in the Ukraine is the most famous early example, completed in 1932. Since then many others have been built, including two post-war colossi in Siberia: those at Bratsk and Krasnoyarsk.

Railways play an important part in the transport system. They still have their 'magnificent mystique' and 'old first-class wagons, with their faded, wine-colored curtains, quaint lamps and doilies on the writing tables and curved brass handles on the doors'.[1] Russian rail travel traditionally inspires a delicious sense of timelessness, not least during the week-long haul along the Trans-Siberian line through a span of plains and taiga unparalleled anywhere else in the world. Railway stations are everywhere apt to become congested with delayed travellers.

The same is true of airports, air transport having been developed with particular intensiveness in the USSR owing to the country's immense distances and to the slowness of other forms of transport. The routes of Aeroflot, the USSR's huge civil airline, radiate from Moscow – the centre of this, as of most other Soviet activities – to near and distant parts of the country, the longest haul being that to Vladivostok via Sverdlovsk, Irkutsk and Khabarovsk (4,700 miles). Air travel is cheap, but subject to particularly frequent and unpredictable changes in timetable.

Demography

Despite the wars, and the other calamities to which reference has been made above, the USSR's population has increased rapidly during the six post-revolutionary decades. It approximately doubled in the three quarters of a century since 1897, when it was recorded at nearly 126 million (excluding Finland) in the only systematic census ever taken in Imperial times. An interim figure is that for 1920, and was celebrated by Mayakovsky in a poem written in the same year, *One Hundred and Fifty Million*. With this may be compared the total of 250 million attained in August 1973. Since then the population has continued to increase, but without remotely approaching the figures for India and China, at about 600 and 800 million respectively.

The preponderance of women over men is a striking feature of Soviet population statistics in the later decades of the period. On the eve of the First World War the balance stood almost even, but by 1959 females outnumbered males by over twenty million. The reasons for this include the many casualties from military operations, from executions, from concentration camp conditions and even from alcoholism – all misfortunes afflicting the men to a greater extent than the women. It is also possible, as has been claimed by one literary widow far from unique in surviving her husband by forty years, that women possess extra built-in durability.[2] Be that as it may, the numerical disparity between the sexes remains, though it has gradually declined since 1959. In January 1977 the figures were: 119·9 million males to 138·0 million females, and that out of a population larger by nearly fifty million than in 1959.

The most spectacular shift in population statistics is from country-side to town. Traditionally a peasant community with an overwhelmingly rural population, Russia entered the First World War with less than twenty per cent of its people rated as town-dwellers. The proportion changed fairly rapidly with intensive industrialization, parity between town and country being attained in the early 1960s, since when the trend has continued, as is reflected in the following table.[3]

Population (in millions)

Year	Urban	Rural	Total
1913	28·5	130·7	159·2
1939	63·1	131·0	194·1
1959	100·0	108·8	208·8
1970	136·0	105·7	241·7
1977	159·6	98·3	257·9

As in the nineteenth century two great cities continue to dominate Russia: Moscow and Leningrad. The latter has twice undergone a change of name: after being founded as St Petersburg in 1703, it became Petrograd in August 1914 and Leningrad on 26 January 1924.

As population figures illustrate, both cities have greatly increased in size since the end of the nineteenth century – Moscow twice as much as Leningrad.

Population (in thousands)

Year	Moscow	St Petersburg/Leningrad
1897	1,035	1,267
1959	6,044	3,321
1970	7,061	3,950

These cities continue to dwarf all others. Despite a general continuing increase in the population they were still, as late as 1954, what they had been in 1897, the only two cities in the country with a population exceeding a million; but by 1970 eight others had passed

the million mark, with Kiev as the largest of them at 1,632 thousand.
In 1970 the RSFSR's largest provincial cities were: Gorky and
Kuybyshev in eastern European Russia; Sverdlovsk and Chelyabinsk
in the Urals; Novosibirsk in Siberia. The largest Soviet cities outside
the RSFSR include Kiev, Kharkov, Odessa and Donetsk, all in the
Ukrainian SSR, Kiev being its capital; Minsk, capital of the Belorus-
sian SSR; Tashkent, Baku and Tbilisi, the capitals respectively of the
Uzbek, the Azerbaydzhani and the Georgian SSRs.

Some confusion has been created by the common practice of
changing the name of a Soviet town to honour some political leader
eminent at the time, but later disgraced – whereupon the relevant place
name has either reverted to its original form, or has undergone a second
rechristening. We therefore list some of the most important towns for
which different names have been current at earlier periods of Russian
or Soviet history.

Current name	Previous name(s)
Chkalov	Orenburg
Dnepropetrovsk	Yekaterinoslav
Frunze	Pishpek
Gorky	Nizhny Novgorod
Kalinin	Tver
Kaliningrad	Königsberg
Kirov	Vyatka
Krasnodar	Yekaterinodar
Kuybyshev	Samara
Leninabad	Khodzhent
Leningrad	St Petersburg, Petrograd
Sverdlovsk	Yekaterinburg
Tbilisi	Tiflis
Zhdanov	Mariupol

Among the cities that have changed their name more than once the
following three reflect Stalin's rise and fall in official esteem:
Donetsk (1924–61, Stalino; before 1924, Yuzovka);
Dushanbe (1929–61, Stalinabad; before 1929, Dyushambe);
Volgograd (1925–61, Stalingrad; before 1925, Tsaritsyn).

The disgrace of Voroshilov and Molotov respectively is reflected in the following instances of a city reverting to its original name:

Lugansk (1953–58, Voroshilovgrad);

Perm (1940–57, Molotov).

Finally, a triple change of name reflects the rise, fall and posthumous rehabilitation of a close political ally, and later victim, of Stalin's:

Ordzhonikidze (until 1932, Vladikavkaz; 1932–44, Ordzhonikidze; 1944–54, Dzaudzhikau).

Though the towns and cities mentioned, and innumerable others too, figure as settings in modern narrative fiction, the USSR has failed to generate important urban centres of Russian literary activity outside Moscow and Leningrad. Otherwise only Kiev and Odessa (both in the Ukraine) have provided a habitat of any significance for Russian writers, even though obscure branches of the Union of Writers of the USSR will be found in many provincial cities such as Ryazan and Rostov-on-Don.

We have referred to the USSR loosely as Russia, but it must be stressed that Russians are not the country's only inhabitants. They are of course the dominant nationality, but constituted a bare majority of about fifty-three per cent of the population as a whole in the mid-1970s. Since the Russian birth rate is low, and that of certain other peoples (especially those of Central Asia) is higher, the Russians may be expected to lose their overall majority in the next few years. This will not, however, be a new experience for them, since they formed a mere forty-three per cent of the population of the Empire in 1897, the lower proportion being partly due to the inclusion of Poles and Finns in the census figures of that year. So ethnically varied is the USSR that it contains over a hundred national groups, each speaking its own language and each possessing some degree of cultural autonomy. Most are so small that we shall not even list their names. Others constitute large and important nationalities that must be mentioned individually with some indication of their size.

The largest national group after the Russians is that of the Ukrainians, at just over forty million in 1976, to which date figures in this and the following paragraph refer. They are related to the Russians as fellow-members of the East Slav group, and speak a language closely akin to Russian. So too do members of the third East Slav nationality of the USSR, that of the Belorussians, numbering just over nine million. The Slav component of the USSR accordingly stands at roughly 180 million, about three quarters of the whole, leaving a balance of up to eighty million non-Slavs.

The most numerous of the non-Slav group of peoples is that of Central Asia, especially the Turkic-speaking Uzbeks and Kazakhs, at over nine million and over five million respectively, to which may be added the Kirgiz and Turkmens (both Turkic-speaking) at about one and a half million each; and the Tadzhiks (just over two million), whose language belongs to the Iranian family. These five peoples accordingly number some twenty million in all. The next group in order of size is that of the Caucasian peoples, especially the Azerbaydzhanis (over four million), the Armenians (over three and a half million) and the Georgians (about three and a quarter million). Then come the three Baltic peoples – Estonians, Latvians and Lithuanians – comprising together over five million. To them must be added the Rumanian-speaking Moldavians, at 2·7 million.

Each of the fifteen peoples so far mentioned is sufficiently important to possess its own Union Republic, and there are accordingly fifteen of these in all, each named after the nationality that constitutes the core of the population. Three are Slav: the Russian Soviet Federative Socialist Republic (RSFSR); the Ukrainian and the Belorussian Soviet Socialist Republics (SSRs). Five are Central Asian: the Kazakh, Uzbek, Tadzhik, Kirgiz and Turkmen SSRs. Three are Caucasian: (the Azerbaydzhani, Georgian and Armenian). Three are Baltic: the Lithuanian, Latvian and Estonian. Finally, one is Rumanian: the Moldavian. Of these units the RSFSR is naturally by far the largest.

Turning to smaller administrative divisions, we find that special provisions have been made wherever a minority nationality within a given Union Republic is sufficiently numerous and cohesive to qualify as the nucleus for an eponymous territory. It thus comes about that there are, encapsulated within the Union Republics, certain units named after their leading nationality. The largest and most important of these territories are the Autonomous Soviet Socialist Republics (ASSRs). Then there are the Autonomous Oblasts ('districts'), which are smaller than the ASSRs; and there are the still smaller National Okrugs ('regions') for still less populous nationalities. On 1 January 1977 the USSR contained the following numbers of these territorial divisions in descending order of their size and importance: fifteen Union Republics; twenty Autonomous Republics; eight Autonomous Oblasts; ten National Okrugs. The Union and the Autonomous Republics are subdivided into Oblasts ('districts') and Krays ('provinces'), totalling 126 in all at the same date. These in turn are further split into Rayons ('areas'), of which 3,117 were rural and 572 were subdivisions of certain larger cities; the country as a whole then having a total of 2,040 towns or cities.

Among the larger minority nationalities are the USSR's numerous Finnic peoples – the Karelian, the Komi, the Mari, the Mordva and the Udmurt, each of which has its own ASSR situated within the territory of the RSFSR: the Karelian ASSR etc. Besides these numerous Finnic peoples, whose association with the Russians goes back into the mists of prehistory, we must also mention the Tatars, whose historical links have lasted a mere three quarters of a millennium since the Tatar-Mongol conquest of Russia in the thirteenth century. Though the modern Tatars will be found in many parts of the USSR, and numbered nearly six million in 1970, they are most numerous in the Tatar ASSR, which has its capital at Kazan on the middle Volga. Lower down, near Saratov, was once situated another ASSR, that of the Volga Germans; but they were deported to the Far East in 1941 as a wartime measure, and their republic was dissolved. A similar fate befell what had been the second largest agglomeration of the USSR's Tatars – those of the Crimean ASSR, which was also dissolved when the Crimean Tatars were deported to the east *en masse* in 1945.

Of such ethnic connections the pseudonyms of Russian writers may sometimes remind us. Anna Akhmatova, for example, was born as Anna Gorenko, but she did not invent the pseudonymous and characteristically Tatar surname under which she became famous, since it had been borne by one of her great-grandmothers, a Tatar. The name Pilnyak is also pseudonymous; the author's true name was the Teutonic 'Wogau', and he was descended from German settlers on his father's side. Here are two prominent authors of whom one sought to flaunt non-Russian origins while the other was concerned to conceal them.

A special position is occupied by the USSR's Jews, who differ from other comparably numerous peoples in lacking any national home or geographical base within the country. The census of 1970 gave the total number of Soviet Jews at just over two million, but despite their comparatively small numbers the Jewish impact on modern Russian literature has been enormous and will be discussed at greater length below.

The Economy

The economy is highly centralized, all the major means of production, agencies and institutions being controlled by the State even when they are nominally independent co-operative enterprises, as is true of the Collective Farms. Virtually all Soviet citizens are, accordingly, paid directly or indirectly by the State, and at rates controlled by central authority, the economy being nationalized in an extreme degree. It is sometimes known as a command economy since it is directed by decisions taken at the centre and is influenced only in a lesser degree by the operation of market forces. It is also a production economy in which maximum priority is given to the needs of the military and of heavy industry, while the consumer tends to receive little consideration. One consequence is this: that though the USSR is second only to the USA in total output, and is the USA's only world rival in military and industrial power, the standard of living of the average Soviet citizen lags behind that of his opposite number in the USA and in all other advanced countries outside the Soviet bloc.

In transport and communications the contrast is also striking. The Soviet road network is, for example, only a quarter as extensive as that of the United States, and even then only forty per cent of Soviet roads have paved surfaces; the number of private cars is still more disproportionate: three million in the USSR to about a hundred million in the USA, as is also that of telephones at about eleven million to 120 million (early 1970s).[4] Moreover, as any visitor to the USSR can easily confirm, wooden brooms, hoes and abacuses are regularly used for functions performed in other advanced industrial countries by mechanized means. Then again, Soviet citizens are as a whole worse housed than the citizens of any other leading industrial nation, though housing is perhaps cheaper in the USSR than in any other advanced society. For their food Russians pay more, yet have an inferior diet.

Within the overwhelmingly preponderant State-controlled sector of the economy four major branches may be distinguished: defence, heavy industry, consumer industry and agriculture. The first of these is by far the most effective and enjoys overriding priority, followed by heavy industry, while consumer industry and agriculture are, despite recent improvements, comparatively neglected and noted for their inefficiency. One result is that though the USSR is, as mentioned above, second only to the USA in total output, its *per capita* output lags far behind, coming somewhere between fifteenth and twenty-fifth in the world (1973).[5]

Since 1929 the State-controlled industries have been organized through a series of national plans, mostly of five years' duration. The Five Year Plans lay down targets, known as norms, for all official sections of the economy, the operation being partly directed by the State Planning Agency (Gosplan) and the plans being parcelled out, down to individual enterprises and units. 'Fulfilling the norm' is, accordingly, a major ambition of all Soviet workers and managers. But so too is the aim of not overfulfilling it by more than a narrow margin, lest it be revised upwards: a common penalty for excess of zeal. Nor must we ignore the common procedure of padding, or even of falsifying outright, production statistics as submitted in periodical reports to higher authority. To this practice, colloquially known as *tufta* or *tukhta*, Solzhenitsyn devotes a memorable passage in Part Three of his *The Gulag Archipelago*. We also encounter it in Vladimir Voynovich's Export Only novel *The Life and Extraordinary Adventures of Private Ivan Chonkin* (unfinished, begun in 1963), where a Collective Farm Chairman is found compiling a routine report on haymaking activities during the previous ten days. 'Needless to say the report was a fraud, since there had been practically no haymaking at all.' But similar reports were being compiled by all the Collective Farm Chairmen of the Area for submission to Area Headquarters: an accretion of *tukhta* eventually destined to be collated with innumerable other accretions, and to snowball on and on 'all the way up to the top'.

For the achievements (*dostizheniya*, a key concept), notional or not, of the economy the system demands from all citizens repeated affirmations of enthusiasm, productivity statistics – whether relating to pigs, pig-iron or any other index of material progress – being widely advertised on hoardings and in the media. In periods of severest regimentation literature has been obliged to contribute directly to such publicity programmes, and even in more relaxed phases attempts by authors to deride, belittle or ignore the country's economic organization have been discouraged or prevented.

Besides the above-mentioned four major nationalized branches of the economy the USSR possesses a fifth, variously known to foreign observers as the counter-economy, the shadow economy, the secondary economy or the unofficial economy. It is represented by those who work, either part-time or full-time, for their own support or profit, without remuneration from the State, and its largest sector is that of food-growing on private allotments, including the private plots tilled by collective farmers. This produce is either consumed by the grower and his family, or may be sold at commercial prices in special markets. Here is an institution on which more will be said below, whereby a tiny proportion (about 1·6 per cent) of the cultivated land produces up to a third of the nation's food other than grain: a state of affairs, unpalatable to official ideologists, that arises from the notorious lack of incentives in the public sector of agriculture. Apart from widespread allotment farming the unofficial sector of the economy also embraces domestic service, private teaching, and private medical and dental work. In a sense it also includes our main subject, the profession of letters, since this is, as mentioned above, based on individual contracts negotiated between an individual author and a State-controlled publishing enterprise.

Besides the above-listed activities, none of which contravenes legality, the unofficial economy also embraces the operations of those who regularly flout the law: 'moon-lighting' taxi-drivers; builders, plumbers and other skilled workers who accept assignments *na levo* ('on the side'). They too have a rough literary equivalent in writers who circulate their work privately or have it published abroad, though generally without the financial rewards available to the other kinds of 'moon-lighters'; nor are these literary activities in themselves illegal (but see also page 248).

For the extremely prevalent system of unofficial contacts by which restrictive bureaucratic controls are circumvented, and without which the social and economic fabric might cease to cohere, the slang term *blat* is employed; it combines the concepts of a black market with that of an 'old boy network', together with a hint of Mafia-style potentialities.

One striking feature of the economy is the enormous disparity in access to real benefits between the small, privileged section of society and the mass of the unprivileged. The privileged include high officials in the Party and government apparatus, together with leading scientific, industrial and academic administrators, and also outstanding figures in the performing and creative arts. The unprivileged consist of humbler employees, including the majority of teachers and doctors;

ordinary industrial workers; and above all the peasantry.

There is a large earnings differential between the average industrial wage (1,728 roubles per annum in 1975) and top salaries, which go up to nearly fifteen times that amount, but without any large or progressively rising income tax to level out the difference. This disparity is increased in real terms by a hierarchy of graded perquisites, access to which is regulated according to the individual's importance to the system. Among them are: concessionary shopping in special closed stores containing superior or otherwise unobtainable products; preferential housing, including both town apartments and dachas (country cottages); chauffeur-driven or private cars; easy and cheap travel facilities inside the Soviet Union; foreign travel; superior medical facilities. These advantages are conceded to writers, as to others, in accordance with their acceptability to authority. Consequently writers have included some of the most, but also some of the least, privileged members of Soviet society.

Owing to the subtle grading of emoluments and perquisites we cannot easily count the élite, which has been said to number 'well over a million' members excluding dependents.[6] Nor can we determine the precise point at which privilege shades into under-privilege. But we can be confident that the allotment of high rewards to favoured individuals achieves its purpose. It elicits from the élite – consisting largely of controllers, custodians, policemen, propagandists, cheerleaders and activists of one kind or another – effective co-operation in manipulating the average citizen, and in persuading or intimidating him into accepting smaller recompense for his labour than is received by those doing comparable work in other advanced countries of the world.

2 History and Literature

To attempt a comprehensive view of post-revolutionary Russia is to be impressed by the dominant influence exercised, over writers and over every aspect of their society, by the dictatorship of a single individual, Iosif Stalin. The subject accordingly falls into three major periods: that preceding Stalin's imposition of a fully developed totalitarian dictatorship (1917–29); that of the Stalin dictatorship (1929–53); that following Stalin (1953 onwards). In the brief review that follows we shall first consider the pre-totalitarian period as a whole as it developed before, during and after the Civil War of 1918–20. Then Stalin's rule from 1929 to 1953 will be reviewed, also in three phases (pre-war, wartime and post-war). The post-Stalin period will involve considering the rise and ascendancy of two successive leaders, Khrushchev and Brezhnev. The effect will be to provide, in the present chapter, a synoptic view of political and literary developments to many of which (for example, the collectivization of agriculture, Socialist Realism, the rehabilitation of Stalin's victims) we shall return in greater detail at a later stage.

Before Stalinism

First Months

An interval of about eight months separated the October Revolution of 1917 from the development of a large-scale Civil War in the summer of 1918. This comparatively quiescent phase witnessed the consolidation of Bolshevik rule under Lenin's leadership through the Communist Party's Politburo and through People's Commissars (in effect Ministers) united in a Council of People's Commissars (Sovnarkom:

in effect a cabinet). A Soviet security police authority, the Cheka, was established on 7 December 1917.

In the following January a severe blow was dealt to any lingering hopes that the Bolsheviks might be willing to make way for a form of parliamentary government. Before the October Revolution arrangements had been made to hold nationwide free elections to a Constituent Assembly: that is, to a representative body charged with creating a constitution for the country as a whole. The elections had been duly held, chiefly in November, and had produced a total of 707 deputies. Of these less than a quarter were Bolsheviks, and they were heavily outnumbered by the Socialist Revolutionaries – the party of the numerically preponderant peasantry, who had more than twice as many representatives. Faced with a choice between yielding power and defending their form of government by force, the Bolsheviks decided on the second course, and so they put the Assembly permanently out of commission by violently dispersing its one and only session, in Petrograd on 18 January 1918.

At the end of January 1918 the Old Style (Julian) Calendar was replaced by the New Style (Gregorian) Calendar used in Western Europe; the effect of this was that, in 1918, Russia's 31 January was immediately followed by 14 February. The thirteen-day discrepancy thus abolished incidentally explains why Russia's 'February' and 'October' Revolutions occurred in what were, in other parts of the world, March and November respectively. Further events of 1918 included the signing of the peace treaty of Brest-Litovsk with the Germans on 3 March; the transfer, also in March, of the Soviet seat of government to Moscow, which had lost its place as the Russian capital city in 1712; the slaughter, on Lenin's instructions, of the ex-Emperor Nicholas II and members of his family at Yekaterinburg in the Urals. Occurring in July, this last episode heralded the intensification of hostilities in the Civil War.

The Civil War

The military campaigns of the Civil War mainly consisted of defending the Soviet heartland, based on Moscow, against attacks mounted by White armies on the periphery of the former Empire: through the Ukraine, the Caucasus, Siberia and the far north of European Russia. Though this was, in a sense, an ideological war, the troops on both sides were largely politically apathetic peasants press-ganged into the

Red or White armies at gun-point, besides which many private armies, composed of anarchists or brigands, also fought against or for the main contestants. After two years of hostilities the Reds signalled their victory in all the major campaigns by enforcing the evacuation of General Vrangel's forces from the Crimea in November 1920. This Bolshevik victory was due to a variety of causes: better co-ordination based on their central strategic position; a more positive-sounding political programme contrasting with that of the Whites, who were united by little more than hatred of Bolshevism; the peasants' fear that a White victory would restore landlords' holdings appropriated by themselves; the odium incurred through widespread ineffectual military intervention on the White side by foreign forces – those of Britain, France, Japan, the USA and other countries.

By no means were the privations imposed by the Civil War confined to combatants. Lack of food, and of fuel in the especially bitter winters, imposed acute suffering on civilians, and conditions were especially harsh in the former capital, Petrograd. That city had turned into the diametrical opposite of itself, Akhmatova recorded in her diary, what with typhus, famine, shootings, apartments plunged into darkness and people so swollen from famine as to be unrecognizable; 'Yet they still loved poetry.'[1] Another observer has written, of Kiev, that 'streams of blood actually flowed down the street, outside every window. We had all seen bullet-riddled corpses in the roads and on the pavements, but more than bullets we dreaded the indignities and tortures inflicted before death.'[2] Books too suffered in these terrible years, for many a private library was fed into the stove by its owner when the alternative seemed to be death by freezing.

The Civil War period witnessed the completion by the Bolsheviks of their suppression of all other political parties within their jurisdiction. They had begun in 1917 with 'bourgeois' (non-Socialist) movements, including that of the liberal Kadets, and then moved on to crush rival left-wing groups: those of the Socialist Revolutionaries and Anarchists. They also eliminated the Mensheviks – fellow-Marxists who had split away from the Bolsheviks within the Russian Social Democratic Party, to which both belonged, in 1903. The publications of these parties were banned, some of their members going over to Bolshevism, while others were arrested, held as hostages and shot.

During the Civil War the Bolsheviks operated a system of severe economic and social control to which the name War Communism was

given. It involved the complete nationalization of industry and com-
merce, compulsory levies of foodstuffs from the peasants, payment
in kind for workers and the imposition of compulsory labour on the
bourgeoisie.

Literature could not flourish under these conditions, also being
hampered by an acute paper shortage. But poetry at least was relatively
unimpeded, and was often declaimed at the various 'poets' cafés' of
the period by authors – Mayakovsky and Yesenin among them – who
carried over into the early post-revolutionary years the Bohemian and
bourgeois-baiting life style that they had already evolved earlier in the
century.

The New Economic Policy

In 1921, with the Civil War virtually at an end and the economy in
chaos, War Communism was abolished as no longer workable. It was
replaced, as an emergency rescue operation, by the New Economic
Policy (NEP), which remained in force until the adoption of the First
Five Year Plan in 1928. NEP restored a measure of private trade,
permitting the peasants to grow crops for the market. It also allowed
small businesses, including publishing firms, to operate under private
ownership. Though the State always retained its control of heavy
industry, the more doctrinaire Bolsheviks interpreted this temporary
retreat as a betrayal of the revolution. Others welcomed it as a relief
from wartime rigours. In Moscow, Petrograd and other cities 'The
recently boarded-up shop windows once again glittered with lights. . . .
Cafes and restaurants dotted the streets. Instead of machine-gun fire,
the streets resounded with the hammering of boilermakers, bricklayers
and carpenters.'[3]

The year of NEP's introduction coincided with a working-class
rebellion against Bolshevism in the naval port of Kronstadt, near
Petrograd, and with an anti-Bolshevik peasant revolt in Tambov
Province in the south-east of European Russia. Both were ruthlessly
suppressed by armed force. At the same time measures were introduced
to stiffen Party discipline. In March 1921 the Tenth Party Congress
outlawed any form of concerted opposition within the Party to decisions
taken at the top. Soon after the same Congress, which also adopted
NEP, the extensive famine of 1921–2 erupted in the south and east
of European Russia. NEP did, however, prove successful to the extent

that the economy had been restored, by 1928, to approximately the level of 1913.

With the restoration of a measure of prosperity and the return to a limited form of capitalism under NEP came the rise of the 'Nepman' or small-scale businessman. This development was accompanied by a revival of the acquisitive 'bourgeois' mentality of cliché, as utterly abominated by enthusiasts for Bolshevism, to whom NEP was at best a regrettable necessity and at worst a betrayal of all that the Revolution stood for. Such was the attitude of the non-Party bolshevizer Mayakovsky, who had been a scourge of the bourgeoisie since long before the Revolution, and whose onslaughts on the Nepman mentality include some ingenious scenes in his play *The Bedbug* (1928).

One important feature of early NEP was the death of Lenin on 21 January 1924 after a series of incapacitating strokes beginning in May 1922. Meanwhile Stalin was preparing his rise to power. It was he who, as People's Commissar for Nationalities, first established the new State – on 27 December 1922, under the title 'Union of Soviet Socialist Republics' (USSR) – by uniting the Russian Federation (RSFSR) with the three other existing Soviet Socialist Republics: those of the Ukraine, of Belorussia and of Transcaucasia. Appointed Secretary-General to the Party's Central Committee earlier in the same year, Stalin encouraged more flamboyant colleagues to write him off as a plodding mediocrity while he brought all the key interlocking Party organs under his own control. Stalin outmanœuvred (in triple alliance with Zinovyev and Kamenev) his greatest rival, Trotsky, before entering a quadruple alliance with Bukharin, Rykov and Tomsky, and ousting Zinovyev and Kamenev in turn. In the end all these figures, including his three more recent allies, met a violent death as the result of their opposition to the Stalin who seemed comparatively harmless in the middle 1920s.

One feature of the early Communist regime had been the belief that there were 'no fortresses which the Bolsheviks could not conquer': in other words, that all things were possible, including the total transformation of social life along new and radically permissive lines. Extreme sexual licence was accordingly encouraged by making divorce and abortion available on demand. Parental authority was undermined within the family, as was teachers' authority within the schools, which went through an extravagantly experimental and anti-disciplinarian phase. Patriotism, and even the use of the words 'Russia' and 'Russian', were officially discouraged.

The pre-1930 period was one of comparative freedom for writers. Negatively censored in that they might not publish material directly attacking the new political and social dispensation, they were otherwise free to write as they pleased and in whatever style they chose. Such was the general situation during the 1920s, especially in the first years of the decade, which have come to be regarded in retrospect as a Golden Age. But this sentimentalizing of the past has often been overdone, as Solzhenitsyn has warned in *The Gulag Archipelago*, pointing out that the 1920s also witnessed persecutions and oppressions, mild only by comparison with what was to follow.[4] Among those affecting the literary world was the tyranny imposed on the writing fraternity as a whole by a single authors' association, RAPP, from the late 1920s until its dissolution in 1932 (see page 192). The most dramatic episode in this phase of regimentation occurred when Pilnyak and Zamyatin were subjected, in 1929, to a ferocious campaign of vilification in the media and in public meetings for having published ideologically inadequate works, and outside the USSR at that: Pilnyak's story *Mahogany* and Zamyatin's novel *We*. The affair is notable as the first full-scale Soviet literary witch-hunt – a process whereby preselected scapegoats have been publicly denounced (often in pairs) as a device for disciplining the writing fraternity in general.

Stalin's Dictatorship

The Stalin dictatorship falls into three main phases: pre-war (1929–41); wartime (1941–5); post-war (1945–53).

Pre-War Stalinism

As already indicated, one casualty of the early 1920s had been the Bolsheviks' widespread belief that their rule, at first recognized as precarious even by themselves, would be rescued by a more general revolution erupting on a world-wide scale. When it became obvious that this hope was not to be fulfilled, a policy of self-sufficiency was adopted by Stalin under the title 'Socialism in One Country'. After obtaining power as the main advocate of this approach, he further developed the USSR's ability to stand alone by embarking on a crash programme of industrialization imposed through a series of Five Year Plans, the first of which began in 1928. He also collectivized agriculture by breaking up individual peasant homesteads, of which there were some twenty-five million, and compelling peasants to amalgamate in *kolkhozy* (Collective Farms) and *sovkhozy* (State Farms) with an average of some seventy-five households to a farm.

Though industrialization was enforced with great stringency, and through harsh labour legislation, it also evoked considerable enthusiasm. In this it contrasted with collectivization – universally unpopular and ruthlessly imposed by military and police power. Many millions of peasants perished, whether slaughtered in armed clashes with the authorities, executed or freighted in bulk to concentration camp and exile. The severe famine of 1932–3, which Stalin failed to relieve as a matter of policy while maintaining the export of Soviet-grown grain, completed the subjugation of the peasantry. Collectivization was thus a political success, since it broke the resistance of a traditionally conservative and uncontrollable element, but an economic failure.

In view of the scale of peasant sufferings one can only marvel that Stalin largely succeeded in concealing them at the time, both from world opinion and even from his own urban population. As for writers, themselves largely town-dwellers, they were obliged to ignore or distort the numerous discreditable aspects of Stalinism, which now included the growing use of forced labour (at this stage largely that of imprisoned peasants) on massive industrial projects.

The year in which the great famine began, 1932, was also that in which the Party dissolved all existing writers' associations, ordering the establishment of a single, all-embracing Union of Writers of the USSR, which held its first congress in 1934. This new body was set up in an atmosphere that seemed to promise a degree of freedom and tolerance denied to authors in the period from the late 1920s to 1932. But the promise proved illusory. Though not formally compulsory, membership of the new Union was virtually inescapable for professional authors. Henceforward they were also under a formal obligation as Union members to write in accordance with a newly enunciated and obligatory literary method, that of Socialist Realism, adherence to which still remains a condition for publication in the Soviet press. Amongst other requirements Socialist Realism demands from authors 'a truthful, historically concrete depiction of reality in its revolutionary development'. The formula has proved admirably imprecise from the point of view of Soviet authority, and the requirements which it has been used to enforce have accordingly varied considerably from time to time. In periods of strictest control, especially 1946–53, Socialist Realism was to foster the composition of crudely optimistic and xenophobic propaganda on behalf of the Soviet dispensation. At other times, and especially in recent years, the doctrine has been imposed so tolerantly that it has been compared to the Church of England's Thirty-Nine Articles; see further, page 203 ff.[1]

By the mid-1930s Stalin had begun to re-establish certain traditional features of social life that had been overthrown or undermined in the 1920s. He encouraged Russian and Soviet national pride, also restoring school discipline and supporting the exercise of parental authority, while further strengthening family ties through restrictions on divorce and abortion. But it is also true that he divided families by encouraging children to report their parents for politically aberrant views and conduct.

December 1934 witnessed the assassination of the Leningrad Party leader Sergey Kirov. It is thought likely that Stalin himself ordered the killing, thus simultaneously removing a popular junior rival and providing a pretext for the vast new wave of arrests and executions that reached their peak in 1937. To these and to their period Russians gave the unofficial name Yezhovshchina, derived from that of the reigning security police boss Nikolay Yezhov. The terms Great Purge or Great Terror are also commonly applied to the years 1936–8 by non-Soviet specialists, while the victims are often described in Western sources as having been liquidated (originally a Soviet term). The commonly employed phrase 'liquidated in the purges' is admittedly imprecise. But its very imprecision makes it particularly apt for describing a process on which, as it affected the fate of individuals, hard information is rarely forthcoming: arrest coincident with disappearing from circulation for ever under circumstances which remain unclarified except in certain cases by sparse, uncheckable and often mutually contradictory information later published in official sources such as encyclopedias and rehabilitation documents.

The Great Purge was comparable in scale to the assault launched on the peasantry some six or seven years earlier, but differed in being chiefly directed against town-dwellers, and with particular emphasis on those holding high positions in the professions: officers in the armed forces, ministers and senior civil servants, economic managers, scientists, engineers, scholars, professors. Since nearly all highly-placed persons, in whatever walk of life, were Party members, the new attack fell with particular severity on the Party. Nor did the Yezhovshchina spare the Party Apparatus, consisting of those whose principal activity was within the Party organization itself; on the contrary, the Apparatus suffered at least as severely as any other major category. So too did the very security police (now called the NKVD) on which the dictator depended to implement the Terror. However, despite the high proportion of victims among members of the Party and security forces, we must not forget that the overwhelming majority of the sufferers consisted of ordinary citizens lacking Party or police affiliations. Writers suffered along with all other sections of the community, Mandelstam, Pilnyak and Babel being the best-known among several hundred who lost their lives through the Terror.

The main device for initiating, symbolizing and excusing the un-acknowledged death of so many millions was that of the Stalinist show trials. They had begun in 1928 on a comparatively humble level with the arraignment, on charges of economic sabotage, of various engineers and managers: non-Party specialists whom Stalin made scapegoats for the many shortages and economic disasters of the period. A few years later, with the excuse of the Kirov assassination, he was ready to move publicly against Party members of the highest degree. The most important of the judicial pageants were the three great Moscow trials of 1936–8, at which fifty-four defendants appeared in all, and were mostly sentenced to death. They included Lenin's senior surviving associates, among them his veteran allies Zinovyev and Kamenev (at the first trial) and Bukharin (at the third). Here were publicly staged and widely publicized dramas, all the defendants – prominent and not-so-prominent – having been carefully selected and processed to confess, in accordance with prearranged scripts, to a series of crimes: sabotage, terrorism, plots to kill non-disgraced Soviet leaders, espionage on behalf of foreign powers, support of the exiled Trotsky and the like. The charges appear to have been entirely false from beginning to end, co-operation having been enlisted by lengthy pre-trial softening up through torture, and threat of torture, menaces to families, promises of remission in return for compliance and appeals to Party loyalty. As for the most illustrious of all Stalin's rivals, Trotsky, he was to be assassinated in Mexico City on 20 August 1940, almost certainly on the dictator's orders, after being driven into foreign exile in 1929.

Such was the fate of a few dozen public victims. Meanwhile comparable methods were being secretly applied to the several million unpublicized martyrs of the Yezhovshchina, most of whom were eventually terrorized into confessing imaginary and absurd crimes. 'Who recruited you?' and 'Whom did you recruit?' These were the questions to which answers were persistently demanded by interrogators themselves menaced with arrest, enforced confession and torture should they fail. Thus the Great Purge became self-perpetuating, and was threatening to engulf the entire country by the time that Stalin decided, in 1938, to reduce the quota of arrests, eliminating his chief enforcer Yezhov and appointing Lavrenty Beria to head the security police in his place. Some interrogators and police officials were now indicted for excess of zeal, but only a small minority of concentration camp inmates appears to have been released.

Since it was unsafe to allude to the Terror, except in certain permissible guarded formulas denouncing kulaks, traitors and the like, these spectacular events could only be reflected by imaginative literature in distorted form; or in works published many years later, usually outside the USSR.

Wartime Stalinism

Hitler's unprovoked attack on the USSR was unleashed on 22 June 1941, and took Stalin by surprise. Launching a series of colossal German victories, it revealed the outstanding incompetence with which the Soviet leader had organized the military defence of his country – probably because he had banked heavily on Hitler not mounting an invasion as early as 1941, and also because subordinate Soviet generals and officials no longer dared to inform their leader of the true state of military unpreparedness. In the first winter of the war the Germans came near to capturing Moscow, but retreated in the face of bitter weather and stubborn resistance. In 1942 they penetrated far into the south-eastern regions of the European USSR, but were held and routed at the Battle of Stalingrad. The defeat of another massed German onslaught, at the great tank battle of Kursk in central European Russia in mid-1943, was the prelude to the rout of the Axis Powers by the USSR and her Western allies in 1944-5.

The four years of war between the USSR and Germany represent the largest campaign known to military history. What with the fighting, the horrors of occupation by Germany and her allies, the freighting of Soviet citizens as forced labour to the West, the extermination of Soviet Jews, and the general policy of treating the USSR's inhabitants as members of an inferior race, Hitler accomplished the remarkable feat of killing Soviet citizens more rapidly than even Stalin had contrived over any comparable period of time. The result was to rally popular enthusiasm to Stalin; whom no one, surely, but a Hitler could have converted into the symbol of Russia's freedom and national pride.

Hence the strange paradox whereby Soviet censorship controls were relaxed rather than tightened in wartime, indoctrination in Marxism and ideological intimidation being substantially reduced, while Russian nationalist fervour was officially encouraged, and the Orthodox Church was exempted from the severe persecution to which it had been subjected in time of peace. For these reasons, and through the sense of national unity created by defence against a universally identifiable enemy, the general morale rose during wartime, having sunk to abysmal depths during the days of the Yezhovshchina and through the successful pre-war policy of dividing citizens against each other in an atmosphere of intense mutual suspicion. 'However terrible it may seem, the Second World War conferred spiritual relief on some, since it exempted them from the divided feelings typical of peace.'[2] Such is Nadezhda Mandelstam's witness. Pasternak has put the same point more forcibly in *Doctor Zhivago*: 'When war flared up its real horrors and real dangers, the threat of a real death, were a blessing compared to the inhuman reign of fantasy, and they brought relief by limiting the magic force of the dead letter.'[3] Among other wartime relaxations was the opening of contacts, rigorously supervised by Soviet authority, between the USSR and her Western allies, notably the USA and Great Britain.

The relaxations of the period affected literature too. Pasternak and Akhmatova, neither of whom had published original work for some years, were able to bring out books and to place some of their verses in the press. No less remarkable was the publication of *Before the Sunrise* (1943), an essay in semi-autobiographical self-examination by Mikhail Zoshchenko, otherwise chiefly known for his humorous writings. Such episodes were exceptional, and Zoshchenko's work was severely censured shortly after publication as an example of acute individualism:[4] a foretaste of the far more virulent attacks to be made on him in 1946. In any case the majority of writers were concerned with recording the war – either in journalistic despatches or in novels and poems praising the wise leadership of Stalin in the accepted formulas.

Post-War Stalinism

In the immediate post-war period the Soviet leader dismayed the non-Communist world by adopting policies no less harsh and militant, in their very different way, than those of the 1930s.

Rejecting further co-operation with his wartime allies, Britain and the USA, Stalin imposed Soviet control on seven European countries (Albania, Bulgaria, Czechoslovakia, Hungary, Poland, Rumania, Yugoslavia) and also on Soviet-occupied eastern Germany. Of these Yugoslavia (in 1948) and Albania (in 1961) were to escape Kremlinite dominion; the others, nominally independent, were called People's Democracies by the Kremlin, and 'Soviet satellites' by those unsympathetic to the Kremlin. Operating through his security police and agents, Stalin compelled the leaders of these newly dependent states to arraign some of their chief political rivals at show trials tailored to the Soviet model that had already proved its worth as a device for intensifying political control by terror. Stalin also sponsored the blockade of Western-occupied Berlin from August 1948, and he either provoked or failed to countermand the war between North and South Korea that began in June 1950. Conscious of his lack of nuclear weapons, he intensified research that led to the explosion of the first Soviet atom bomb in 1949 and of the first hydrogen bomb in 1953. While promoting these policies, whether through fear of the USA or through a desire to extend his empire, Stalin was also fostering the Soviet international Peace Campaign, in which Ilya Ehrenburg and other writers participated, and which unavowedly sought to persuade foreigners to equate the interests of world peace with support for the aims of Soviet foreign policy.

Internal policies were comparably harsh, leading to the widespread incarceration in concentration camps of returning prisoners of war released from German captivity. Several million Soviet citizens, both military and civilian, had found their way to the West during the war, and were now repatriated, often forcibly and against their will as the result of Soviet diplomatic pressure and of a desire on the part of Western statesmen not to offend the Soviet dictator. But those repatriated were in many cases summarily shot, or consigned in bulk to outposts of the camp empire. There is no more eloquent witness to these events than Solzhenitsyn. Himself arrested in 1945 as a prelude to more than a decade's imprisonment and exile, he protests with especial vigour in *The Gulag Archipelago* against the consignment to concentration camps of so many Soviet servicemen whose only crime had been to defend their motherland. Nor does he withhold all sympathy from the defecting Red Army troops who fought on the German side, their best-known formation being the army of General Vlasov.

Besides housing innumerable Soviet returners from the West, the post-war Soviet concentration camps were also extensively replenished with prisoners from the satellite countries and from newly reoccupied Soviet territory, notably the western Ukraine.

The severities of post-war Stalinism did not spare those citizens who remained at liberty. A decision was taken to disrupt the relatively relaxed and ideologically neutral atmosphere of wartime, to which reference was made above, and which continued for about a year after the end of hostilities against Japan. That literary policy became the main vehicle for proclaiming this change of course was characteristic of Stalinist conditions, as emerged when two ideologically suspect writers, Akhmatova and Zoshchenko, were singled out as scapegoats and subjected to extravagant officially orchestrated abuse. Here was a signal to the community as a whole that a new era of harsh regimentation had dawned. Each of the victimized authors has been mentioned above as having temporarily benefited from wartime easements to publish works focused on their personal experiences to an extent exceeding that normally permitted. Now they were to pay the penalty, the attack being sprung in the form of a Party decree dated 14 August 1946. It denounced two Leningrad-based journals, *Zvezda* ('The Star') and *Leningrad*, for publishing items by the two pilloried authors. Akhmatova and Zoshchenko were also expelled from the Union of Writers, but were not imprisoned. As for the choice of location for the campaign's initial impact, we are reminded that the city once called St Petersburg had, for more than a quarter of a century, been particularly suspect to Muscovite and Stalinist authority as the Soviet Union's most international city and Russia's former capital – and thus as a potential source of ideological and cultural contamination.

The decree of August 1946 was followed by harsh policy statements from Andrey Zhdanov, the high Party official responsible for cultural affairs, and to such effect that the years 1946–53 are sometimes called the 'Zhdanov Era', even though Zhdanov himself died in 1948.

At no other time have the Soviet communications media been so strictly regimented. Literary style was homogenized, and subsided into lifeless officialese lacking the imprint of individual authorship, while stylistic or structural experiment became more stringently taboo than ever. Authors were required to lavish inordinate praise on everything Soviet, while societies outside the Kremlin's orbit, especially that of the USA, were to be viciously abused. Any writer showing insufficiency of zeal in these matters was liable to be denounced and persecuted for 'kow-towing to the West', and for being a 'rootless cosmopolitan'. Since the latter term was often applied to Jews – though also, not uncommonly, *by* Jews – the campaign acquired an anti-Semitic flavour. The new campaign also placed unprecedented stress on optimism as an essential ingredient in literary works, and so the sufferings of the average citizen in the post-war years were passed over in silence. This period also saw the adoption by writers of the so-called No Conflict Theory: that Soviet society had attained such a pitch of perfection and harmony as to exclude the possibility of all clashes, either between citizen and citizen, or between the citizen and the State. Typical of the period, and of the treatment of even so intimate a theme as love, were the portraits of ecstatic, norm-exceeding, handsome lathe-operators and milkmaids exchanging details on production statistics by the light of the moon in novels that won Stalin Prizes and accompanying privileges for their authors, while others attained comparable renown by accusing the USA of slaughtering North Korean babies through germ-impregnated spiders broadcast from the skies.

All this led to intellectual and cultural stagnation so extreme that even the authorities who imposed it, led by Stalin himself, began to show mild signs of dissatisfaction with what they had wrought. One symptom of their unease was an official demand for new satirical works ridiculing the shortcomings of Soviet society: a *Pravda* article of 7 April 1952 called for the emergence of Soviet-style Gogols and Shchedrins (the two chief literary scourges of Russian nineteenth-century society). But those who dared attempt a response predictably found themselves under attack for slandering Soviet society.

So closely had the arts been harnessed to the needs of political propaganda that they had become ineffectual even in their propaganda role. But despite not a few indications that Stalin himself was toying with the desire to mend matters, nothing short of his death, on 5 March 1953, could end the deep freeze that he had ordained.

After Stalin

The post-Stalin period falls into two phases – those associated with the rise and ascendancy, first of Khrushchev and then (from 1964) of Brezhnev. Each of these leaders followed in Stalin's footsteps by holding the chief secretaryship of the CPSU Central Committee as the most important among their many offices. However, neither did Khrushchev nor (to date) has Brezhnev ever attained power remotely comparable to that exercised for a quarter of a century by Stalin. As for their comparative standing, Khrushchev probably enjoyed a greater degree of ascendancy over his colleagues, especially after he had assumed the premiership (Chairmanship of the Council of Ministers) in 1958, than Brezhnev has ever attained. But the latter's prestige and influence have steadily increased over more than a decade.

Khrushchev's Ascendancy

Stalin's death brought a sense of relief to the country as a whole, and led to the widespread release, over the next few years, of prisoners who had survived concentration camp conditions. The concentration camp system was not abolished, but reduced to considerably smaller dimensions, while the ever-present danger of unheralded arrest was largely removed from the population in general. The powers of the security police (entitled, since 1954, the KGB) were curbed too, but the organization was not dismantled, merely brought under more stringent Party control.

Khrushchev's supremacy was notable for sharp policy oscillations in conformity with the man's capricious temperament. Relaxations of Stalinist rigours were instituted, partly owing to a widespread reaction against the methods of the past, and partly because Khrushchev sought to gain political credit by espousing the cause of reform. But these reliefs were received with such excitement and enthusiasm that they seemed to threaten the system's ultimate stability, thus requiring correction by the reimposition of restrictions. Hence the image so often invoked to describe post-1953 developments: as a thaw or, better, a series of thaws separated by intervals of re-refrigeration. It is typical of Soviet conditions that these climatic variations were more faithfully recorded in imaginative literature than in any other documentary source.

The first phase of relaxation occurred in 1953–4, taking its name from Ehrenburg's short novel *The Thaw* (Part One, 1954). Here the author departs from extreme Socialist Realist practice in favour of a cautiously optimistic attempt to describe Soviet life as observed from an ideologically neutral standpoint. Meanwhile certain articles of literary criticism, notably by Vladimir Pomerantsev ('On Sincerity in Literature') and Fyodor Abramov, attempted to claim for imaginative writers a greater degree of freedom to reflect their individual vision of the world than had been permitted during the previous quarter of a century and more. However, even these cautious probings seemed dangerous to the leadership. They were enough to cause the temporary dismissal of Aleksandr Tvardovsky from the chief editorship of the leading reformist or 'liberal' journal, *Novy mir* ('New World'), which had carried the offending items.

Less optimistic than Ehrenburg, Pasternak found it hard to take comfort from the Thaw, to which he alluded as follows:

> Kneading clayey ice like dough,
> I plod through liquid goo.[1]

Nor, though he welcomed Khrushchev's relaxations, was the poet greatly impressed by the personality of the new ruler: 'For so long we were ruled over by a madman and murderer – and now by a fool and a pig.'[2]

A second Thaw followed Khrushchev's so-called Secret Speech of 25 February 1956 to the Twentieth Congress of the CPSU, in which he guardedly denounced Stalin – largely for causing the death of leading Communists, and for failing to take adequate defence measures before the war. Of Stalin's oppression of the population as a whole, of the concentration camp network, of the muddle and suffering associated with collectivization virtually nothing was said. Still, to criticize Stalin at all, even in this covert and limited fashion, was to suggest that a glorious new era might be dawning. Writers accordingly began to bring out material of a type that had not attained Soviet publication for many years, with the result that 1956 became known to foreign specialists as the Year of Protest. The year's most out-standing publications included two symposia entitled *Literary Moscow*, the second of which was highly critical of Soviet conditions, while the most notorious individually published work was Dudintsev's novel *Not by Bread Alone*. In this the complacency and excessive privileges, and even (in effect) the bourgeois mentality of the Soviet ruling class came under attack.

The new liberties of 1956 were abruptly curtailed late in that year after the unsuccessful Hungarian revolt against subjection to the Soviet Union. Erupting in October, this was partly inspired and led by Hungarian writers (as did not escape the Kremlin's notice) and was suppressed by Soviet armed intervention. The episode helped to bring on a renewed literary and cultural freeze at home, and it was main-tained with minor variations of temperature until the Twenty-Second Party Congress in October 1961. Khrushchev then unexpectedly mounted a further attack on Stalin, one that differed markedly from the Secret Speech of five years earlier in being officially reported by the Soviet press. It was followed by an event of still greater symbolic significance: the removal of the deceased dictator's embalmed remains from the Red Square mausoleum, where they had reposed for eight years alongside the mummified Lenin. This episode marks the political high water mark of 'de-Stalinization', as the process came to be called.

The sequel was yet another Thaw (the third), of which the most notable single manifestation was the publication, by *Novy mir* in November 1962, of Solzhenitsyn's story of concentration camp life, *One Day in the Life of Ivan Denisovich*. It contains the frankest account of the camps, and surely the best, ever to have appeared with a Soviet imprint, and its appearance represents the furthest point ever attained by the post-Stalinist relaxation of literary controls. A renewed freeze soon followed, provoked through Khrushchev's rage at being confronted with specimens of 'modern' (i.e. non-representational) art at a Moscow exhibition in December 1962. Further oscillations and tantrums, provoking further minor thaws and minor freeze-ups, followed during the two years of power remaining to Khrushchev. Against this background an unusual degree of licence was extended to literary-political controversy in the press, albeit conducted in charac-teristically veiled terms, between liberals (reformists) and conservatives (conformists).

Not the least beneficial feature of the Khrushchev years was the rehabilitation of many leading figures purged and liquidated under Stalin. Deceased writers falling into this category could not be restored to life, but at least their works could be republished. In keeping with the policy of de-Stalinization as a whole, literary rehabilitations were implemented selectively, hesitantly and with many delays.

Brezhnev's Ascendancy

The keynote of the Brezhnev administration, which followed the dismissal of Khrushchev in October 1964, has been extreme caution. One early outcome of this was a brief period of relaxation, lasting from late 1964 into 1966, during which the new leadership was still feeling its way. This phase saw the publication of remarkably outspoken material, less in the form of imaginative literature than in that of memoirs, particularly military memoirs, and also of articles by historians and military experts. They contained revelations about early Soviet history and criticism of Stalin's, and also of Khrushchev's, military activities. Meanwhile many of the latter's more inspirational measures, to which the new authorities referred as 'hare-brained schemes', were being swiftly dismantled.

Once the Brezhnev administration was firmly established it began to impose controls more effective, if less fussy or newsworthy, than those of the previous dispensation. From 1966 onwards the literary censorship was unobtrusively strengthened and rendered more sophisticated, being applied with special rigour to works and periodicals enjoying a large circulation. As for Khrushchev's devious and limited brand of de-Stalinization, it was replaced by a contrary policy: that of discreetly rehabilitating the great dictator while yet keeping public comment on him to the minimum. Even the soothing Khrushchevite formulaic euphemism for the horrors of the Great Purge ('phenomena associated with the cult of the personality of I. V. Stalin') ceased to be employed, while Khrushchev himself became a virtual unperson – someone to whom reference could no longer be made in print. The general effect of this policy has been to remove the pall of uncertainty under which the USSR had lived during the period when Khrushchev's sudden bouts of rage or benevolence were at any moment liable to initiate a sudden switch in policy.

The Brezhnev era has by no means avoided literary scandals. The first noteworthy example was the trial, in Moscow in February 1966, of two writers, Andrey Sinyavsky and Yuly Daniel, on the basis of literary works by them which had somehow come to be published abroad under the pseudonyms, respectively, of Abram Tertz and Nikolai Arzhak. Hard labour sentences of seven and five years imposed on the two authors caused considerable indignation throughout the world; it was noted that never previously, even under Stalin, had writers been overtly prosecuted on the basis of what they had written and 'after a trial in which the principal evidence against them was their literary work'.[3]

The year of this double trial coincided with a great increase in the particular kind of transaction that the accused had conducted: the spiriting abroad, for foreign publication, of Export Only literary works found or assumed to be ineligible for publication in the USSR. One reason for their proliferation since 1966 has been the imposition of more effective censorship controls at home. After 1966 writers could be fairly certain that works of a certain character had no hope of Soviet publication; under Khrushchev, by contrast, it was difficult to be absolutely certain that any item must inevitably be excluded, besides which the possibility of a radical transformation of the Soviet system was easier to credit under Khrushchev than under Brezhnev.

The most prominent Russian writer of the Brezhnev era is Solzhenitsyn, whose literary career began in 1962 with the Khrushchev-sanctioned *One Day in the Life of Ivan Denisovich*. Solzhenitsyn became an Export Only author only after it had proved impossible to publish certain other works, notably the long novels *Cancer Ward* and *The First Circle*, in his native land. His forcible ejection from the Soviet Union in February 1974 turned him into an émigré author operating henceforward in the third of the three possible frameworks in which modern Russian writers have created their work.

One of the main differences between the Khrushchev and the Brezhnev eras has been the disappearance from the Soviet press of the controversy between liberals and conservatives who had attacked each other in the oblique and veiled language of Soviet public utterance under the Khrushchev dispensation. After 1966 such public political controversies were far less in evidence, except that a leading journal *Molodaya gvardiya* ('The Young Guard') was able to campaign for a degree of Russian nationalism greatly exceeding the limits set to this trend by authority. From 1970, however, this ultra-patriotic movement was discouraged through dismissals and arrests. Other post-1966 nonconformist material has tended to be diverted into *samizdat* and

Export Only channels to a greater extent than was found necessary in the Khrushchev period. It would, however, be most misleading to suggest that politically *risqué*, critical and ambivalent themes have disappeared entirely from the pages of recent Soviet-published literature.

In dealing with writers considered obstreperous, Brezhnevite policy has shown great flexibility. Some offenders have been tried and sentenced to concentration camps, only to be permitted to emigrate later; others have been incarcerated in psychiatric clinics; expelled from the Union of Writers; thrown out of the country. Not a few have been induced by these means, or by the threat of their application, to assume more conformist postures. Others have continued defiant. Meanwhile, though Socialist Realism still remains the mandatory literary doctrine to which all writers are obliged to defer, many of its most exacting requirements, as imposed under Stalin, have been unavowedly abandoned: especially the insistence on portraying Positive Heroes and on purveying ebullient optimism.

As for scandals in the international arena, the most acute of these occurred in the spring and summer of 1968 when the new Czechoslovak leadership, still nominally Communist, began to show marked signs of emancipating itself from Kremlinite control. Soviet military intervention rectified this indiscipline, but aroused worldwide protests, including demonstrations in the USSR itself.

The dissident movement appeared to be flourishing in the early 1970s, when its three principal spokesmen – Solzhenitsyn, the nuclear physicist Andrey Sakharov and the publicist Roy Medvedev – were even able to engage in semi-public controversy through *samizdat* and Export Only channels. But the publicity given to their pronouncements outside the USSR helped to conceal a decline in the dissident movement as a whole. This has partly succumbed to the official policy of repressing the minor dissidents while allowing some latitude to those whose names are known to the West: usually as a preliminary to procuring their expatriation. But though some dissident activities, and especially the signing of protest letters, have been severely restricted, the main outlet for literary dissidence – the spiriting abroad of Export Only literature – has somehow continued to prosper.

3 Russian Authors and the World

East-West Contact

Cultural contacts between Russia and the West have followed the general configurations of the period as outlined above. Once again three phases are to be noted. The first was a period of relative freedom in the 1920s, decreasing and virtually disappearing by the end of the decade. In the second, that of fully developed Stalinism, association with foreigners not only became taboo, but could easily prove lethal. So intense was Stalin's suspicion of all communion across national barriers that the merest hint of any foreign connection could become the pretext for arrest on a charge of espionage. From this extreme position the Khrushchev and Brezhnev years have provided relief – to the point where over a million foreign tourists have come to visit the USSR annually, while a fair number of Soviet tourists are permitted to journey to the West. Both classes of visitor are, however, regularly freighted around in bulk under the eye of Soviet supervisors; they are discouraged from following up uncontrolled contacts; and they are kept under particularly close scrutiny such as was not exercised in the 1920s and early 1930s, when travel and tourism were in any case not so prevalent.

More recent Soviet tourists are intensively briefed before their departure for foreign countries, and are even rehearsed in offering answers to questions about the USSR that may be put to them on alien soil. Once abroad they are under instruction to go about in groups, never alone, and there is a tendency for them to concentrate their efforts less on visiting cultural monuments than on scouring supermarkets for consumer goods unavailable at home.

Permission to travel to the West has become a major Soviet status symbol virtually restricted to those in good political standing. Not only is a foreign passport expensive, costing 300 roubles, but it is also difficult to obtain owing to the severity of the preliminary security checks. And yet, strict though security vetting is, it has not been universally successful. So effectively did one prominent author, Anatoly Kuznetsov, simulate a hyper-loyalist posture over the years that he was granted, in 1969, a place on a London-bound Soviet delegation, and seized this long-sought opportunity, as he had all along intended, to claim political asylum.

In the first post-revolutionary decade leading writers could tour Western countries free from official Soviet custodianship, give recitals of their work and publish their travel experiences. Among the most enterprising was the globe-trotting Pilnyak, who not only visited America, but twice went to Japan. He was able to make the following boast in a travel book, *Roots of the Japanese Sun* (1927): 'I have visited the brothels and dives of Moscow, Berlin, Constantinople, Smyrna, Shanghai.' But in a revised version (1934) of the same remark we find Moscow expunged from the list and the more prudish 'have inspected' substituted for 'have visited'.[1]

Mayakovsky went abroad at least once a year between 1922 and 1929, commemorating many of these escapades and their attendant love affairs in verse. His most notable expedition took him to the USA in 1925, where he reputedly fathered an American daughter, also begetting a remarkable cycle of poems on America. In one of these, *Brooklyn Bridge*, he pays tribute to a triumph of capitalist engineering in one of many fine poems showing that literary talent has never been a monopoly of Bolshevism's opponents.

Yesenin's expedition to America of 1923 provoked a chain of disasters that began when he and his American wife (the dancer Isadora Duncan) were detained and interrogated on Ellis Island as suspected Bolshevik agents. Ignorant of English, as of all other foreign languages, Yesenin felt professionally humiliated by his consort's success. Her art being independent of language, she had previously enjoyed triumphs comparable to his own in Russia; but now, in the USA, the monoglot peasant husband's only means of communicating with Americans was to stage one drunken brawl after another.

Neither Yesenin nor Mayakovsky, nor even – despite his lengthy foreign residence – Gorky commanded any Western language, and so there was a considerable contrast between these missionaries of Bolshevik culture and writers reared in pre-revolutionary professional families where knowledge of French, German and English was habitually instilled into the children. Such, for example, were Akhmatova, Mandelstam, Pasternak and Tsvetayeva, all nurtured within the traditions of European culture as a whole, and all with experience of foreign travel during the pre-revolutionary years. With Mayakovsky's stirring verses *Notre Dame* (1925), in which he incidentally urges Parisian mobs to smash their local police stations, may be contrasted Mandelstam's calmer poetic invocation of the same cathedral (1912).[2] Fascinated by Mediterranean culture, including that of classical Greece, Mandelstam wove many references to these themes into his poems. Tsvetayeva's verse too draws extensively on classical myth; nor should we forget that she and Rilke each respected the other's work, and addressed poems to each other.

Pasternak attended Marburg University in Western Germany before the First World War, and commemorated his emotional experiences in that delightful town with a famous lyric, *Marburg* (1916). After revisiting Marburg in 1922 he was to travel abroad only once more, when ordered by Stalin to attend an international writers' congress in Paris in June 1935. Here he met an old friend and correspondent – Tsvetayeva, who had left Russia in 1922 and whose talent he admired above that of all his contemporaries. She asked him whether he thought that she should return to her mother country, and Pasternak gave a non-committal answer.[3] For this he was later to reproach himself after Tsvetayeva had indeed returned in 1939;[4] her suicide in 1941, following two years of acute suffering, suggested that he had been wrong in not urging her to remain abroad.

Akhmatova's travel experiences were interrupted between 1912, the year of her last pre-revolutionary visit to western Europe, and 1964, when she travelled to Taormina in Sicily to receive an Italian literary prize. In the following year she went to Oxford University, where she received an honorary degree and was compared to Sappho by the University's Public Orator. Akhmatova's other foreign involvements have included writing a poem inspired by the London Blitz and a cycle of verse, *Cinque* (1946), commemorating a meeting with an Oxford philosopher, Isaiah Berlin.[5] The poet unfortunately died shortly after her visit to Oxford, and at the advanced age of seventy-six, which reminds us that the Soviet authorities seem to make a practice of relaxing exit restrictions in the case of eminent writers who have reached the evening of their lives. Fyodor Panfyorov and Konstantin Paustovsky were each permitted to visit the West shortly before they died, and another distinguished elderly writer to do so, fortunately without any fatal sequel, was Viktor Shklovsky.

In difficult times politically suspect writers could earn their living by translation: a form of cultural cross-fertilization that did not become an automatic pretext for arrest even in the years of severest oppression, though translation contracts could be revoked as a means of putting pressure on non-approved writers. Moreover, several important poets have spoken of translation as an irksome chore inimicable to creative writing.

Among authors more closely identified with Soviet official policies – and who could therefore uninterruptedly earn their living from original work without having recourse to translation – Konstantin Fedin had a thorough knowledge of Germany, based partly on internment in that country during the First World War. Foreign themes accordingly figure prominently in his early novels, from *Cities and Years* (1924) onwards. Ilya Ehrenburg, the Soviet Union's most cosmopolitan leading writer, contrived to combine French and American settings with deference to the literary canons of rampant Stalinism in his long novels, *The Fall of Paris* (1942), *The Storm* (1947) and *The Ninth Wave* (1951).

Though Stalin had sought to insulate his subjects from contact with the polluting foreigner in the pre-war years, wartime conditions disrupted this enforced quarantine. Liaison with the USSR's allies, including the USA and Britain, involved considerable contact. So too – on a far larger, more intimate and mutually destructive scale – did involvement with the invading Germans, with the result that many millions of Soviet citizens were exposed to foreign influence behind German lines, as prisoners of war, civilians under military occupation and forced labourers. It was largely in order to neutralize the political disadvantages of such extensive communion with the non-Soviet world that Stalin reimposed a stringent return to discipline in the post-war USSR.

During the post-war period Ehrenburg continued to travel abroad and to make public appearances as a combined spokesman of Stalinism and 'licensed liberal' (see page 233); he has been succeeded in the latter capacity by the poet Yevtushenko and others. However, by no means all cultural expeditions by Russia-based writers of the post-

Stalin years have taken place under unremitting scrutiny by the agents –
interpreters or diplomats – of the home country so often attached to
touring literary celebrities, for these have also enjoyed erratic and
unpredictable opportunities to relax and speak their minds. Indeed,
it so happens that I personally had the privilege of a long private conversation with Ehrenburg during one of his foreign visits. More
recently, in 1977, the novelist Yury Trifonov was able to give a lecture
tour of American universities unaccompanied by any of the Soviet
interpreters, embassy officials or other watchdogs and custodians who
are commonly – but by no means invariably – attached to travelling
Soviet notabilities at the behest of their own authorities.

One basic feature of East-West contact, as moderated by the Soviet
authorities, is the unavailability of Western-published literature in
Soviet bookshops. Not that such works are entirely unobtainable, for
they are sometimes to be had at inflated prices on the black market,
but also through official channels by those whom the authorities may
consider entitled to such access. It is probable, for example, that
members of the Union of Writers in good standing can now obtain
individual copies of virtually any work of foreign literature through
their professional association. To this it must be added that foreign
authors have extensively received Soviet publication in Russian translation, not excluding such original talents as Joyce, Kafka and Beckett
together with other twentieth-century authors almost comparably
eminent. So extensive has this programme been that foreign experts
have been known to interpret it as the beginning of a cultural breakthrough to East-West contact of a more natural and unsupervised
character than has in fact been permitted to occur. On a less exalted
level translations of Conan Doyle's Sherlock Holmes stories were
printed in over a million copies in 1956-7. But the decision to under-
take this publication was censured in a Party decree dated 5 April
1958, as also was the issue of writings by Alexandre Dumas and Upton
Sinclair.[6] In general translations are wider in range, and more extensive,
than is often realized, but suffer from the disadvantage that all are
chosen for the reader by authority; that they are often published in
restricted editions; that they are often difficult to obtain; and that
Soviet conditions offer little scope for spontaneous pressure by readers
as a spur to publication. Nor must it be forgotten that translated literature often appears in texts rigorously pruned and distorted by Soviet
censors in order to reduce the level of ideological unacceptability.[7]

Radio broadcasts have become an important channel for surmounting barriers to East-West cultural contact. While affording the Soviet government a means of making its claims widely known to the non-Soviet world, they also permit the broadcast to the USSR of Russian material of a type banished by censorship from the Soviet media. This has included extensive extracts from Pasternak's *Doctor Zhivago* put out by the BBC's Foreign Service, and other Export Only literature. Such broadcasts have been extensively received in the Soviet Union even in the days when they were jammed. Jamming was suspended in 1963, reimposed after the Czechoslovak crisis in 1968, and again relaxed in 1973 – but not for Radio Liberty, while the station Deutsche Welle was also jammed when it began broadcasting extracts from Solzhenitsyn's *The Gulag Archipelago* in 1974.[8]

A feature of East-West contact is the special responsibility undertaken, as noted above, by those foreign scholars who contribute towards determining modern Russian literary reputations. From the organic process whereby a Western author's standing rises or falls in accordance with readers', reviewers' and critics' fluctuating estimates, and with all manner of other influences – not least the commercial – Soviet conditions are almost immune owing to the close control maintained over literature by authority. So long as these conditions continue the comparative rating of modern Russian authors will continue to rest with a restricted audience consisting of such Russian émigrés and foreign readers as possess (or are able to simulate) literary sensitivity together with competence in the Russian language.

No discussion of East-West literary contact can be complete without reference to the highly technical issue of foreign copyright. During most of our period this has raised relatively few problems, since the USSR was not during the years 1917–72 a signatory to either of the relevant international copyright agreements: the Berne Convention of 1886 (revised 1948) and the later Universal Copyright Convention (1956). This meant that Soviet-based authors could protect their foreign rights only by arranging for their works to obtain publication in copyright-protecting foreign territory on a date preceding publication in the USSR. Otherwise foreign publishers have been free to pirate or less dishonourably appropriate Soviet-originating works, issuing them in the original or in translation, often without the permission of an author whom it may have been impracticable to consult, and also without incurring any legal obligation to pay him. In practice, however, the more reputable Western publishing houses have usually set aside royalties in the name of any author with whom negotiation has been rendered impossible by the barriers placed in the USSR on communication between Soviet citizens and foreigners. Meanwhile Soviet publishing houses have been equally free to appropriate and publish foreign works, payment for these being on a similar *ex gratia* basis and made, if at all, in unexportable Soviet currency.

A fundamental change in these relations occurred in 1973, when the USSR accepted the Universal Copyright Convention. In the same year a new body, VAAP (standing for 'All-Union Copyright Association'), was set up in Moscow. To this organ all USSR-based authors are now formally obliged to entrust the negotiation of their foreign rights. However, one of those concerned (Vladimir Voynovich) has sarcastically complained that writers are not represented on VAAP's control apparatus, and that it consists exclusively of high-ranking functionaries. As this indicates, the nominally independent VAAP is in practice an instrument of the Soviet State. Its establishment, together with the acceptance of the Universal Copyright Convention by the USSR, therefore seems to threaten the extinction of the branch of officially disapproved literature that we have here labelled Export Only. In fact, however, Export Only literature does not, to date, seem to have been affected by VAAP's operations. On the contrary, it has continued to reach the West from the Soviet Union, and to achieve foreign publication, for all the world as if VAAP had never been set up. Some authors of Export Only works have, however, been expelled from the Union of Writers since the institution of VAAP, their unofficial foreign involvements being no doubt the prime cause of their disgrace. Among them has been the outspoken Voynovich, whose very exported publications include a derisive open letter (1973) to VAAP's Chairman, a certain B. D. Pankin. Voynovich amusingly suggests that the organization should be renamed VAPAP, these being the initials of the Russian for 'All-Union Association for *the Appropriation of Authors' Rights*'.[9]

As must also be stressed, the sale of Soviet books to foreign countries is a source, however modest, of foreign currency much needed by the USSR. The commercial interests of the Soviet State must, therefore, not be ignored as a factor influencing its literary policies in the international arena. Indeed, there is even evidence to suggest that VAAP is prepared, under certain circumstances, to sell the foreign rights of works that have been denied publication at home because of their controversial ideological implications.

Emigration

An important part has been played in post-revolutionary cultural life by the country's millions of expatriates scattered over the face of the globe. Three main waves are to be distinguished in Russian emigration: 1917–23; 1941–5; the 1970s. Attention will chiefly be devoted to the first, since it is the most important from a literary point of view.

White military defeats in the Civil War caused three major evacuations in the south of troops and civilians numbering hundreds of thousands: they left with the retreating French interventionists from Odessa in 1919; from Novorossiysk in the spring of 1920 after the defeat of General Denikin; and with Denikin's successor, Vrangel, from the Crimea in November of the same year. Some quitted the Petrograd area with the retreat of Yudenich in 1919 and settled in or passed through the Baltic countries. Others flooded out from eastern Siberia, many of them to Harbin in North China, which became a Russian town. After the war they continued to leave as individuals up to the end of 1923, which concluded a period when it was possible to cross and recross the frontier with any degree of freedom. We also note an isolated instance of collective expulsion: over a hundred and sixty intellectuals, considered hostile to the new dispensation, were driven into exile – initially to Berlin and Constantinople – in autumn 1922.[1]

Always numbering several million, but subject to progressive denationalization through assimilation to their host countries, the scattered Russian expatriate community has enlivened many quarters of the globe. Between the two world wars its main political and cultural centre was Paris. But Berlin was culturally pre-eminent in 1921–3. Prague too was important and became the seat of a Russian émigré university. In these and other centres expatriate writers settled down, worked and indulged in political or literary controversies. Reference has been made by one foreign scholar to 'the vertiginous scope afforded to malice in the community of Russian literary exiles';[2] but this only lent extra spice and panache to the numerous émigré Russian newspapers, journals and publishing houses.

Before 1923 no rigid barrier was drawn between Russian writers resident within and outside Soviet territory. Members of both fraternities could attend literary meetings in Berlin cafés, and were free to place their work with either Soviet or foreign publishers, or with both. Nor was the line between Soviet and émigré citizens sharply drawn during this period when expatriates could still look upon their foreign residence as temporary, being at liberty to return to the home country without fear of reprisals or inconveniences. Meanwhile Soviet-based writers often published material abroad, especially in Berlin, as well as in Russia, being careful (as is mentioned above) to ensure that the imprint of their foreign-published work should antedate the Soviet, thus protecting their copyright.

Emigration involved Russian writers in varied adventures that cannot be discussed in detail. But we can at least indicate their range. Not a few authors, established or nearly established in the profession at the time of the Revolution, quitted their homeland never to return. Prominent among them was Bunin, who left Russia in 1920 and died in Paris in 1953; owing to the decline in émigré creativity in the years after his death his passing has sometimes been considered the symbolic death of expatriate Russian literature as a whole. Bunin is said to have contemplated returning to Russia towards the end of his life, but to have been deterred by the cultural crackdown imposed by Zhdanov in 1946.[3] That the expatriate Bunin retained cultural links with his home country has already been noted, as also that he continued to write in his native language during a quarter of a century's exile, and that he has been extensively published in the USSR since his death. We have also mentioned another celebrated non-returner – Nabokov, who emigrated in 1919, aged twenty, and wrote several novels in Russian before transferring to the English language and adding to his phase as a Russian writer a second and better-known phase as an American writer. Non-returning authors have further included the prolific novelist Mark Aldanov, now somewhat neglected but sufficiently popular in his day to be translated into over twenty languages. Other non-returners, working principally in prose, included Dmitry Merezhkovsky, Aleksey Remizov, Ivan Shmelyov and Boris Zaytsev. 'Almost all that was best in Russian pre-revolutionary prose turned out to have crossed the frontier.'[4]

In poetry the advantage rested with the home country, since it retained so many of the best-known major poets: Blok, Mayakovsky,

Yesenin, Akhmatova, Mandelstam and Pasternak. Yet the émigré poets were far indeed from being eclipsed, including as they did Konstantin Balmont, Zinaida Gippius, Vladislav Khodasevich and the Ivanovs, Georgy and Vyacheslav, who all became permanent expatriates, while Tsvetayeva remained in emigration for seventeen years. These were only a few among many, for so remarkably did the poetry flourish on foreign soil that nearly 400 volumes of Russian verse were published by over 250 émigré poets during the forty years after the Revolution,[5] and this despite the fact that verse, lending itself less easily to translation than prose, was denied the financial sustenance that vogue with a non-Russian reading public could provide. By contrast with the much-translated novelist Aldanov, the leading Symbolist poet Balmont became an obscure refugee, active but unnoticed; far from being translated *into* a score of foreign languages, he is said to have translated works into Russian *from* at least thirty foreign tongues.[6]

Short-term emigrants include three particularly important names: Andrey Bely, Aleksey Tolstoy and Maksim Gorky. Of these Bely, renowned before the Revolution as a Symbolist poet, returned in 1923 and lived out his last ten years in Russia, engaged principally on autobiographical writing and without notably contravening or fulfilling the demands made on writers by the Soviet authorities. Aleksey Nikolayevich Tolstoy, by contrast (a hereditary count and a distant cousin of the great novelist Count Lyov Tolstoy), became a Soviet literary potentate. Adapting his style with great aplomb, after returning home in 1923, to the conditions of nascent and rampant Stalinism, he triumphed over the seeming disadvantage of aristocratic birth. He was commonly addressed in pre-revolutionary style as 'My Lord' (*vashe siyatelstvo*) by his Soviet chauffeur, and would even give his name as '*gr.* A. N. Tolstoy', explaining to the curious that the prefix '*gr*', which they naïvely took for the obsolete *graf* ('count'), in fact represented the revolutionary title *grazhdanin* ('citizen'), the common mode of address that had replaced pre-revolutionary *gospodin* ('mister'). Glorifying Stalinism and Stalin in his novels and plays, Tolstoy enjoyed the many luxuries available to politically acceptable writers of the period and won several Stalin Prizes for literature before and after his death in 1945.

Of all temporary emigrants the most notable was Gorky, who was to become the doyen of Soviet-based Russian letters, and who is in some ways the most significant literary figure of the whole period.

Possessing the authority to behave more independently than others, he had, we remember, opposed Lenin in print in 1917–18. After that he helped to find work for starving writers; and he even determined, in this period of acute shortages, which of them deserved to be issued with trousers or sweaters. When Gorky emigrated, in 1921, he did so partly for health reasons (he suffered from tuberculosis), but partly because Lenin found him a political embarrassment. Gorky remained in exile, largely at Sorrento in Italy, for ten years; he paid visits to Russia in 1928 and 1929, and resumed permanent residence there in 1931, living out his last six years in a new role: that of the senior literary apologist of Stalinism. Honoured beyond all other living writers, but now presumably a prisoner of the regime, he died in 1936 under obscure circumstances; according to an official announcement, which can neither be confirmed nor refuted, he was murdered at the orders of the disgraced secret police chief Yagoda. Both in emigration and after his return to Russia, Gorky continued to write prolifically, but his fiction is largely set in the pre-revolutionary world. He is still honoured as the founder of Soviet literature, but largely in respect of works written before the Revolution, notably his novel *Mother* (1907).

Among other prose writers well established before the Revolution the novelist Aleksandr Kuprin – like Gorky, a friend of Chekhov's in youth – became an expatriate for many years. Having left Russia in 1919, he took up residence in Paris. But he did not thrive in exile, and his fiction of the period is markedly inferior to his earlier work such as his novel *The Duel* (1905). When seriously ill and in his late sixties he received permission to return to his native land, where he died a year later. Kuprin has since achieved a measure of recognition by the Soviet literary establishment, and his works have been published fairly extensively in the USSR since 1947.

As we remember, Ilya Ehrenburg's political experiences and cultural contacts on both sides of the Soviet frontier were particularly varied. After living in Russia under both Red and White jurisdiction during the Civil War, he spent most of the years 1921–41 in Western Europe, but decreasingly in the role of expatriate and more and more as a commuter mysteriously privileged to travel between the two worlds. He remained miraculously unscathed during the worst years of Stalinism, when even perfunctory contact with foreigners could provoke liquidation on a charge of espionage. Until his death in 1967 Ehrenburg continued to commune with both East and West, and to explain each to the other within the limits available to him as a licensed, yet wholesomely unpredictable, spokesman.

So much for Russian writers who temporarily or permanently quitted Russia with the First Emigration. But we must also mention 'internal emigrants' – authors who stayed behind, yet without accepting the aims of the new dispensation. Some firmly rejected emigration, believing their place to be in their homeland, however uncongenial and dangerous. Akhmatova expresses this view in a celebrated lyric of pre-October 1917, speaking of a mysterious voice that called on her to 'leave your remote and sinful country, abandon Russia for ever'. But her answer was to block her ears 'calmly and equably so that my grieving spirit should not be polluted by words so ignoble'.[7] Akhmatova rejected emigration on principle, believing it more important to die *with* than *for* one's country;[8] expatriate life, however safe and comfortable, would have been a deprivation. That this view is shared by her close friend Nadezhda Mandelstam, premier memoirist of our period and widow of a foremost poet, seems a legitimate deduction from her comment on Nabokov, the era's most renowned expatriate writer after Bunin. She describes Nabokov as 'separated from his homeland and the vital element of its language and history...living as an outcast'. For these reasons Nabokov was, in her view, 'prevented from growing up to manhood'.[9] Before his expulsion from the USSR Solzhenitsyn put the same point still more forcibly when he described the prospect of deportation to the West as 'spiritual castration'.[10]

Other 'internal émigrés' were less spiritual, less high-minded in their rejection of expatriation. Pilnyak, whose alleged indifference to political issues made him a target for abuse and persecution, was once asked why he did not take up residence in London, and rejected the idea on purely financial grounds. 'What can I do there? I earn a great deal at home, and so does my wife. But refugees live poorly.'[11]

The First Emigration ended in 1923 with the imposition of restrictions on leaving the country that virtually stopped self-expatriation until the Second World War. However, the leading poet Vyacheslav Ivanov successfully emigrated in 1924, settled in Rome, embraced Catholicism and held aloof from the international community of Russian expatriates. A still more exceptional case occurred in 1931, when Yevgeny Zamyatin, author of the anti-Communist satirical fantasy *We*, made personal application by letter to Stalin, asking that he should be permitted to go abroad and practise the profession of letters, which had been made impossible for him in Russia.[12] His outspoken appeal was risky in the context of growing persecution; but it provoked one of the dictator's isolated acts of clemency, for Zamyatin did indeed receive permission to emigrate, and he died six years later in Paris. His legally permitted act of self-exile is unparalleled in the 1930s, when Soviet citizens, whether writers or not, were prevented from travelling abroad except on official missions. A similar request, addressed to Stalin by the novelist and playwright Mikhail Bulgakov, was turned down.

The Second Emigration resulted from the Second World War, during which some five million Russians moved or were transported into areas west of the pre-war Soviet frontier, whether as refugees, forced labourers or prisoners of war. The majority were restored to Soviet residence, and in many cases to renewed persecution, by the advancing Red Army and through harshly implemented repatriation agreements with the Western allies. But many hundreds of thousands avoided repatriation, constituting a formidable addition to the now ageing ranks of the First Emigration. The Second Emigration has tended to establish itself in America, with New York as its main cultural centre. Here, by contrast with Paris of the 1920s and 1930s, assimilation to the host country has been fairly intensive. Second-wave Russian emigrants have been active in American academic and other cultural life, and have contributed to émigré Russian-language periodicals. But though they have included a number of original imaginative writers, none of them has yet become established as a leading name in modern literature.

By contrast with the first two waves of emigration, that of the 1970s has been carefully controlled by the State, and has principally affected members of non-Russian nationalities: over a hundred thousand Jews have been permitted to leave, largely for Israel; some ten thousand Soviet citizens of German stock have also been permitted to emigrate during the same period. Together with this relatively large efflux the State has simultaneously permitted or contrived the expatriation of certain prominent Russian or Russian-Jewish writers. Only a dozen or so have been affected, but their literary importance makes this aspect of the Third Emigration more relevant to our study than the exodus of Jews and Germans. The policy of expelling or releasing individuals has been applied to authors considered trouble-makers after offending by publishing works abroad, by engaging in protest movements and the like. Most had already been subjected to persecution on Soviet soil – arrest, imprisonment, incarceration in psychiatric clinics, general harassment – during the years preceding the decision to sanction or impose expatriation.

The first such action occurred in 1966, when the fiction-writer Valery Tarsis unexpectedly received permission to travel abroad, only to find his Soviet citizenship revoked during his absence, so that he had in effect been exiled. In 1972 the poet Iosif Brodsky was forced to leave the USSR, to be followed in the next year by Andrey Sinyavsky, who was permitted to emigrate with his wife and child; both Sinyavsky and Brodsky had previously served penal sentences as a result of their literary activities. The most notable of all the third-emigration expulsions occurred in February 1974, when the premier literary rebel Solzhenitsyn was forcibly flown out of his native country under escort and dumped in Frankfurt-am-Main; he has since resided in Switzerland and the United States. Among other important writer-dissidents, permitted to leave and take up residence outside the Communist orbit, have been Andrey Amalrik, Aleksandr Galich, Anatoly Gladilin, Natalya Gorbanevskaya, Naum Korzhavin, Vladimir Maksimov, Vladimir Maramzin, Viktor Nekrasov and Aleksandr Zinovyev, to which important names may be added that of the distinguished literary scholar Yefim Etkind.

The third-wave emigrants have continued culturally active, and they publish a remarkably rich and varied array of literary journals in Paris, Tel Aviv and other parts of the globe.

4 Writers and their Work

In this chapter an attempt is made to trace the general shape of the modern literature within each of its major genres: poetry, prose fiction, memoirs, drama and criticism. The need for such a survey is dictated by the complexity of the material, and by the fact that even the leading modern authors are far less familiar to Western readers (as is noted in the Introduction) than are the great Russian novelists of the nineteenth century. So numerous, indeed, are the important authors of the Soviet period that not a few significant names will be mentioned only perfunctorily or not at all – a form of self-denial without which the material would have degenerated into a skeletal catalogue or bald bibliography. The review is designed to include the most important authors enjoying the blessing of Soviet authority, but also non-approved figures widely admired by those, in Russia and abroad, who are indifferent or opposed to the official processing of literature in the USSR. High reputation in one or other of these areas, and not infrequently in both, has been the main criterion for deciding how to site and move the spotlight. That connoisseurs of the literature may find parts of this idiosyncratic, and neglectful of their own particular favourites, is likely; but it is impossible to keep the chart clear and helpful without passing over many intricate ramifications that cannot be unravelled in a brief study.

Poetry

Many connoisseurs regard modern Russian poetry as superior in originality and aesthetic appeal to modern Russian prose, and a leading specialist has made a claim for the verse such as few would make for its prose: 'From, roughly, 1895 to 1930 great poetry was uninterruptedly written by no less than twenty first-rank poets.'[1]

As this date span emphasizes, the political revolutions of 1917 had been preceded and overrun by the poetical revolution that had begun in the 1890s. It was pioneered by the Symbolist movement which arose in opposition to Russian Realism and to theories sometimes associated with the Realist School: that art should purvey instruction, either fostering social reform or teaching individuals how they could best live their lives. The Symbolists, by contrast, proclaimed the primacy of art over life, often associating poetry with religious or metaphysical conceptions; they pioneered new technical devices, attaching supreme importance to poetic language, to metrics and to imagery. Often obscure in meaning and purport, their work took its place as part of the European Symbolist movement and of modernist and *avant-garde* currents in the arts as a whole: trends that some Russians lumped together under the disrespectful title *dekadentstvo* ('decadence'). The most renowned of the Symbolist poets is Aleksandr Blok, other leading figures being Konstantin Balmont, Valery Bryusov and Zinaida Gippius.

By 1910 Symbolism itself was in decline, but experimental and *avant-garde* tendencies remained in vogue among the movement's successors and rivals, who largely abandoned Symbolism's religious and transcendental elements: Acmeists, Imaginists and Futurists. War and revolution struck Russia at a point when a score of major poets of these and other schools were producing or about to produce some of their most original work. Far from inhibiting their activities, the upheavals of the period were for many a stimulus. As we have seen, Civil War conditions even benefited verse production in that short poems could be published or circulated at a time of paper shortage, also lending themselves to recital at public assemblies and the numerous poets' cafés of the period. Here the impassioned declamation of new verse punctuated heated arguments about who, among those present, must be considered the world's greatest living genius.

For a few years poetry enjoyed a near-monopoly, and many poets briefly flourished. Eventually, however, 'Soviet cultural policies brought total tragedy to every single one of the ... major poets who were active at the time of the Revolution.' Such is the claim, slightly exaggerated perhaps, of a literary scholar whose own tally of major poets active in 1917 is eighteen.[2] Two of these, Blok and Bryusov, survived the Revolution by only a few years. Blok died in 1921, disillusioned with the new society that he had helped to acclaim with *The Twelve* (1918); this is the most famous of all poems celebrating the Revolution, and its enigmatic conclusion appears to associate the onward march of Bolshevism with the leadership of Jesus Christ. Bryusov joined the Communist Party in 1920; and he became, during the years left to him before his death in 1924, one of those literary functionaries who were charged with adjudicating the scale of food rations assigned to their colleagues.[3] Another leading Symbolist, Bely, has already been mentioned as returning from emigration to live relatively undisturbed in Soviet Russia, occupied largely with memoir-writing during the decade preceding his death in 1934.

One of the chief schools to succeed Symbolism was Futurism, which stressed experiment with language, specialized in shocking the bourgeoisie and advocated a total break with the art of the past. The movement's main pioneer, Velimir Khlebnikov, died in poverty in 1922, leaving Mayakovsky as the leading Futurist. He had more popular appeal than the excitingly obscure Khlebnikov, and successfully harnessed his verse to the purposes of Bolshevism. Many, including his friend and admirer Pasternak, have preferred his personal poetry, for much of his political versifying was ephemeral agitation; but he also composed impressive long and (in his own style) heroic poetic eulogies of the Revolution and its leaders, notably his *Vladimir Ilyich Lenin* (1924). Mayakovsky was too unruly an individual to suit an age of increasing regimentation, and his suicide in 1930 probably saved him from liquidation a few years later. By the time of the Yezhovschina he was already enjoying what is an overwhelming advantage in the USSR where officially determined literary reputation is concerned: that of being dead. His promotion as, in effect, the country's posthumous poet laureate took place after Stalin had been persuaded to sponsor him in 1935. Once the dictator had stated that 'Indifference to his [Mayakovsky's] memory and his works is a crime,' canonization became automatic. According to Pasternak, the compulsory cultivation of Mayakovsky resembled the enforced introduction of potatoes under Catherine the Great. A feature of the cult was the naming of tractors, minesweepers, tanks, streets, squares and an underground railway station after the poet.[4]

An earlier suicide had been Yesenin's in 1925 – an act held up to contempt in one of the future suicide Mayakovsky's most famous lyrics, *To Sergey Yesenin* (1926), as contravening the ethics of the

Bolshevik era. The great drunkard, lover and self-proclaimed hooligan Yesenin had, in life, been a successful rival *prima donna* to Mayakovsky. A peasant poet, writing on peasant themes, he denounced the urban civilization into which he had plunged, and which tantalized, revolted, uprooted and ultimately killed him.

Yesenin was the leading figure in the group called Imaginists from their emphasis on the importance of poetic imagery, and he has perhaps been the most widely popular of all the major modern Russian poets. Describing him as a writer 'for wide, general consumption', one critic goes on to specify Pasternak as, in effect, a poet for middle-brows, while, 'at the top, where he is available only to those who aspire to membership in a poetic elite, is Osip Mandelstam'.[5] As the phrasing suggests, Mandelstam offers great rewards to patient application. Much of his verse is difficult to assimilate without repeated re-reading and the aid of commentaries, of which several are now available. His life has been well called 'a paradigm of modern tragedy',[6] and he is significant as a subtle artist uniquely vulnerable to the pressures of a brutal age. The object of increasing official persecution from the mid-1920s onwards, he was congenitally incapable of simulating political conformism, possessing the considerable force of character that is not necessarily incompatible with a high degree of sensitivity. When, in the early 1930s, he wrote a notorious lyric disparaging Stalin – in one version as 'a mass murderer and destroyer of peasants'[7] – and did not take steps to prevent this from being circulated, he was possibly choosing a more complex form of suicide than Mayakovsky's bullet and Yesenin's noose. The poet died during the Terror, probably in a transit camp and probably in December 1938, after writing his 'Voronezh Notebooks' (1935–7) and other late lyrics that have come to light only in recent years; they form what is perhaps the most valuable Russian poetic contribution of their period.

Mandelstam belonged to the Acmeist group. It stressed precision of poetic expression and sought to take its place in the general cultural tradition of Western Europe, and of the ancient Greek and Roman civilizations from which that tradition stems. An earlier leading Acmeist, Nikolay Gumilyov, was executed in Petrograd in 1921. He perished for alleged participation in counter-revolutionary activity, being the first notability among Russian poetry's long list of post-1917 martyrs. As for the third noted Acmeist, Anna Akhmatova, she survived to die a natural death in 1966 after suffering privations and discomforts that included the imprisonment of her son and her starring role as scapegoat in the literary witch-hunt launched by Zhdanov in 1946. Despite long periods of silence she continued writing poetry up to her death. It includes the cycle of laments entitled *Requiem*, based on her experiences during the Terror; and a longer work, *Poem without a Hero*, in which she more elusively attempts to sum up the experiences of her era.

Boris Pasternak, who once said that he could make no sense of Akhmatova's *Poem without a Hero*,[8] was outstanding among poets less closely associated with specific schools. Though his name became a household word in the West in the late 1950s, with the foreign publication of his novel *Doctor Zhivago*, he is chiefly known as a lyric poet of great originality and force. His posthumous treatment by Soviet literary authority has involved a differentiation between his verse and his prose. As a prose author he is officially despised, rejected or ignored, but his poetry is praised and widely read, having been repeatedly published in selections.

These are some names from the older poetic generation, all of whom began publishing verse before the Revolution. All died in the USSR, as also did Marina Tsvetayeva after returning from emigration. As mention of this important poet reminds us, Russian verse long flourished abroad, and some of the most prominent expatriate poets have already been mentioned: Gippius; Khodasevich; Vyacheslav and Georgy Ivanov.

Rightly or wrongly, none of the poets who began publishing after the Revolution, whether in Russia or abroad, has been accorded the stature of the above, except that Eduard Bagritsky and Nikolay Zabolotsky, both USSR-based, stand particularly high in critical esteem. A prominent place among officially approved authors of verse has been occupied by Aleksandr Tvardovsky, who wrote in a peasant idiom reminiscent of the nineteenth-century poet Nekrasov, and whose work is easily understood and assimilated by non-intellectual readers; besides short lyrics it also includes *The Land of Muraviya* (1936), *Vasily Tyorkin* (1941–5) and other long narrative poems. Tvardovsky was no less renowned in his last years as Chief Editor of the leading monthly *Novy mir*.

It is less to these representatives of an earlier generation of poets than to their successors, who began publishing in the post-Stalin era, that attention has recently been directed. The most widely-advertised is Yevgeny Yevtushenko; a gifted versifier, he came to prominence under the poltical showman Khrushchev, with whom he sometimes engaged in public cross-talk acts. As was appropriate to that flamboyant age, mass poetry recitals were given before audiences of many thousands; for example in the Luzhniki Stadium in Moscow. Adjudged suitable for export, such performances have also been staged before smaller audiences in cultural centres outside the Soviet orbit, by Yevtushenko, Andrey Voznesensky and others.

Though such foreign visits have continued into the Brezhnev era, mass recitals have been severely curtailed at home in keeping with the new dispensation's 'low profile'. Poetry has, accordingly, largely reverted to the private plane. The process may be traced back to the trial, on a charge of 'parasitism', of the Leningrad author Iosif Brodsky towards the end of the Khrushchev era. Widely admired as the most talented poet of the younger generation, Brodsky has barely been published in the Soviet Union, but his work began to be issued abroad before his enforced emigration to the West in 1972.

USSR-domiciled Russians have had varyingly restricted access to their own poetry. During the Stalin era only Blok, Bryusov, Yesenin and Mayakovsky, among major poets, enjoyed full official recognition, all of them being conveniently dead. Other poets were banned, and even killed, but later rehabilitated, belatedly republished in slanted selections with slanted introductions and in printings that fell far below the demand and were largely sold abroad. But these restrictions have only stimulated the educated Russian's poetic thirst, which patently exceeds that of his Western counterpart. Volumes of verse exchange hands for large sums on the black market, recent Soviet-published editions being far more easily purchased in the West than in the USSR.

What of Russians' attitude to their own poetry? Reporting an American translator's opinion, that Blok was a 'highly overrated' poet, a Russian scholar has added that to make this remark in Russia would be to risk being lynched on the spot.[9] A similar point was once made in a different way by Mandelstam, in his bitterly ironical and prophetic comment on official cultural policies. 'Only in Russia is poetry respected – it gets people killed. Is there anywhere else where poetry is so common a motive for murder?'[10] Poets done to death by authority, readers threatened with lynching for expressing a deviant opinion on prosody – here are indexes of a literary culture exalted beyond the aspirations of more humdrum civilizations.

From the early post-revolutionary years with their café poets, to the later mass meetings of poetry-lovers in the Luzhniki Stadium, verse recitals have occupied a prominent place in post-revolutionary, as in pre-revolutionary, social life. They have often developed into public scandals or demonstrations. In the winter of 1921 Tsvetayeva gave a recital including several poems praising the White Army in the Civil War – and that to audiences of Red Army men, Communists and revolutionary students.[11] On other occasions – recitals by Mandelstam in 1933 and by Pasternak in 1948 – the audience has eagerly participated in turning a poetry reading into a public display of non-conformist political sentiment.[12] That many of those who attend these performances do so for love of poetry we do not dispute. But it must also be added that they go to enjoy a public display of nerve by the poet. How far will he venture in challenging by implication the political and other assumptions imposed by Soviet authority? How skilful will he prove in deploying the language of oblique hints and ironical innuendo inevitable on these occasions? Expert beyond the dreams of any Western audience in monitoring such refinements, the Soviet poetry-lover is kept in a delicious state of tension: his idol may delicately taunt the Kremlin and remain unscathed; or (even more gratifying to some) he may find himself in serious trouble. It is not surprising that these displays also provoke the enthusiastic frenzy of 'bobby-soxers' who are liable to rend the poet's handkerchief into shreds and even to make off with his cigarette ends.[13]

Not always has close rapport been achieved between audience and poet on such occasions. In April 1930, five days before his suicide, Mayakovsky gave a recital that revealed a total lack of sympathy between himself and a new type of audience largely drawn from the communized younger generation. Disillusionment over this fiasco presumably contributed to his decision to kill himself a few days later.[14]

Before leaving the verse form we must note that Russians make a formal distinction between two kinds of writing jointly embraced by the English term 'poetry': short lyrics (*stikhotvoreniya*) and longer poetical works (*poemy*). The former are, on the whole, the better known both at home and abroad, being also the more suitable for public recitation. But most leading poets other than Mandelstam have practised both genres, and longer poems by Akhmatova, Mayakovsky and Tvardovsky have been mentioned above. Among poets who particularly excelled with *poemy* may also be instanced Bagritsky, Bely and Khlebnikov; but Pasternak's long poems written between 1923 and 1931 (*The High Malady, The Year 1905, Lieutenant Shmidt* and *Spektorsky*) have not on the whole enjoyed a vogue comparable to that of his lyrics.

Prose Fiction

In this brief literary survey poetry has been given pride of place, but without any intended disparagement of prose fiction; nor has it been forgotten that many writers, including Bunin, Mandelstam, Nabokov and Pasternak, have practised both genres. Whatever the comparative value of the verse and the prose may be, the latter inevitably has the greater importance for foreign readers ignorant of Russian, owing to the greater effectiveness with which the prose-writer's statement can be conveyed in translation. It is natural, therefore, that no verse of the period has attained best-seller status abroad, whereas not a few works of modern Russian prose fiction have been widely read all over the world. Many have succeeded in terms of critical as well as commercial esteem – especially the writings of Bunin, Gorky, Nabokov, Pasternak, Sholokhov and Solzhenitsyn.

One feature of Soviet-published belles-lettres will already be familiar to students of the nineteenth century. Literary works still normally receive their first publication in periodicals, novels of any length being issued in serialized instalments – usually as a prelude to appearing in book form after an interval of a year or two. In its inordinate length (as it is sometimes felt) the modern Russian novel preserves, if in nothing else, the traditions of Dostoyevsky and Tolstoy. With regard to some inferior works, which need not be named here, cynics may feel that excess of bulk has owed less to creative inspiration than to a system of remuneration based chiefly on length, by contrast with the sales-determined royalty system prevalent in the West.

However high or low the motives inspiring individual writers may have been, the monumental novel reasserted its status in the early 1920s as the Russian literary genre *par excellence*. Its introduction or revival was pioneered by Konstantin Fedin with his *Cities and Years* (1924). It held sway for over three decades, entering a state of decline in the late 1950s; for though the earlier monumental fiction includes much of what is most memorable in the modern literature, 'Nearly all the large novels of the past twenty years have been stodgy, formula-ridden and ponderous', according to a recent (1978) authoritative statement.[1]

There is a tendency not only for individual novels to be extremely long, but also for strings of thematically linked novels to be grouped together under separate titles in couples, trilogies, tetralogies and so on. Though such Western authors as Marcel Proust and Anthony Powell furnish a rough parallel, the multi-volume novel is more a tradition of the Soviet than of the Western publishing world. Many of these extensively articulated works have appeared over periods stretching into three decades, and the time span of their overall narrative may be still more extensive.

An example is Valentin Katayev's Odessa-based tetralogy, first published as a whole in 1961 under the blanket title *The Waves of the Black Sea*. It had begun life in 1936 as a single novel about two boys, set against the background of the 1905 Revolution and entitled *Lonely White Sail*. This was later to become Part One of the tetralogy. The succeeding parts carry the narrative into the Second World War, and are as follows: *A Small Farm in the Steppe* (1956); *Winter Wind* (1960); *The Catacombs* (1961). As for the twenty-year hiatus (1936–56) between the publication of the first two parts, this is paralleled in the work of many others. We may compare, for instance, the dating of Galina Serebryakova's trilogy of historical novels on the life of Karl Marx under the general title *Prometheus*. It first appeared as follows: *Marx's Youth* (1934–5); *The Theft of Fire* (1961); *Life's Summits* (1962). With Serebryakova, as with Katayev, the gap of two or more decades is obviously due to inhibitions imposed by the Stalin dictatorship; in the former's case these included prolonged imprisonment.

That a novel sequence may not only straddle two epochs, but even two worlds, is shown by Aleksey Tolstoy's trilogy *The Way through Hell*. The first part, eventually entitled *Sisters*, was written in emigration and published in 1920, being later revised and dovetailed into the sequels *The Year 1918* and *A Dull Morning*, with which the author continued the work after his return to Russia in 1923. Not until 1943 was the complete canonical text established by Tolstoy.[2] The trilogy covers the years of the Revolution and Civil War, portraying four members of the pre-revolutionary middle classes as they learn to live with the new dispensation.

Though Tolstoy's trilogy remains a major monument, it has never equalled the status of Mikhail Sholokhov's *The Quiet Don*. That was first published between 1928 and 1940, a comparatively small time span in the context, and is another phenomenally bulky work. But though its 1,500-odd pages are grouped in four 'books', Sholokhov did not give them separate titles, and so the work is not strictly speaking a tetralogy. An additional complication derives from a decision by the novel's first English publisher to bring out the work – as translated by 'Stephen Garry' (H. C. Stevens) – under two titles, thus suggesting that two separate works are involved: *And Quiet Flows the Don* and *The Don Flows Home to the Sea*. About a quarter of the text was omitted from this version, so that it diverges considerably from any of the numerous Russian recensions. A fuller English text, closer to one of the original recensions (the 1956 Russian edition), is that by Robert Daglish as published in Moscow without dateline in 1960.[3] Despite the variety of its various manifestations *The Quiet Don* represents one of the principal literary achievements of the period. It is another panoramic survey taking in the First World War, the Revolution and the Civil War, but is geographically and ethnically restricted by comparison with Tolstoy's trilogy, in that the Don Cossack people and lands dominate so much of the narrative. The writing of Sholokhov's other major novel, *Virgin Soil Upturned*, was interspersed with that of *The Quiet Don*. The second work is a study of collectivization, and appeared in 1932 (Part One); but the long-awaited Part Two was delayed until 1959, and is generally regarded as inferior – as is *Virgin Soil Upturned* as a whole, for all its merits – to *The Quiet Don*.

Among novel sequences first published in the post-war period an important place is occupied by Fedin's trilogy (*Early Joys*, 1945; *No Ordinary Summer*, 1947–8; *The Bonfire*, 1967). Fedin had been a member of the fellow-travelling group called the Serapion Brothers, who cultivated literary independence in the 1920s. Having been interned in Germany during the First World War, he was well versed in German and Western European culture – themes prominent in his early writing. His first major novel, *Cities and Years*, is to some extent an *avant-garde* work, owing to the deliberate shuffling of the time sequence in the narrative – a device such as the more mature Fedin has dutifully avoided in accordance with the practice of Socialist Realism. Other important early novels were Boris Pilnyak's *The Naked Year* (1921); Fyodor Gladkov's *Cement* (1925); Dmitry Furmanov's *Chapayev* (1923). As the last-mentioned work reminds us, this was a period when individual heroic leaders were accorded particularly close attention in fiction, by contrast with later attempts to give more emphasis to collective responses. Nor was Fedin the only author of the 1920s to use impressionistic and experimental verbal or structural ornamentation such as later became taboo. On the contrary, 'ornamental' prose was for a time extensively cultivated.

Among the novelists who avoided such methods was the straightforward Aleksandr Fadeyev, who also eschewed sequences of thematically linked novels; his three major works – *The Rout* (1925–6), *The Last of the Udege* (1929–41) and *The Young Guard* (1945 and 1951) – are all self-contained. But the second remained unfinished at the time of the author's death, which may have been hastened by his tribulations in rewriting the third at the behest of the Party.

The early 1930s witnessed an officially imposed concentration on Five Year Plan novels – works advertising the achievements of Stalinism in intensifying industrialization and collectivizing agriculture. The better-known examples include Sholokhov's above-mentioned *Virgin Soil Upturned*, Marietta Shaginyan's *Hydrocentral* (1930–1), Valentin Katayev's *Time, Forward* (1932), Ilya Ehrenburg's *The Second Day* (1934) and two (*Sot* and *Skutarevsky*) by Leonid Leonov, another author to avoid the articulated chain-novel.

Leonov's *œuvre* includes as its major component a sequence of six independent novels of great originality and subtlety which, in combination, make him the foremost USSR-based contributor to the genre during the Stalin period. His peculiar skill lay in cultivating an ingeniously oblique approach that enabled him to work within the censorship, while yet continuing to present a world all his own and to project a markedly individual literary personality. He covers many facets of Soviet life and society, which makes him an author of great importance to the present study, and the following is a brief indication of his range as illustrated in the six long novels. *The Badgers* (1924) deals with peasant unrest during and after the Civil War, stressing the conflict between town and country. *The Thief* (1927) studies the fringes of the criminal underworld in the NEP period. Of Leonov's two Five Year Plan novels *Sot* (1931) depicts the construction of a paper mill in the far north, while *Skutarevsky* (1932) studies the world of scientists and managers as newly evolved under intensive industrialization. *Road to the Ocean* (1936) is a long semi-fantasy uniting many of the above themes. Finally, the last and the longest – *The*

Russian Forest (1953) – is partly an allegory in which Leonov voices a conservationist's protest against the wanton destruction of the country's timber resources, while daring to make it clear that he wishes the mass annihilation of Russia's woodlands to be interpreted as a symbol for the mass liquidation of her peoples under the Terror.

To the many long novels of the period also belongs Gorky's four-part saga, *The Life of Klim Samgin* (1925–36). It describes the hesitancies of a liberal intellectual, the lawyer whose name appears in the title; he is shown falling short of the demands of his epoch between the mid-1870s and 1917 in an epic of non-fulfilment that still remained unfinished after extending to some 1,700 pages of print. In an earlier, shorter novel, *The Artamonov Business* (1925), the same author reviews the rise of a pre-revolutionary commercial enterprise and its collapse in 1917. We therefore note that all Gorky's major fiction of the Soviet period is set in the pre-Soviet era, and though we can hardly call either of the above-mentioned works a historical novel, since the action is set in the author's own lifetime, they may serve to remind us of the important part played in the modern fiction by studies located in the more distant past. The vogue of the historical genre is partly due to the fact that events remote in time have tended to be relatively safe, politically, by comparison with contemporary themes, with which authors need to tread particularly warily.

Notable historical fiction includes Vasily Yan's trilogy on the Mongol-Tatar invasion of Russia in the thirteenth century: *Genghis Khan* (1939); *Baty* (1942) and *To the Last Sea* (1955). A fourteenth-century Russian national hero is commemorated in Sergey Borodin's *Dmitry Donskoy* (1941), while the seventeenth-century leader of a peasant rebellion against the Tsar of Muscovy is the subject of Aleksey Chapygin's 1,000-page *Stepan Razin* (1926). A theme of the later seventeenth century inspired Aleksey Tolstoy's *Peter the First* (1929–45), describing the childhood and early manhood of Peter the Great. Among historical novels devoted to the early nineteenth century we may note the trilogy by Yury Tynyanov: *Kyukhlya* (1925), *The Death of Vazir-Mukhtar* (1927–8) and *Pushkin* (1935–43); the last is devoted to Russia's national poet and the first two to his author-contemporaries, Küchelbecker and Griboyedov respectively. More recently Bulat Okudzhava has also published historical novels set in Russia of the same period, while Yury Trifonov has portrayed the revolutionary terrorists of the later nineteenth century, and their assassination (in

1881) of the Emperor Alexander II, in his *Impatience* (1973). Another nineteenth-century setting, and a foreign one too, is that of Serebryakova's trilogy on the life of Karl Marx, mentioned above. Nor have military themes of the early nineteenth and twentieth centuries been neglected. In his 1,600-page *The Martydom of Sevastopol* (1936–8) Sergey Sergeyev-Tsensky portrays a key amphibious operation of the Crimean War, as a prelude to commemorating a notable feat of Russian arms on the Austrian front in 1916 with his *Brusilov's Breakthrough* (1943). Naval warfare, and the annihilation of the Russian fleet by the Japanese in 1905, is the theme of Aleksey Novikov-Priboy's *Tsushima* (1932–5).

We have now considered some of the bulkiest items, and the time has come to review less extensive works: shorter novels and short stories. We shall also take the opportunity to glance at material in which the full, frontal, serious exposure of stark reality is avoided: humorous works, satire, fantasy, science fiction and writing for children.

Short items of fiction are called either *povesti* or *rasskazy*, partly according to their length, the former tending to be longer than the latter. *Povest* is also regarded as a more ennobling designation than *rasskaz*, for which reason Solzhenitsyn's *One Day in the Life of Ivan Denisovich* was billed under the former heading to 'give it weight', on the insistence of his editor and to his own later regret.[4] The work was long enough to be published as a self-contained book in English translation, for which reason English readers may easily think of it as a short novel. Some attempt has been made, by Solzhenitsyn and others, to differentiate the *povest* from the novel (*roman*) on the basis of technique. The former has been called paratactical, the latter syntactical; the former has been said to deal with mono-linear, the latter with multi-linear themes. But the fact is that no hard and fast distinction betwen these allegedly separate genres is maintained in practice; it is simplest and most helpful to regard a *povest* as either a long story or a short novel.[5]

As the consideration of shorter items of fiction will indicate, there is some correlation between a work's brevity and its political unacceptability. The monumental novels mentioned earlier have had their troubles, and were in some cases subjected to politically dictated revision. But the mere fact that material so extensive could secure Soviet publication at all, and in many cases over a long span of years, is an index of its respectability. The shorter a work is the better adapted it is likely to prove for infringing political taboos, besides which shorter works also lend themselves more easily to duplication in the form of *samizdat*.

Whether termed *rasskazy* or *povesti*, short stories and novels have been contributed over the years by many of the novelists previously mentioned. But the period's most celebrated exponent of fictional brevity has been Isaak Babel, who avoided the novel while contributing sequences of very brief, thematically linked anecdotes or sketches, documentary rather than imaginative in content. In his collections *Cavalry Army* (1926) and *Odessa Stories* (1927) scenes of extreme violence are viewed through a veil of idiosyncratic irony. The writing is sparse, economical and highly polished, its author being regarded by many as the most significant of all post-revolutionary Russian prose writers.

Babel's writings were much acclaimed in Russia of the 1920s, but failed to satisfy the demands of rampant Stalinism in the following decade, presumably because of the author's highly individual approach and insistence on viewing the world through his own pair of spectacles. In the 1930s he virtually abandoned creative writing, practising what he called the 'genre of silence' and thus becoming a suspect figure before being liquidated in the Terror. Another noted prose ironist, Andrey Platonov, escaped the severer forms of persecution, contributing both short stories and novels that were either never published in the USSR, or were suppressed in the 1930s after earlier publication, but then posthumously and selectively revived in the post-Stalin era.

Among shorter fictional works of the early Soviet period none has had more impact in the USSR and abroad than Yury Olesha's *povest* of about 120 pages, *Envy* (1927). It is remarkable for the insight with which the author explores the clash between the demands of Communist society, personified by one Babichev (an expert in the manufacture of sausages), and the strivings of the individual as represented by Babichev's *protégé*, the indecisive Kavalerov. In course of time *Envy* proved unacceptable to fully-fledged Stalinist authority owing to its lack of ideological clarity, besides which it also erred in employing symbolism and a mixture of narrative angles. For these reasons it was consigned to neglect in the 1930s, but republished in 1956 with other works by Olesha.

Together with Ilf and Petrov, to be mentioned below, the leading humorous author of the period is Mikhail Zoshchenko, whose most characteristic writings are short, comic sketches depicting the petty tribulations of everyday life. *The Poker* (1940) does so while portraying a dilemma such as is familiar to many a foreign student of the Russian language. It describes the chaos created in a Soviet office when the time comes to indent for five new pokers, the difficulty being that none of those involved knows the genitive plural (obligatory after the number five) of the word for 'poker', *kocherga* (the correct form is *kocheryog*). Zoshchenko's most typical work avoids the faintest hint of the heroic and idealizing style that became *de rigueur* by the mid-1930s, when he somewhat modified his approach. Official disapproval of his work culminated in his public disgrace in 1946: partly for a story (*Adventures of a Monkey*, 1945) allegedly implying that life was better for the inmates of Soviet zoos than for the country's human citizens. Zoshchenko was a complex individual, who also wrote introspective fiction incorporating tragic themes and lacking the humorous approach of his best-known work. As a result of his individualism and inability, despite efforts on his part, to meet official requirements, he lived out his later years in obscurity and poverty, but was not subjected to the harsher forms of persecution practised under Stalin. That it was not impossible to keep humour within the bounds of the permissible, though with considerable loss of effectiveness, is shown by the career of Leonid Lench, who continued publishing his humorous sketches in the Stalin period, having cultivated a skill in manœuvring denied to Zoshchenko.

Among humorous writings various picaresque novels of the 1920s and early 1930s are outstanding, and describe the adventures of amiable scoundrels who exploit Soviet dispensations to their personal advantage. The most celebrated is Ostap Bender, described as the Great Operator; his ingenious confidence tricks enliven two particularly renowned works: *Twelve Chairs* (1928) and *The Golden Calf* (1931) by Ilf and Petrov. The latter contains a scene set in a Soviet lunatic asylum where an accountant has taken refuge after simulating insanity, but only to discover that the other inmates are also malingerers; the true lunatics are, of course, those who continue to inhabit the world outside. An earlier picaresque novel is *The Embezzlers* (1926) by Valentin Katayev, whose younger brother Yevgeny happens to have been the pseudonymous 'Petrov' in the combination 'Ilf and Petrov' mentioned above.

Fantasy and science fiction also flourished in the 1920s. Such a work is Aleksey Tolstoy's novel *Aelita* (1923), depicting an expedition to Mars which witnesses that planet undergoing a proletarian revolution. A still more successful fantasist was Mikhail Bulgakov. His imaginative flights include *The Fatal Eggs* (1925), describing a world terrorized by giant reptiles; *The Heart of a Dog* (1925), in which a dog lectures his owner on civil rights; and above all the multi-level *The Master and Margarita* (1928–40), embracing both the crucifixion of Jesus Christ as it may have taken place in about 30 AD and the activities of the Devil as deployed in the Soviet Union of the 1930s. The work also satirizes writers' associations, portraying an imaginary organization entitled Massolit, and thereby ridiculing literary-bureaucratic activity as deployed in Herzen House in Moscow, a centre for authors and journalists.[6] These works by Bulgakov have met a variety of fates. *The Fatal Eggs* appeared in a Soviet publication; *The Master and Margarita* was rescued from oblivion and given posthumous Soviet publication in 1966–7; *The Heart of a Dog* has never been published in the Soviet Union, and so comes in the Export Only category.

Still more escapist in character are the fantasies of Aleksandr Grin set in an imaginary world, 'Grinland'. His works fell under a ban at about the time of his death in 1932, but were extensively and successfully published in large editions from 1956 onwards. Among more recent fantasists are Ivan Yefremov, and also the Strugatsky brothers, Arkady and Boris; they have published some memorable science fiction in the 1960s and 1970s, by no means abandoning the tradition of Bulgakov, whereby fantasy, like the picaresque novel, easily veers into satire.

Another form of literary escapism has been practised by Mikhail Prishvin, a much-travelled author who was in his ninth decade when he died in Moscow in 1954. In his numerous sketches and stories he has chronicled the flora and fauna of North Russia, the Urals, the Far East and Central Asia, adroitly eluding the obligation to incorporate political messages by avoiding, often enough, human themes altogether.

Children's literature has provided yet another refuge from political pressures and has been successfully cultivated by the literary historian and critic Korney Chukovsky, whose works in this genre include *The Adventures of Krokodil Krokodilovich* (1921) and *From Two to Five* (1925). Samuil Marshak, author of the comic verse published under the title *Mister Twister* (1933), is also renowned as a children's writer.

A younger epigone of these two masters, Sergey Mikhalkov, has succeeded so well financially with his writings for the young that the phrase 'rich as Mikhalkov' has become proverbial.[7]

As has already been indicated, techniques of fiction-writing have undergone considerable modification from the mid-1950s onwards. Since then many of the most notable authors have come to favour the short story or *povest* rather than the novel, or the short novel of manageable length rather than the multi-volume 'block-buster' of the Stalin era; which is not by any means to say that the novel has died out, or lost all its importance, in recent years. Meanwhile the post-Stalin reduction of ideological pressures, combined with a relaxation of the requirements enforced in the name of Socialist Realism, has freed authors from the obligation to infuse their work with optimistic political messages. This has made possible descriptions of everyday life, of urban and rural conditions, and of domestic and moral predicaments – all portrayed without militantly improving overtones such as were obligatory under Stalin. Among such politically detached works are the short stories of Sergey Antonov, Irina Grekova, Yury Kazakov, Yury Nagibin, Vasily Shukshin, Vladimir Tendryakov and Yury Trifonov. Several of these authors have taken Chekhov as their literary model, being comparatively laconic where their major predecessors were verbose. No longer, moreover, does fiction exclusively purvey the plain, straightforward – albeit lengthy and often blatantly falsified – statements of the Stalin era, since scope now exists for hints, half-statements and narrative creatively blurred to the point where the author's intentions may even become a matter for heated dispute. Alongside this more sophisticated, less explicit narrative technique – which to some extent represents a return to the traditions of the 1920s – practitioners of the more direct approach, as familiar from the Stalin era, continue to ply their trade.

The politically neutral area of Soviet-published post-Stalin fiction includes one particularly flourishing genre, that of Village Prose. Its main achievement is to chronicle rural life affectionately and faithfully, with respect for traditional features and in an elegiac spirit utterly at variance with former practice; see pages 162–4. Mention must also be made of the more evanescent movement known as Youth Prose, which arose in the early 1960s, and of which Vasily Aksyonov, author of *A Ticket to the Stars* (1961), has been an outstanding exponent. This specialized in the portrayal of the cynical young in revolt against the older generation, and was especially notable for contravening established canons by the use of racy dialogue. There is a lavish infusion of slang expressions such as were taboo under fully Stalinized Socialist Realism, and not a little 'stream-of-consciousness' first-person narrative. However, as has been well noted, the youthful heroes usually contrive to overcome their mutinous urges, their wining, wenching and other forms of anti-social activity, only to end up dutifully toiling away at some Siberian hydro-electric station like any run-of-the-mill Positive Hero.[8] After Brezhnev's rise to power, followed by a tendency to cultivate colourlessness in all walks of Soviet life, Youth Prose, with its jazzy, off-beat, 'do-your-own-thing' flavour, died a natural death, at least in its most extreme form.

Some of the best-known and most admired fiction of the period falls into the Export Only category. Bulgakov's *The Heart of a Dog* has already been mentioned, and so too has by far the most celebrated early specimen of the type, Zamyatin's *We*. So harshly critical of early Soviet dispensations was this inverted Utopia that it could not be brought out in Russia even in the early 1920s, but was published abroad in English and Czech translation; not until 1952 was *We* first published in full in Russian, in New York. Of other novels, written on Soviet soil but published only in the West, we remember Pasternak's *Doctor Zhivago* (1957) as the first notable post-war example. It has been followed by many others, among which those of Solzhenitsyn, *Cancer Ward*, *The First Circle* (both 1968) and *August 1914* (1971), have attracted most attention. Both authors have been awarded Nobel Prizes, Pasternak in 1958 and Solzhenitsyn in 1971. Sholokhov received a Nobel Prize in 1965 – the only Russian author enjoying the fairly consistent approval of Soviet authority to have obtained that honour. The remaining Russian Nobel Prize for Literature has already been mentioned: that awarded, in 1933, to Ivan Bunin, the leading émigré Russian author of his day.

Among Export Only satirical fantasists Andrey Sinyavsky and Yuly Daniel made their mark in the West with stories published (under the pseudonyms 'Abram Tertz' and 'Nikolai Arzhak' respectively) in the 1960s. A more recent outstanding Export Only satirist and humorist is Vladimir Voynovich, whose *The Life and Extraordinary Adventures of Private Ivan Chonkin* was begun in 1963 and is still unfinished; the first two parts were published in Paris in 1975. Another, still more recent – and far more sharply satirical – work is the fantasy

The Yawning Heights (1976) by Aleksandr Zinovyev, which ridicules the Soviet Union in the guise of an imaginary country – Ibansk. This represents the *reductio ad absurdum* of the closed society, its political leaders being those of recent Soviet history under recognizable pseudonyms, while the eventual doom of the Ibanskians as a whole is to perish from sheer boredom. The Export Only publication of this work resulted in its author's dismissal from his post as Professor of Logic at Moscow University's Institute of Philosophy. A little later he received permission to leave the USSR, and did so in August 1978. The same year also saw the publication, in Switzerland, of his second novel, *The Brilliant Future* – a satire depicting the tribulations of the Moscow intelligentsia in recent years.

Memoirs

It is difficult to exaggerate the importance to our subject of the vast corpus of memoir material – autobiographical and descriptive of writers and their society – by established authors and others. If we ask which foremost writers have contributed memoirs it might almost be easier to reply by listing those who have not. Many of these writings possess high literary merit, and one Western scholar has claimed Russians as 'indubitably the greatest memoirists in the world'.[1] The verdict is firmly supported by the best samples of the material. But what of the worst? They suffer from obvious defects: distortion of the facts, repetitiousness, vagueness, the self-congratulatory jactitation of emotion *à la russe*, and a tendency to reproduce in verbatim form, many years after the event, long conversations such as only the most exceptional human memory could have retained for five minutes, let alone for several decades. Nor are the best-written memoirs necessarily the most revealing and reliable.

The value of any memoir must partly depend on the extent to which its author has been controlled or intimidated by outside forces. Whereas Soviet-published material of the 1920s is particularly useful, that dating from Stalin's dictatorship can offer little more than vague intimations and indirect clues, while the post-1953 era has been highly informative by comparison with the preceding quarter of a century. But the best insights naturally come from those who have eluded or defied official controls by writing in emigration or by permitting work written in the USSR to be spirited abroad for publication.

Among celebrated earlier memoirists, writing in the Soviet period but largely on pre-revolutionary themes, is Maksim Gorky. His *My Universities* (1922) – a sarcastic title since his higher education was exclusively in the 'university of life' – concluded an autobiographical trilogy begun before the Revolution with *Childhood* (1913–14) and *In the World* (1915–16). This tripartite work is regarded as one of the author's finest. He has also left individual memoirs of figures from the literary and political world, those of Chekhov, Lyov Tolstoy and Lenin being outstanding. Other notable chronicles of childhood include a work largely set in pre-revolutionary Russia, but written and published in emigration: Nabokov's *Speak, Memory* (revised, English version 1966), which had already appeared in Russian in an earlier recension as *Other Shores* (1954). An author's youthful experiences also form the material of Aleksey Tolstoy's study of a young boy, *Nikita's Childhood* (1922). Though presented as a work of fiction, it is largely based on his own childhood and is widely regarded as his finest work. It thus continues a tradition represented in the nineteenth century by Sergey Aksakov and Lyov Tolstoy, both of whom also described their own families and childhood under invented names and in the guise of fiction.

Poets too have left their memoirs – some significant despite their brevity, such as those of Mandelstam and Pasternak, while others are valuable through their very bulk and wealth of detail, such as those of Bely. As for the many published memoirs describing poets, two useful accounts of Pasternak by close friends have recently become available as Export Only items: those of Alexander Gladkov (1977) and Olga Ivinskaya (1978).

It is perhaps worth briefly alluding to the indignation naturally aroused in USSR-based authors when they have chanced to read expatriate memoirists whose accounts seem, to survivors most closely involved, mischievously misleading. For example, Akhmatova was moved to protest in old age against versions of her own youthful activities by the expatriate memoirists Sergey Makovsky and Georgy Ivanov. Nor can credit be given to the latter's recollections of Mandelstam. Himself a major poet, Ivanov evidently overworked his creative imagination when offering, in his *St Petersburg Winters* (1928), what purports to be a factual account of the pre-revolutionary literary world.[2]

This kind of offence naturally seems particularly heinous to Soviet-domiciled readers; for *they* are often prevented from telling the truth while émigré memoirists are not – and therefore tend, when misrepresenting the facts, to seem guilty of cultivating mendacity for mendacity's sake.

Among Export Only memoirs the two long volumes *Hope Against Hope* and *All Hope Abandoned* (English editions, 1970 and 1974) by Nadezhda Mandelstam, widow of the poet who died in 1938, are especially revealing. They cover the entire span of our study except its last few years. Inside knowledge of the literary world, feeling for social pressures, lack of sentimentality, refusal to fictionalize – all these qualities help to give her work its special value, compensating for much repetitiousness and vagueness, especially about dates. One also notes a degree of bias, for the memoirist's contemporaries are sardonically weighed in the scale according to whether they harboured or sustained herself and her husband during their years of tribulation; not that this is, incidentally, the worst criterion of human worth.

Equally valuable in its different way is Solzhenitsyn's literary memoir *The Calf and the Oak* (1975). This is of greater technical interest than Nadezhda Mandelstam's books, for it takes the reader behind the scenes into editorial offices and literary-political committees to reveal a world of complex relationships more fully than previous disclosures had contrived. Moscow of the 1960s and early 1970s is the main arena, and the dominant character (after the author himself) is the poet and Chief Editor of the monthly *Novy mir*, Aleksandr Tvardovsky. He emerges both as a heroic figure of Shakespearian dimensions and (if the expression can be forgiven) an archetypal Russian 'slob': a muzhik Falstaff turned literary bureaucrat; see further, pages 234–60.

In *The Calf and the Oak* Solzhenitsyn records his contempt for the voluminous reminiscences, published in the Soviet press, of Ehrenburg (*People, Years, Life*; 1960–5) and Paustovsky (*The Story of a Life*; 1945–63). 'Writers who have witnessed a great and tragic age keep trying to creep through it in a crouching position while failing to say what really matters, offering a few trifles and smearing up our eyes with a palliative unguent to stop us seeing the truth.'[3] Solzhenitsyn asks what on earth they were afraid of, these established writers who were not personally threatened. The answer is, of course, that substantial self-censorship was an inevitable precondition for Soviet publication, and that these important memoirs would, if written with greater frankness, have remained unavailable unless their authors had been willing to launch them on the Export Only network.

For all the excess of caution in his *Peoples, Years, Life*, Ehrenburg at least broke certain taboos in that work. He was probably the first to refer in print to the Terror of the late 1930s by the common colloquial name Yezhovshchina, and he spoke of the purges more freely than many another contemporary in the age of so-called de-Stalinization: a timid operation even at its peak. Yet his references to the horrors of Stalinism have an air of remoteness – when he mentions the defunct dictator one might suppose him to be invoking an Aztec Emperor or Pharaoh, not someone who had occasionally spoken to him on the telephone. Moreover, valuable though Ehrenburg's witness is when he discusses his many writer friends, even Mayakovsky and Pasternak seem ghostlike on his pages, where Babel comes most fully to life. Babel also figures, with Bagritsky, Valentin Katayev, Olesha and other writers, in Paustovsky's six-part reminiscences covering some fifty years of pre-revolutionary and Soviet Russia.

An unusual position is occupied by Yevtushenko's *Precocious Autobiography*. As has been noted above, this was first brought out abroad in 1963, without having been published in the USSR; and it consequently became ineligible for publication in the author's homeland. The special feature is that Yevtushenko retained his position as an officially tolerated author and *enfant terrible* despite this brief excursion into the Export Only business.

Drama

After October 1917 Russia's Bolshevik rulers quickly showed that they regarded the stage as a vital formative influence in a society still largely illiterate. Theatres were speedily nationalized and used for propaganda purposes, free tickets being issued to visiting peasants, while many new actors were recruited and audience participation was elicited. The most extravagant of all these early productions was Nikolay Yevreinov's *Storming of the Winter Palace*, staged on location in the huge square before the actual building in Petrograd on 7 November 1920, exactly three years after the event, and culminating in the hoisting of the Red Flag on the Palace while a hundred thousand voices joined in singing the *Internationale*;[1] shortly afterwards the author and producer emigrated.

The further evolution of the stage followed that of the Soviet cultural world as a whole. Under NEP private theatres were permitted to re-emerge alongside those sponsored by the State, and the 1920s became famous for creative experimentalism and spectacular *avant-garde* productions in accordance with new techniques termed expressionist. A high point was Vsevolod Meyerhold's production, in 1929, of Mayakovsky's satirical comedy *The Bedbug* with incidental music by Shostakovich. The same author's *The Bath-House*, also directed by Meyerhold, followed in the next year. Other original producers of the period included Yevgeny Vakhtangov and Aleksandr Tairov.

Under the Stalin dictatorship the experiments of the 1920s were discouraged. Meyerhold was arrested and liquidated, and the theatre reverted to realism, sometimes called 'grey' realism, under the supervision of two veteran producers, Konstantin Stanislavsky and Vladimir Nemirovich-Danchenko. Both had been friends and associates of Chekhov in the distant past, and had revolutionized the Russian stage of their youth with the foundation of the Moscow Art Theatre in 1898. However, by the time of the Stalin dictatorship their techniques, once so original, had become ossified, while the Moscow Art Theatre, now named after Gorky and itself converted into a major cult object, was presenting Russia's nineteenth-century stage classics (predominant in the repertoire) as statuesque pageants rather than as living drama. As for modern plays by Russian authors, by the mid-1930s they had been emasculated under rampant Stalinism, being devoted to Positive Heroes and the like, with a few stage traitors and villains thrown in. During the war this didactic bias was naturally directed to military needs, as when Aleksandr Korneychuk's drama *The Front* (1942) portrayed the contrast between outmoded generals, whose methods had not changed since the Civil War, and pioneers of a new military philosophy geared to winning the campaigns that were proceeding even as the play went on to the stage.

Immediately after the war works by foreign, 'bourgeois' dramatists tended to dominate the Soviet theatre, provoking the Party decree of 26 August 1946, 'On Theatre Repertoires', whereby theatres were required to stage new, ideologically acceptable dramas portraying Soviet Man. In the outstandingly authoritarian years 1946–53 the theatre accordingly tended to concentrate on eulogies of everything Soviet and denunciations of foreigners, being especially hampered by the No Conflict theory; see pages 45 and 200-1.

A revival has followed in the post-Stalin years, which have seen many imaginative productions and restagings of successes of the 1920s, together with the disinterring of forgotten dramas from that earlier period. Though the *élan* of the early Soviet theatre has never been fully recaptured, there has at least been no return to the total paralysis of late Stalinism. Indeed, one recent observer believes that 'drama was the most lively and popular of the Soviet arts in the early Seventies', adding that no other medium lends itself so readily as the theatre to the 'duel between artist and censor'.[2] This gladiatorial contest between visible performers and the invisible force of authority lends piquancy to not a few Soviet cultural occasions, and especially to the theatrical.

The theatre of the Soviet period has been more remarkable for its actors, producers and designers than for its playwrights. There have, for example, been remarkably few authors of any stature writing chiefly or exclusively for the stage; Aleksandr Afinogenov and Aleksey Arbuzov are perhaps the most important. But many leading prose works of the period have been successfully dramatized – Leonov's *The Badgers*, for instance, and Vsevolod Ivanov's *Armoured Train 14-69*, adapted from the same authors' works of prose fiction with the same titles; and Bulgakov's *Days of the Turbins* (1926), based on his novel *The White Guard* (1924). Bulgakov also wrote several original dramas in the late 1920s, but these were banned from the stage after he had been repeatedly attacked by spokesmen of RAPP at the end of that decade. The author was then astonishingly rescued through the patronage and intervention of Stalin himself, who was so taken with *Days of the Turbins* that he ordered a special performance of it for his individual benefit in 1932, and is said to have sat through it fifteen times in all.[3] Bulgakov also wrote, in 1936-7, a notable fictional study of the theatre extensively based on his own experiences: *A Theatrical Novel*; it was first published in *Novy Mir* in 1965, twenty-five years after the author's death.

Among established authors Zamyatin enjoyed some success with his play *The Flea* (1925), as did Babel with his *Sunset* (1927); both authors wrote other plays too, and showed considerable capacity to develop before arrest (Babel) and emigration (Zamyatin) radically changed their slant towards the Soviet stage and existence in general. We must further add that Leonid Leonov, mentioned above as having dramatized his novel *The Badgers*, also wrote several original plays for the theatre, showing a flair for stage dialogue and retaining some of the capacity to surprise that characterizes his fiction. Other authors made more concessions to the political requirements of their age: Aleksey Tolstoy incorporated implied homage to Stalin in his drama in two parts *Ivan the Terrible* (1941–3); in his *The Unforgettable Year 1919* (1949) Vsevolod Vishnevsky magnifies Stalin's Civil War record out of all recognition.

Besides Mayakovsky, whose *Bedbug* and *Bath-House* have been mentioned above, the most significant of the era's fantasizing stage satirists was Yevgeny Shvarts. His dramatized tales for children, including *The Naked King* (1934) and *The Dragon* (1943–4), were easily interpretable as indictments of Stalin. They therefore remained unstaged during the dictator's lifetime, but were revived, in print and in the theatre, in the 1950s and 1960s.

Criticism

Literary criticism has followed the general cultural contours of the period: it operated with relative and increasingly impaired freedom in the 1920s; it was severely restricted during the Stalin dictatorship; and it has since been permitted greater liberties – erratically under Khrushchev and decreasingly under Brezhnev.

The 1920s saw the flowering of Formalism, a movement founded during the First World War and incompatible with Marxism owing to its rejection of sociological literary criticism. Within the movement Viktor Shklovsky was prominent, as also were Yury Tynyanov, later to become a celebrated historical novelist, and the influential émigré scholar Roman Jakobson. Formalists were indifferent to any political or social messages that a work might contain, as also to its biographical and historical background, preferring to concentrate on aesthetic factors – especially on the nature of poetic language, and also on the structure of works of art. The movement lost ground in the late 1920s under attack by RAPP, and was virtually extinguished by 1930, despite attempts by Shklovsky and others to achieve a measure of *rapprochement* with the sociological school of criticism. Accused of believing in Art for Art's sake, a theory flagrantly contravening Marxist doctrine, adherents of Formalism were viciously denounced; but it must also be noted that the word Formalist soon lost any precise connotation and became a mere term of abuse applied without discrimination to all disgraced or non-approved authors. One curious feature of official policy towards literary criticism was a tendency to exempt genuine Formalists from varieties of persecution more severe than mere abuse.[1] Aberrant Marxist critics, by contrast, tended to perish in the purges. Such was the fate of some who represented the more tolerant wing of their doctrine, as did the important editor and critic Aleksandr Voronsky. But such too was the fate of Marxists who had gone to the opposite extreme, proclaiming that true art could only be created by, for and about manual workers – as did Vladimir Pereverzev and others. These were officially abused as 'vulgar sociologists', often as a prelude to being liquidated.

Disembarrassed of these deviants, critics rallied behind the newly enunciated doctrine of Socialist Realism after 1932, their interventions assuming an increasingly inquisitorial tone. The debasement of criticism culminated, in the post-war Stalin period, in the No Conflict theory, mentioned above, according to which Soviet dispensations had eliminated evil from society, and with it the struggle between Good and Bad. By 1952 art had become so emasculated, partly through adherence to this doctrine, that the very Party began to call for the reintroduction of conflict; but with small success. Meanwhile literary criticism had become a vehicle for abuse and witch-hunts; critics, literary scholars and imaginative writers all came under attack, or busily attacked their colleagues, for 'kow-towing to the West', for being 'rootless cosmopolitans' and so on.

The first notable attempt by a post-Stalin literary critic to claim a measure of intellectual freedom was the article 'On Sincerity in Literature' by Vladimir Pomerantsev, published in Novy mir in December 1953. It called for a literature truthful in the ordinary everyday sense, rather than in the ideal sense ordained by the Party, and alarmed the authorities. It was partly for publishing such material that the Chief Editor of Novy mir, Tvardovsky, was replaced in 1954, to be reinstated four years later. By that time some of Pomerantsev's aims had been achieved – particularly in the year 1953, when writers took the opportunity to express themselves with a degree of freedom unknown for a quarter of a century.

Though most officially sanctioned criticism has remained narrowly sociological, some latitude has recently been allowed to deviant literary studies, care being taken to ensure that they are published in strictly limited quantity. There has, accordingly, been a discreet but significant

revival of Formalism in the Brezhnev period. But literary criticism
in general still suffers from the obligation to interpret works of art
within a prescribed ideological framework, with the result that critics'
findings are of limited interest to those who reject the ideology, as also
to many of those who must simulate acceptance of it. There have
been times, moreover, when the obligation to simulate conformity
has been blithely cast aside, even on a Soviet public occasion. In 1958,
when answering questions after giving a lecture at Moscow University's
Philological Faculty, I was – to my astonishment – greeted with vigor-
ous applause on revealing that I made little use, in my lectures on
literature at Oxford University, of contributions by post-1932 Soviet-
published critics of Chekhov. I explained, to the evident delight of
the audience, that this was partly due to the difficulty that I would
have in accepting those critics' philosophical assumptions as helpfully
applicable to the study of literature, and partly because it was impossible for me to agree with them in measuring the significance of an
author such as Chekhov by the extent to which his work furnishes
models of conduct to the young.

Among contributions made to the study of literature since the early
1930s literary criticism has been less valuable than literary scholarship.
This has involved the preparation of many detailed and comprehensively documented critical editions of authors of the classical period,
including Chekhov, Dostoyevsky, Saltykov-Shchedrin and Lyov Tolstoy. We may further note the practice of publishing detailed chronicles
of the lives of individual authors; their day-by-day activities, painstak-
ingly listed in diary form, are an invaluable aid to biographers – for
example, of Chekhov and Dostoyevsky. Scholarly publications have
also embraced the series *Literary Heritage*, containing much hitherto
unavailable archive material and published by the Academy of Sciences
of the USSR. Even in this area, however, editors must tread warily.
On one occasion the Academy's Department of Language and Literature was publicly rebuked by the CPSU Central Committee: for
including, in Volume 65 (*New Light on Mayakovsky*, 1958) of *Literary
Heritage* 'materials which distort the image of . . . [this] outstanding
Soviet poet' together with 'correspondence of a profoundly intimate
nature and of no scholarly interest'. The Central Committee went on
to complain that 'the reactionary foreign press' had picked out from
this publication items exaggerating elements of conflict between Mayakovsky and Soviet society, and had made use of them 'for . . . anti-Soviet

propaganda'. The allusion was probably to the useful volume *Vladimir Mayakovsky: The Bedbug and Selected Poetry*, edited by Patricia Blake (New York, 1960).[2]

Owing to the various limitations mentioned above the more stimulating Soviet-published biographies and critical studies of Russia's greatest authors tend to be products of the relatively free 1920s. Where later work is concerned, valuable critical and biographical insights are less likely to be found in home-produced articles than in émigré or Export Only studies. Among post-Stalin critical works belonging to the latter category Andrey Sinyavsky's spritely and irreverent essay, 'What is Socialist Realism? – first published in Paris under the pseudonym 'Abram Tertz' (1956) – is perhaps the most noteworthy. However, the same author's Soviet-published study *Poetry of the First Years of the Revolution*, brought out under his true name in collaboration with A. Menshutin (Moscow, 1964), is also a valuable contribution that may warn us not to seek critical enlightenment exclusively outside the Kremlin's sway. One Soviet-published critic, Vladimir Lakshin – a member of the staff of the liberal monthly *Novy mir* – attained considerable prominence for his articles of the mid-1960s, and not least for his spirited defence of Solzhenitsyn entitled 'The Friends and Foes of Ivan Denisovich' (1964). As the Solzhenitsyn controversy of that period illustrates, Soviet-published critics do not always present a united front, nor are lively polemics by any means excluded from the Soviet literary press.

Part Two
THE SOCIAL
AND POLITICAL
SPECTRUM

5 Peoples and Regions

The RSFSR

Only one of the fifteen Union Republics concerns us in any detail – the Russian. Known as the RSFSR (Russian Soviet Federative Socialist Republic), it dwarfs all the others, and incorporates all the territory predominantly inhabited by Russians. From Smolensk in the west to the Pacific Ocean in the east the RSFSR spans some six thousand miles, and reaches about half that distance from north to south at its widest point, containing nearly three quarters of the USSR's territory. But the RSFSR is far less densely populated than the other parts of the Soviet Union, since so much consists of the uninhabitable wastes of the north, and so it contains little more than half of the total population (about 134 million out of about 255 million in 1976). It includes within its boundaries sixteen Autonomous Republics and numerous lesser units.

The designation RSFSR was adopted in 1918, antedating the creation of the Soviet Union (USSR) by four years. Though the USSR itself, and the RSFSR within it, are both notionally federative, the Russian component has naturally dominated both – yet not so as to exclude the tenure of dictatorial power over a quarter of a century by a non-Russian individual, the Georgian Iosif Dzhugashvili (Stalin).

Russians

Loyalist or disaffected, most Russian citizens of the USSR think of their motherland as Russia rather than as the RSFSR, a sequence of letters lacking emotional resonance. Russian patriotism remains a powerful sentiment that can unite the most extreme of political dissidents.

Official policy on Russian patriotism is based on compromise. As a Marxist – and therefore internationalist – creed, Soviet Communism is opposed in principle to all forms of exclusive nationalist sentiment, including the Russian. But it has never been expedient to abjure Russian nationalist feeling altogether, since this has always been one of the most powerful consolidating forces on which the regime can rely. The most anti-nationalist phase was the earliest, when even the use of the terms Russian and Russia was discouraged in favour of 'Soviet' and 'Soviet Union'. Then came the fully established dictatorship of Stalin, who began restoring Russian patriotism to respectability in the 1930s, and who allowed it particularly free rein in the Second World War. As one feature of this campaign official approval was conferred on fiction, drama and films lauding such national heroes as St Aleksandr Nevsky, Ivan the Terrible and Peter the Great. Tsarist territorial expansionism, denounced in the earlier post-revolutionary years, was now proclaimed a progressive development, while such a persistent opponent of Russian colonialism as the nineteenth-century Caucasian guerrilla chieftain Shamil reverted, in historical allusion, from the status of tolerated local anti-imperialist hero to that of imperialist agent and rebel against the rightfully established order. Among other concessions to Russian nationalism was Stalin's restoration, from the late 1930s, of certain military traditions that had been abandoned for some twenty years. For example, he reintroduced the title 'officer' – hitherto anathematized in Soviet Russia as typifying the *ancien régime* – in place of 'commander', as so far used in the Red Army; see further, page 14.

In recent years revived Russophile sentiment has led to a fashion for collecting icons and *objets d'art* of the Tsarist period, as also to effective campaigns against the demolition of pre-revolutionary architectural monuments. Affection for the Russianness of Russia has been extensively expressed in two Moscow monthlies, *Molodaya gvardiya* ('Young Guard') and *Nash sovremennik* ('Our Contemporary'). It has helped to inspire the writings of representatives of Village Prose, who praise the traditional features of the Russian countryside. Among the Russophiles Vladimir Soloukhin has been prominent, having published a eulogy of old Russian culture in *Letters from the Russian Museum* (1966), and a sequence of essays on icon collecting, *Black Boards* (1969). For excessive nationalist fervour, and for bringing out *samizdat* journals overpraising traditional Russian values, the underground publicist Vladimir Osipov has suffered arrest and exile. Another officially disapproved champion of traditional Russia is Solzhenitsyn, who has occasionally made strenuous attempts to base the vocabulary of his published work on etymologically Russian words while avoiding the extensive stock of alien borrowings long established in the language.

To those expressing such Russophile sentiment the colloquial term *russity* ('Russia-fanciers') is sometimes applied.

Moscow and Leningrad

The Revolution brought a change in the relative status of Russia's two chief cities when, in March 1918, the seat of government was transferred to its earlier site, Moscow, after more than two centuries during which the city now called Leningrad had been the capital as St Petersburg/Petrograd. Russia's two greatest cities are still unofficially called the two capitals, as in Tsarist times, and the contrast between them has been drawn again and again.

St Petersburg's citizens were conscious of residing in an imperial capital, a thriving port with its boulevards, wealth of fine eighteenth-century architecture and unmistakeably cosmopolitan atmosphere. St Petersburg was an artificial creation, originally called into being by a single dominant will, that of its founder Peter the Great – a city of uniforms, order, regulations and ambition. But Moscow was a sprawling, ramshackle settlement, more an overgrown village than a town. It looked to Russia's past, being the focus for the Slavophile and nationalist movements, a place of priests and merchants, while St Petersburg was the abode of financiers, bankers and businessmen. Moscow had more churches and tumbledown log cabins, whereas St Petersburg had more tenements and palaces, also abounding in canals, mists and islands. When St Petersburgers criticized the cut of Muscovites' whiskers, Muscovites would retort that St Petersburgers could not speak proper Russian.

Much of this changed with the Revolution, which relegated the former St Petersburg from the status of capital to that of chief provincial city. Despite much wartime destruction and post-war reconstruction, the former capital still retains much of its majestic nineteenth-century appearance; one may still visit such historic sites as the quayside where Tsar Alexander II was assassinated in 1881 and the quarter in which Dostoyevsky set the murders of his *Crime and Punishment*. Moscow has been more extensively rebuilt; many of its mouldering log cabins have been pulled down and replaced with concrete cubes, and with the 'wedding-cake' architecture of the Stalin era. This rears itself cumbrously into the sky – for example, Moscow State University; or it may be pursued into the bowels of the earth – the luxuriously appointed stations of the Metropolitan Underground Railway. Many an onion-domed church has been converted into a bicycle factory or used as a vegetable warehouse; but many too are those, including the Kremlin cathedrals, that have been carefully restored as monuments of Russian culture.

What of the literary fortunes of the two capitals? For the first decade and a half after 1917 the scene has been described in an essay, 'Moscow-Petersburg' (1933), by a leading Leningrad writer, Yevgeny Zamyatin – expertly, but with a natural bias in favour of his native city. Zamyatin claims that Leningrad, as St Petersburg, had long been the country's literary capital, while Moscow was a mere provincial town. In St Petersburg all the most influential journals had been printed. Here the Symbolists of the 1890s and 1900s had supplanted the last Realists, Bunin and Gorky; here too the last spokesmen of the literary Silver Age – Blok, Bely and Remizov – had carried into the revolutionary period the traditions of the Golden Age (also based on St Petersburg) of Pushkin, Gogol, Dostoyevsky and Lyov Tolstoy. Re-established in 1918 as the seat of government, Moscow forgot its age-old traditions, says Zamyatin, and began to march in the van of modernity. Even before the Revolution the city had been the centre of the Futurists, who desired to jettison the culture of the past. To them were added other hyper-modern literary groups – the Proletkult and the Imaginists, who competed with the Futurists for political influence and state subsidies. Meanwhile revolutionary Petrograd was more conscious of traditional values, and Zamyatin stresses its importance as the home of literary movements less strident: of the Acmeist poets (notably Gumilyov, Akhmatova and Mandelstam) who emphasized the significance of Western European culture; of the 'Serapion Brothers', authors of politically uncommitted prose fiction (Vsevolod Ivanov, Venyamin Kaverin, Mikhail Zoshchenko); of the – later officially condemned – Formalist critical school with Viktor Shklovsky as one of its leading representatives. These movements, these important names gave post-revolutionary Petrograd and Leningrad a continuing advantage over Moscow, which – Zamyatin claims – had only produced one original prose-writer (Pilnyak) to set beside its two outstanding poets: Mayakovsky, chief of the Futurists and Yesenin, chief of the Imaginists.

Soon afterwards, Zamyatin notes, 'two first-rate new poets came to maturity', one from each capital: Boris Pasternak in Moscow, Nikolay Tikhonov in Petersburg.[1]

So much for Zamyatin's observations on Moscow versus Leningrad in literature, as seen from his Parisian exile in 1933, when he also greeted the Party's recent intervention in literature (especially the dissolution of RAPP) as 'an unquestionable victory for the civilised, "Petersburg" policy in art'.[2] How wrong he was to be proved – especially as Leningrad then stood on the brink of the sufferings unleashed on the country at large, and on the former capital with especial severity, after the assassination (possibly ordered by Stalin himself) of the local Party boss Sergey Kirov. Some forty thousand Leningraders were deported to the Arctic or Siberia, and other signs began to emerge of a prejudice on Stalin's part against the second city of his empire. He not only purged it again, still more severely, in the late 1930s, but was to do so yet again through a massacre of its notables, termed the Leningrad Affair, in 1949. Leningrad suffered still worse agonies during the seventeen-month blockade by the German forces in 1941–3, when, according to official figures, over 630,000 civilians perished from starvation in the city. Leningrad held out stoically; it was never completely encircled by the enemy, and its wartime agony has been commemorated in three verse publications: Olga Berggolts's collection *A Leningrad Notebook* (1942); Nikolay Tikhonov's epic poem *Kirov is with Us* (1941); and Vera Inber's verse tale *The Pulkovo Meridian* (1942). Meanwhile the city's most distinguished living poet, Anna Akhmatova, had been evacuated from besieged Leningrad to Tashkent, capital of the Uzbek SSR, where she spent most of the war.

By now Leningrad was no longer the chief centre for literary enlightenment, as previously claimed by Zamyatin, for it was Moscow that became the scene for many of the most enterprising developments of the post-Stalin era. Two large literary symposia published in the capital in 1956 (*Literary Moscow I* and *II*) contained much audacious material, breaching taboos that had held since the 1920s – and have since been partly reimposed. Moscow is also the place of publication of *Novy mir*, until 1970 the main vehicle for the liberal movement in literature. In 1956 it published Vladimir Dudintsev's notorious novel, highly critical of Soviet social development, *Not by Bread Alone*; in 1962 it carried Solzhenitsyn's *One Day in the Life of Ivan Denisovich*, the appearance of which has been, by common consent among foreign observers, the high-water mark of post-Stalinist liberalism in letters. At about the same time the Moscow branch of the Writers' Union of the USSR was displaying an astonishingly independent spirit, even contriving, on 4–5 April 1962, to elect a Board without deferring to the customary practice of having all such elections rigged in advance by Party authority.[3]

Though Leningrad still retains its strong local patriotism and special character, Moscow has long been the country's main literary centre, as it is the main centre for everything else in the USSR: Party, government and cultural life in general.

Cossacks

'Cossack' (in Russian *kazak*) comes from a Turkic word meaning 'free warrior'. It was used from the fifteenth century onwards to describe fugitives from central government who established themselves on or near the southern Russian frontiers in independent self-governing communities. They were brought under government control in the eighteenth century, when Catherine the Great ordered the dissolution of their most famous and westerly community, that of the Dnieper Cossacks. By the nineteenth century Cossack units had become the Empire's most loyal troops, and were used for purposes of riot control, being renowned for their horsemanship, and for their skill with the *nagayka* (whip) and sabre. They constituted a special military estate, being obliged to render service on specified terms in Cossack cavalry units, each man providing his own arms, horse and equipment. In return they enjoyed privileged land tenure conditions while retaining their local autonomy, traditional dress, customs and *esprit de corps*. Largely but not exclusively of Russian or Ukrainian origin, they were Orthodox by religion and set great store by their special traditions, despising the muzhiks (non-Cossack peasants) with whom many of their communities lived in close contact.

By the early twentieth century Cossack regions were strung out along many parts of the southern periphery of what is now the RSFSR, the most westerly being that of the Don in the south-east of European Russia. In 1916, when the tally of Cossacks stood at about four and a half million, the Don Cossacks accounted for about a third of the total, while the next most numerous community, that of the Kuban Cossacks to the north of the Caucasus, was almost as large. The remaining third were spread out from Orenburg (south-west of the Urals) to Ussuri in far eastern Siberia, constituting a dozen groupings – all very small when compared with the preponderant Don and Kuban Cossacks. In 1916 the Cossacks had about 285,000 men under arms.[4]

Cossack units stationed in Petrograd played a key role in the February Revolution. During the street riots that precipitated the last Tsar's abdication they held aloof by refusing to discharge their traditional role as riot police. Many Cossacks enthusiastically accepted the February Revolution, hastening to set up their own Soviets; but from 1918 their communities split into warring factions, some rallying to the Bolshevik cause while others became its bitterest enemies. The Don and Kuban areas saw much complex and bloody fighting during the Civil War.

In 1920 Lenin's government abolished traditional Cossack privileges, converting most Cossacks into ordinary peasants – the category that they had always, next to Jews, chiefly despised. Participating, in their own Cossack style, in the hazards and sufferings of the Soviet population as a whole, they also provided their quota of émigrés who drove Paris taxi-cabs, sang in Don Cossack choirs and displayed their superb horsemanship at rodeos, while becoming progressively assimilated to their many countries of domicile. At home they failed to recover their earlier prosperity under NEP and suffered severely from collectivization and famine in the early 1930s, staging revolts that could only be suppressed after military engagements. By the outbreak of the Second World War, Cossack military units had been reconstituted in name, but recruitment was now on a territorial basis, no longer being confined to the descendants of accredited Cossacks. Cossack units showed gallantry in action against the Hitlerite forces, but some fought on the German side, only to suffer extensive forcible repatriation to the Soviet Union after the war. The cause of Cossack separatism – that of seceding from the USSR and forming an independent state ('Cossackia') – has been a sporadic feature in Cossack thinking, and it helps to explain a tendency by the Soviet authorities to play down the role of the Cossacks in Russian history.

It has been necessary to consider the Cossacks at length owing to their importance in the work of a writer who has probably been more widely read, in the USSR and abroad, than any other modern Russian author: Mikhail Sholokhov. Though only one quarter, or not at all, Cossack by birth,[5] he was brought up in a Cossack community, and has lived during most of his life in the Don Cossack *stanitsa* (village) of Veshenskaya. Sholokhov's masterpiece is the long, four-volume novel known in Russian as *The Quiet Don*. It is not only set in the Don Cossack area, but is even written – both narrative and dialogue – in a form of the Don Cossack dialect. Covering the years 1912–22, it portrays Cossack experiences in world war, revolution and civil war with such verve that it may be the most renowned regional novel in literature. It was specifically for *The Quiet Don* that Sholokhov received the Nobel Prize in 1965, the committee apparently concurring with the general opinion of readers, that the author's other works are inferior.[6] Yet Sholokhov's two-part novel *Virgin Soil Upturned* contains some of the best writing on collectivization. He has also written *Tales of the Don* (1925–6) and an unfinished war novel, *They Fought for Their Country* (1959). All these works are set in the Don region.

Earlier Cossack authors of the Soviet period include Aleksandr Serafimovich. He was in his fifties and already an established writer at the time of the Revolution, and he later became a patron of the young Sholokhov. Serafimovich is chiefly known for his Civil War novel, *The Iron Flood* (1924), in which he portrays the agonies of a Bolshevik army retreating with its camp followers from the Caucasus to the north.

Other chroniclers of Cossackdom include Isaak Babel, who served in a Cossack military unit, which he depicts ironically and from the point of view of a comically excluded outsider – a Jew observing a people with a long tradition of anti-Semitism.

The Urals

'The Urals' denotes not only the Ural mountain chain, which forms the division between Russia-in-Europe and Russia-in-Asia, but also a group of Oblasts on both sides of the central and southern part of the range. The population of the Urals was about nineteen million in 1970, and the chief cities include Sverdlovsk, Chelyabinsk and Magnitogorsk. The last-named was founded in 1929 as part of Stalin's industrialization drive. This, followed by the evacuation of much heavy industry from the west to the Urals during the Second World War, led to a great expansion of population and industry in an area that had already become Russia's first industrial centre of any magnitude in the eighteenth century under Peter the Great. The main activities are metallurgical, especially iron and steel plants, together with mining, engineering and chemical works. They formed a natural theme for Five Year Plan novelists of the early 1930s, the best-known of the Urals-based novels being Valentin Katayev's *Time, Forward*, describing the building of a huge industrial plant at Magnitogorsk.

Siberia

The term Siberia is used conflictingly, most commonly to denote the part of the RSFSR that lies east of the Urals – in effect, Russia-in-Asia. A large part of northern Siberia consists of frozen wastes, and the area as a whole, several times larger than European Russia in extent, has always been sparsely populated. Yet the colonization of Siberia has been so intensive that its population has grown more than twice as fast as that of European Russia during the last eighty years. It stood at under six million in the 1897 census, but at twenty-five million in the early 1970s. This increase is largely the outcome of official policy: the deportation, under Stalin, of exiles and political prisoners, including the forcible transfer of whole peoples from European Russia; the evacuation of industries (as also to the Urals) from European Russia during the Second World War; the recruiting of agricultural and industrial workers from European Russia in the post-Stalin era. Siberia's largest city is Novosibirsk, a centre for scientific training and research; it contains an important branch of the USSR's Academy of Sciences, located in a special academic township, Akademgorodok, and its many scientific and technological institutions provide a backing for the economic exploitation of Siberia as a whole. The sub-continent is rich in natural resources: oil, iron ore, coal, timber and water power, and has become the scene of colossal industrial developments. Large hydro-electric stations have been built at Bratsk on the River Angara and at Krasnoyarsk on the River Yenisey. There is also a plan to construct a second Trans-Siberian railway, the Baikal-Amur Trunk Line, running well to the north of the existing line and possessing the strategic advantage of greater distance from the Chinese frontier. In the province of Tyumen in western Siberia extensive oil reserves have been tapped and the territory is now criss-crossed by pipelines carrying oil and natural gas, while boom towns have sprouted to house workers attracted by high wages that are not a little counteracted by the high cost of Siberian living.

Parts of Siberia contain outstandingly fertile soil, and western Siberia accordingly became the main scene, together with north Kazakhstan and the Urals, for the Virgin Lands campaign started by Khrushchev in 1953: huge tracts of hitherto uncultivated territory were ploughed up with the intention, imperfectly implemented, of solving the country's food problem.

Delving into early Soviet history we note that a large area of eastern Siberia, known as the Far Eastern Republic, was the last Russian region to surrender to Bolshevism. The Republic was occupied by the military forces of several foreign interventionist powers, among whom the Japanese were prominent, and it retained its nominal independence until 1922. Aleksandr Fadeyev, novelist and prominent literary functionary, was brought up here, fought for the local Bolsheviks in the Civil War, and has described the adventures of a local band of Red partisans in his novel *The Rout*. He also set his long, unfinished novel, *The Last of the Udege*, in that area; a mere fifteen hundred strong in 1970, the Udege are one of the many indigenous Siberian tribes who inhabit pockets of what has long been a region predominantly Russian in its ethnic composition.

No area of the USSR enjoys more unsavoury repute than that of the Magadan Oblast and the River Kolyma in north-eastern Siberia. Here an enormous area – of undiscoverable extent, but about four times the size of France – was converted, from 1930, into a concentration camp province devoted to mining gold, other precious metals and tin, and was called Dalstroy ('Project Distance'). It was at Vladivostok, in transit to Dalstroy, according to one version, that the poet Mandelstam died in December 1938. Faithful accounts of Dalstroy are naturally confined to Export Only literature. They include Varlam Shalamov's *Kolyma Stories*, published in Russian chiefly in the New York émigré periodical *Novy zhurnal* ('New Journal') from 1966 onwards, and Yevgeniya Ginsburg's memoir *Into the Whirlwind* (1967). The Dalstroy Trust, an organization exploiting mass forced labour on mining projects, was specifically designed to exterminate a high proportion of the labour force through harsh living and working conditions; it was dissolved after Stalin's death.[7]

Among Soviet-published works of the Stalin period devoted to Siberia, Vasily Azhayev's long novel *Far from Moscow* (1948) has been translated into twenty languages. It describes the laying of a pipeline in Siberia by massed workers; these are not, however, portrayed as the forced labourers from concentration camps who in practice performed such work. With its Positive Heroes, political morals and happy ending, the novel represents Socialist Realism in full bloom.

The long autobiographical poem *Winter Station* (1953), with which Yevtushenko originally made his reputation, is prominent among many other works set in Siberia. Himself a Siberian born and bred, the poet describes his birthplace, the small town of Zima ('winter') in the Irkutsk Oblast of Central Siberia. Siberia also figures in an amusingly poignant story by Vasily Aksyonov, *Half-Way to the Moon* (1962). It describes the adventures of a young truck driver employed on the Island of Sakhalin, north of Japan. After celebrating the beginning of his annual leave with a squalid alcoholic and sexual orgy at Khabarovsk on the far eastern mainland, he leaves for Moscow by jet plane and falls in love with one of the stewardesses; but then, after unfortunately losing contact with her, is reduced to commuting to and fro between the capital and Siberia by Aeroflot – all in the vain hope of seeing the young woman again – until in the end his money runs out. The work is a prime example of Youth Prose (see pages 82–3).

For Siberian themes handled in a manner dramatically opposite to that of Youth Prose we may consult the voluminous fiction of the leading literary functionary Georgy Markov, himself a native of the area and the present First Secretary of the Writers' Union of the USSR. Markov's cycle of slow-moving far eastern sagas includes his Lenin Prize-winning novel *Siberia* (1971–3).

The Ukraine

With a population of over forty-nine million (1976) the Ukraine is the most populous, after the RSFSR, of the Soviet Union's Republics. It has its own language and literature, separate from the Russian, and these fall outside our subject. But the fates of the two countries have been so closely intertwined that we cannot consider the culture and history of the one while ignoring the other. Many ethnic Russians have been born and lived for some time in the Ukraine, the political leader Leonid Brezhnev being a well-known example. Another indication of the close association between the two peoples is the activity of the Ukrainian dramatist Aleksandr Korniychuk (in Russian 'Korneychuk') who usually wrote in Ukrainian, but whose plays have been widely produced in Russian; whether in his own versions or in that of a translator remains unclear.[1]

Among authors using Russian as their native language not a few have been born or brought up in the Ukraine. The novelist Viktor Nekrasov is a Russian by birth, but by birth in Kiev, the Ukrainian capital; the Russian Jewish writer Ehrenburg was also born there. Though born in Moscow, Paustovsky attended the pre-revolutionary *gimnaziya* (high school) in Kiev, and has left an account of it in his memoirs. Many Russian novels are set in the Ukraine, or cross and recross the Ukrainian frontier, without the reader necessarily feeling that he is entering or leaving alien territory as he observes the Ukrainian anarchist guerrilla leader Makhno, in Aleksey Tolstoy's description of the Civil War in *The Road to Calvary*; or follows the harrowing experiences of terrorized Krasnodon under German occupation during the Second World War in Fadeyev's *The Young Guard*. To that same period also relate two works each entitled *Baby Yar*: Yevtushenko's short poem (1961) and Kuznetsov's fictional documentary (1966), both of which commemorate the German massacre of Jews during the war in a ravine outside Kiev.

The Crimea
The Crimea is a large peninsula almost surrounded by the Black Sea and the Sea of Azov and separated from the Ukrainian mainland by the isthmus of Perekop. In 1920 this was the scene of a notable White defeat in the Civil War – an event lamented in Marina Tsvetayeva's long poem *Perekop*, first published posthumously in New York. The Crimea has long been renowned as a health resort, with Yalta as its most famous spa, and for the great naval base of Sevastopol which fell after a long and stubborn defence to the besieging British and French in the Crimean War, and to the Germans over eighty years later in the Second World War. Until the late eighteenth century the area was Turkish, and since it retained a large Turkic-speaking population of Crimean Tatars it acquired the status of Crimean (Tatar) Autonomous Republic in Soviet times. When Stalin deported all the Crimean Tatars to Central Asia in 1945, on grounds of their suspected disloyalty and alleged collaboration with the enemy occupier, the Crimea lost this nominal autonomous status, and it has been an Oblast of the Ukrainian SSR since 1954.

Odessa
Odessa is the USSR's second port after Leningrad, being situated on

the Black Sea, and in the Ukrainian Republic. But Odessa is more cosmopolitan than Ukrainian: as noted above, it has been one of the few provincial cities to develop a marked literary personality in a country where the provinces have always been culturally dominated by the capitals.

After being captured from the Turks in 1791, Odessa quickly assumed importance as a major trading channel. It acquired a large cosmopolitan population, and was a centre of Jewish and Ukrainian culture, besides also being the unofficial headquarters of the entire country's criminal underworld. It has retained these characteristics, especially the last-named, in the Soviet period, and has become an important nursery of modern Russian writers.

The best-known of these, Isaak Babel, went so far as to predict, in his article 'Odessa' (1916–17), that his native city would become the base for a flourishing literary movement. Tired of reading 'how people live, love, kill, and conduct local elections' in such bleak and primitive northern provinces as those of Olonets, Vologda and Archangel, Russian readers would turn to the southern port, where people admittedly murdered the Russian language and where half the population was Jewish – but which possessed more charm than any other Russian town. Babel claims Odessans as the very opposite of the fog-bound St Petersburgers. 'In Russian literature there has so far been no real, joyous, and vivid description of the sun.' Odessans would repair that deficiency.[2]

Babel himself recreated the picturesque atmosphere of his home town in his *Odessa Stories*, devoted to Jewish criminal circles in the port. His laconic method contrasts with that of a fellow-townsman, Valentin Katayev, whose novel *Lonely White Sail* is set in Odessa with two boys as heroes and devoted to the events of 1905. It became, as may be remembered, the first part of his tetralogy *The Waves of the Black Sea*, completed a quarter of a century later and consisting of a sequence of novels in which the characters' fortunes, and those of their native city, are taken into the period of the Second World War. In 1941–4 Odessa was under occupation by Rumanian troops, and it is to this phase that the last volume (*The Catacombs*) of Katayev's epic is devoted.

It was Valentin Katayev's younger brother Yevgeny (under the pseudonym 'Petrov') who joined forces with another Odessan, Ilya Faynzilberg (the pseudonymous 'Ilf'), to produce modern Russia's most celebrated picaresque satirical novels, *The Twelve Chairs* and *The Golden Calf*, in which the action ranges over large parts of the Soviet Union. Other notable Odessan writers include Yury Olesha, author of *Envy*, and the poet Eduard Bagritsky, who makes considerable use of southern themes in his work. All these authors were born or brought up in Odessa, and they did indeed introduce a dynamic and exotic element into modern Russian writing. But they also have this in common, that all left their native city in early adulthood to pursue their profession elsewhere, mainly under the grey skies of Moscow. Odessan themes then came to occupy only a secondary place in their work.

Jews

From the Russians and Ukrainians we turn to the Jews, who are the most important people lacking a national homeland within the USSR. This remains true despite the fact that the country possesses, in far eastern Siberia, an Autonomous Oblast entitled Jewish and having its capital at Birobidzhan: the Oblast has never contained more than an insignificant proportion of Jewish residents (under nine per cent in 1959).

By strong contrast with the nineteenth century, prominent authors of the modern age include Jews writing in Russian as their native language. Babel, Ehrenburg, Mandelstam and Pasternak are the best-known, but there are many more to whom reference will also be made below. One authority speaks of several hundred Jewish authors writing in Russian in the 1960s.[1]

This development reflects radical changes in the status of Russia's Jews over the last century. Under the Tsars they were to a great extent a people apart. They were largely confined to a Pale of Settlement in the western and southern provinces, being terrorized from time to time through officially tolerated pogroms, and limited in their access to higher education, as also to officer rank in the army. They almost universally regarded Yiddish as their mother tongue (ninety-seven per cent in 1897);[2] they tended to wear traditional costume and to follow the ancestral customs of their race; most practised their ancient religion or at least had not apostatized from it. Should they wish to abandon Judaism, however, they were free to do so, for one notable feature of

Imperial times was that a Jew could shed his residential and other legal disabilities at any moment by accepting conversion to Orthodox Christianity. As for those who did not embrace this form of assimilation, they remained an identifiably foreign element in the Imperial Russian population, being officially classed with various primitive tribes as *inorodtsy* (aliens). And yet this disadvantage could be ignored in special cases, as it was by Pasternak's father Leonid; a noted painter, he settled down to work and teach in Moscow without going through the formality of registering any change of religion.[3]

The typical Soviet Jew, if such there be, no longer speaks Yiddish. The language has by no means died out, but has been considerably discouraged through the suppression of Yiddish periodicals and a ban on teaching Yiddish in schools: a form of cultural discrimination, 'since the RSFSR alone has forty-five different languages of instruction'.[4] The Jewish religion too has been suppressed, through the closure of synagogues and other means, having been more severely persecuted than any other faith except perhaps for Buddhism and for certain sects that are prohibited outright. No longer confined to any Pale, Jews are now widely scattered throughout the country. Three quarters of them live in the RSFSR and the Ukraine, each of which contains just over a third of the overall Soviet Jewish population. Other, smaller Jewish areas of concentration include Georgia in the Caucasus and Bukhara in Central Asia.

Secularized, no longer for the most part speaking a distinctive language, and less attached to their religious and other customs, Soviet Jews have largely become assimilated to the Gentiles of their area of residence. In the RSFSR many of them are and consider themselves to be as Russian as anyone else. And yet there is an important legal sense in which they can never become fully assimilated. In law a Soviet citizen retains and cannot change his 'nationality' as it is entered in his domestic passport, an identity card mandatory for all except peasants from the age of sixteen. If both parents hold the same nationality the child is automatically recorded as possessing that nationality in his passport. A Soviet citizen born of parents who are both Jewish therefore remains a Jew in law, however Russian he might wish to consider himself by language and general culture. When the parents are of different nationalities their child must, at the age of sixteen, make a choice and commit himself irrevocably to the nationality of one or other parent, so that a young person with one

Jewish parent must choose once and for all to be a Jew or not. Here is a contrast with the Tsarist practice of permitting the renunciation of Jewishness at will, by change of religion. To make these points is not, of course, to imply that a majority of Soviet Jews necessarily wishes to assume another nationality; we merely record the fact that this is not permitted.

Soviet Jews numbered about five million at the time of the Revolution, a figure that had remained fairly constant for about twenty years, for though there was an exceptionally high rate of natural increase between 1897 and 1917 these were also years of mass Jewish emigration from Tsarist Russia. Jewish emigration was severely curtailed, along with all other emigration, in the early 1920s, after which the USSR's Jewish population was greatly augmented in 1939–40 by the annexation of eastern Poland, Bessarabia and Northern Bukovina. Soon afterwards, however, the USSR's Jews suffered devastating persecution by the Nazi invader. Soviet Jewish war casualties, including the victims of Hitler's genocidal policies, have been estimated at about two and a half million – losses four times as severe, proportionately, as the losses of the Soviet population as a whole.[5] One reason for the disproportionate losses among Soviet Jews was the failure of the Soviet government, Hitler's ally from 1939 to 1941, to give warning of the German dictator's policy of exterminating their race. The result was that many Jews failed to seek safety in time through evacuation to the hinterland. Nor, even to the present day, has the virulent anti-Jewish bias of the Hitler government yet been fully revealed in Soviet sources.

These factors have helped to bring about a remarkable demographic change: whereas the population of the country has doubled since 1897, its Jewish component has halved. And we must also note a significant decline, since the 1920s, in the political and administrative status of Soviet Jews. They tended to dominate the early twentieth-century revolutionary movement, and many rose to political prominence as Bolsheviks: Trotsky, Zinovyev, Kamenev, Sverdlov and Radek in particular. Also prominent on the lower levels of the administration, as in the Cheka and later security police apparatuses, Jewish Bolsheviks dissociated themselves from the cultural and religious traditions of their people, being especially active in suppressing Yiddish speech and the Jewish religion. However, Jewish political influence had declined abruptly by the middle 1930s, partly because Stalin was temperamentally anti-Semitic, as his daughter and others have testified, and partly because he suspected all Jews as vulnerable to the appeal of Zionism, a rival ideology that he would not tolerate. Nor would Stalin tolerate potential political rivals, whether Jewish or not, and he accordingly had Trotsky assassinated in emigration after judicially murdering Zinovyev, Kamenev and Radek, among not a few other Jewish victims of the Moscow show trials of the late 1930s.

Stalin's discrimination against the Jews was far less marked than Hitler's, partly because Stalin discriminated against all sections of his community, thus tending in a sense to treat Jews as equals. And yet a special anti-Jewish flavour remained discernible, especially in the post-war Stalinist period, when the campaign against 'cosmopolitans' was given a calculated anti-Semitic twist, though Jews were prominent among the persecutors as well as the persecuted. On 12 August 1952 Stalin had a number of prominent Jews, including Jewish writers, executed on suspicion of planning to turn the Crimea into a Jewish national home.[6] He was also planning to 'frame' certain doctors, chiefly Jewish, on charges of assassinating influential patients by medical means, and to make this the basis for a new nationwide purge. But the intention was frustrated by his death in March 1953.

Jews have continued to suffer certain restrictions since Stalin's death, being virtually excluded from the Soviet diplomatic service and political journalism, as also from the most exalted levels of the Party hierarchy. However, they have the highest proportion of overall Party members of any Soviet nationality,[7] an indication that their influence remains strong at the lower levels even as it has been reduced at the top. Jews are also prominent in the cultural world in general: in the creative and performing arts, and in the scientific hierarchy. They include a high proportion of graduates from institutes of higher education, but there is also evidence of recent attempts to limit their access to higher education by discriminating against them at the admission stage.

A significant and unexpected change in the Soviet government's Jewish policy occurred when large-scale emigration, chiefly to Israel, began to be permitted in the early 1970s. Since then well over a hundred thousand Jews have quitted the Soviet Union. Permission to emigrate has been more readily granted to those Jews who are most culturally alien to the Russians. For instance, Georgian Jews have made up some thirty per cent of the new exodus, though they constitute a mere three per cent of the Soviet Jewish population.[8] Conversely, russified Jewish professional people have been hampered in their desire to emigrate, and in some cases persecuted for expressing the wish to do so.

Despite many disadvantages the Jews of Soviet Russia have not suffered discrimination and persecution as severe as that of the Imperial period. And in one minor respect the Stalinist authorities might seem to have discriminated in their favour: a prohibition on printing the opprobrious term *zhid* ('Yid'). This resulted in the excision of not a few passages from the Soviet-published correspondence of Chekhov and Dostoyevsky, both of whom – like many another nineteenth-century Russian intellectual – freely used the non-approved word. Here was a mechanical and, from the strictly scholarly point of view, regrettable ban that did not affect belles-lettres, and has been rescinded in the post-Stalin period, passages containing the word *zhid* having been restored in recent editions of nineteenth-century Russian authors' correspondence. But the word remains opprobrious.[9]

In 1928, before the ban on *zhid* became operative, Mayakovsky published a poem attacking its use by those Soviet Gentiles who, muttering in the interminable queues of the period, blamed everything on the Jews: '*Zhidy, zhidy*, nothing but *zhidy* – speculators, Soviet officials, members of the government.' Mayakovsky concluded that the loathsome term should be spat out of the language with a volley of the coarsest oaths.[10] Similarly Marina Tsvetayeva, also a non-Jewish author, expressed the solidarity of all poets and Jews (as fellow outcasts) when she wrote that:

> In this most Christian world
> All poets are *zhidy*.[11]

Another Gentile poet to champion the Jews was Yevtushenko. In his poem *Baby Yar* he complains of the Soviet authorities' failure to set up a monument to the Jews massacred by the German occupying forces on the outskirts of Kiev in September 1941. The omission was dictated by the official policy of diverting attention, as far as possible, from the persecution of the Jews by the Hitler regime. It was through this policy that the pre-war Soviet publicity media had not been permitted to mention the harsh anti-Semitic measures adopted by the German government with which Stalin had concluded a pact in September 1939. Moreover, as already noted, the Soviet media also went out of their way to present wartime casualty figures in a form designed to conceal the special degree of martyrdom suffered by the Jews.

As for Jewish authors writing in Russian, their very choice of language implies a degree of alienation from the traditional ethnic background, which would have dictated that they wrote in Yiddish: as not a few did, but they of course fall outside our topic. Many, too, were the Jews who forgot or never spoke Yiddish, failing to practise or abandoning the Jewish religion in which some were brought up. Babel, for example, claims in a brief autobiographical sketch that he had studied Hebrew, the Bible and the Talmud until the age of sixteen, but suggests that he did so unwillingly and on the insistence of his father, an Odessa businessman.[12] Yet Jewish problems and Jewish characters dominate Babel's work. The horrors of the Polish-Soviet war of 1920 are seen through the eyes of a narrator whose Jewishness is constantly stressed, and set in ironical contrast to the barbarous, anti-Semitic Cossacks, the army's main component. Then again, as already noted, Babel's *Odessa Stories* study the Jewish criminal underworld of his native Odessa. It has been said that Babel's Jews are caricatures bearing 'the unmistakable stamp of the ghetto',[13] but they are no less artistically successful for that.

Among Russian Jewish writers least fettered by traditionalism was Pasternak, whose education and culture were broadly international. Himself a Christian by belief, he goes out of his way in two passages from *Doctor Zhivago* to lament Jewish religious and cultural exclusiveness, and to suggest that the Jews should 'merge with all the rest, whose religious foundations they have laid and with whom they would have so much in common if they knew them better'.[14] Another self-emancipator from Jewish tradition was Mandelstam, who writes in his memoirs of his childhood as surrounded by 'the chaos of Judaism . . . that alien womb whence I had emerged, which I feared, about which I felt vague intimations, and which . . . I was always trying to escape'.[15] In about 1911 Mandelstam became a convert to the Russian Orthodox Church – perhaps little more than a formal step designed to free him from the residential and other restrictions imposed on Imperial Russia's Jews. In any case Mandelstam never renounced his Jewish affiliations. Referring to his tribulations as a non-loyalist writer, he compared them to the ordeal of circumcision, and added that 'authorship, as it has developed in Europe, and especially in Russia, is incompatible with the honourable calling of Jew on which I pride myself.' His blood was, he wrote, 'gravid with the legacy of shepherds, patriarchs and kings'.[16]

Ilya Ehrenburg, the most prolific of leading Russian Jewish writers, was the son of the manager of a Moscow brewery. His native language was Russian, but his parents spoke Yiddish and would use it when they did not want the boy to understand them. His father was an unbeliever, yet disapproved of the practice whereby Jews would embrace Orthodoxy in order to make their lot easier. The boy Ehrenburg encountered virtually no anti-Semitism among his Russian playmates, but claimed of himself as a Jew that 'I belong to those whom it is proper to persecute'.[17] The Jewish theme is particularly prominent in one of his early novels, *The Stormy Life of Lazik Roytshvants* (1928). An Export Only work, first published in Paris, it is the story of a Jewish tailor who rejects the traditions of the ghetto, but cannot conform with the new traditions of socialist society either. Escaping to Poland, he is arrested as a Bolshevik spy. His further journeys take him to Western Europe, and he eventually dies in Palestine in a traditional Jewish milieu not so different from that in which he had been brought up.

As this novel illustrates, there has been a tendency for Russian authors of Jewish origin to avoid exclusively Russian scenes and to concentrate on foreign settings and characters. This is a feature of Ehrenburg's prolific work, and not least of his long autobiographical *People, Years, Life*, recording experiences in Spain, Germany and above all France in addition to Russia. This reminds us that Jewish writers, and not least Ehrenburg, are prominent among the numerous memoirists of the period, without whom our understanding of it would be small indeed, and who include Pasternak, Shklovsky and the two Mandelstams, Osip and Nadezhda.

Jewish characters figure prominently in the work of Gentile Russian authors, being recognized by the obviously Jewish surnames or first names attributed to them, but also by their strength of will and dedication to Bolshevism – though they are often described as physically frail. All these traits are united in the person of Osip Abramovich Levinson, hero of Aleksandr Fadeyev's highly successful novel *The Rout*. This physically feeble, red-bearded, indomitable Positive Hero boldly leads a detachment of Red partisans active in the far east during the Civil War. Another intrepid Jewish figure from those days is the nineteen-year-old female machine-gunner Anna Pogudko in Sholokhov's *The Quiet Don*, who perishes in action against the Whites after falling in love with her commanding officer. Moving into the Five Year Plan period we find Davyd Marguliyes, of Valentin Katayev's *Time, Forward*, conscientiously presiding over a concrete-laying marathon as engineer in charge. 'Precise, neat, well-organized', he is another Jewish Positive Hero, though it is characteristic that his origins are indicated cryptically: only in his name and in a reference to his father having been killed in a pogrom.

The Marguliyes tradition is continued in Vasily Azhayev's ultra-Stalinist *Far From Moscow* by the Party organizer Zalkind – Positive Hero through and through, 'with the special strength of logical conviction always so characteristic of experienced Bolshevik political leaders'. The novel's other main Jewish character, the supply chief Liberman, begins as one of those comic little Jews who are more familiar from pre-revolutionary Russian literature, but by the end he too has been transformed into something approaching a Positive Hero.

Other Peoples

Caucasians

The Caucasus consists of the Caucasus mountain range, lying between the Black Sea and the Caspian, together with certain lands on its northern slopes and more extensive territories to the south. As has been noted, they include three separate Union Republics: Georgia, Armenia and Azerbaydzhan. But these are only the three largest units in a complex assortment of Caucasian lands, languages and peoples so varied that they may constitute the most ethnically and linguistically mixed amalgam on the face of the globe. The area passed substantially under Russian control in the first half of the nineteenth century, but remained unruly for many years after the capture of the main Caucasian resistance leader, Shamil, in 1859.

A remarkable instance of Caucasian self-assertion was the rise of the Georgian Stalin to the position of absolute dictator during the quarter of a century preceding his death in 1953. But Stalin's rule did not exempt his native Georgia from the severities imposed on the USSR as a whole, though it is true that other, smaller Caucasian peoples suffered still more from his oppressions. In 1943–4 five small Caucasian peoples – the Chechens, Ingushes, Karachays and Balkars from the north and the Meshketians from the south – were deported wholesale from their ancestral lands into permanent exile; as also were the Crimean Tatars (already mentioned) and the Kalmucks from the steppes north-west of the Caspian.

The Caucasus has had a long literary association with Russia from the days when it figured prominently in the poetry of Pushkin and Lermontov. This link has been less intimate in modern times, but is far from having disappeared. Pasternak paid his first visit to the Caucasus in 1931, travelling to Tiflis on the famous Georgian Military Road, and he has commemorated in his poetry the spectacular scenery of this land where 'the outlines of executed castles rear their Adam's apples into the marbled vault of August like the throats of men beheaded'.[1] Pasternak was the friend of two Georgian poets liquidated under Stalin, Titsian Tabidze and Paolo Yashvili, and his correspondence with them has been posthumously published abroad. Pasternak is also one of several Russian poets who, without knowing Georgian, have translated verse from that language into Russian, using the device of the *podstrochnik* (line-by-line literal translation). Mandelstam used the same method to translate an earlier Georgian poet, Vazha Pshavela, but his major Caucasian poetic contribution takes us to a different Union Republic: the cycle of thirteen original short poems collectively entitled *Armenia* (1931).

Among recent authors stemming from the Caucasus, but writing in Russian, is Fazil Iskander, a native of Sukhumi in the Abkhazian Autonomous Republic, whose literary range includes lyrics hymning the mountain landscape of his homeland, but also satirical prose deriding the absurdities of its bureaucratized agriculture.

Central Asians

Soviet Central Asia consists of the huge complex of Asian lands belonging to the USSR and lying south of the Siberian RSFSR. The peoples are largely Turkic-speaking and traditionally Muslim, and they inhabit the Kazakh, Kirgiz, Turkmen and Uzbek Union Republics, as also the Tadzhik (Iranian-speaking). Most of Central Asia became part of the Russian Empire somewhat later (from the mid-nineteenth century onwards) than did the Caucasus, and though it has been extensively colonized – especially Kazakhstan – by Russians, cultural ties between Russians and Central Asians are less intimate than those between

Russians and Caucasians, who are culturally more occidental. To many Russians Central Asia is known as a place of imprisonment, the concentration camp system having been extensively developed there. Solzhenitsyn describes his own imprisonment at Ekibastuz in Central Kazakhstan (in *The Gulag Archipelago*), as also his exile and confinement to hospital in Tashkent (in *Cancer Ward*). It was to that same city, the capital of the Uzbek Republic, that Anna Akhmatova and Nadezhda Mandelstam were both evacuated during the Second World War. One striking evocation of the Asian scene in literature is Paustovsky's story *Kara-Bugaz* (1932), a Five Year Plan work since it describes the industrial exploitation of a deposit of Glauber's salt in an isolated bay on the eastern shore of the Caspian – but one that more successfully evokes the mystery and isolation of the pre-exploitation phase than its industrializing sequel.

Though literary cross-fertilization between Russians and Central Asians has not been prominent, a recent author, Chingiz Aytmatov, writes both in Russian and his native Kirgiz and has attained some renown for stories and plays set in his homeland. A Kazakh poet, Olzhas Suleymenov, has recently published a study of Russia's anonymous medieval prose poem *The Lay of Igor's Raid*, stressing the importance of Asian themes in that disputed masterpiece. Whether these phenomena herald a new phase of assertiveness by Central Asians in the Russian cultural sphere remains to be seen. But we must not forget, either, that the Central Asians possess their own indigenous and now Sovietized literature, as do the Caucasian peoples – writings that fall outside the scope of the present study.

6 The Power Structure

The Communist Party

The Communist Party of the Soviet Union (CPSU) is the only political party in the USSR. It exercises close control over all aspects of cultural, social, economic and political life, claiming authority in virtually all areas of human activity except that of the liturgy and doctrine of the churches. According to the new constitution of 1977, 'The Communist Party of the Soviet Union is the leading and guiding force of Soviet society and the nucleus of its political system, of all state and public organizations.'[1]

The CPSU has changed its name several times since it was first founded as the All-Russian Social-Democratic Labour Party in 1898, and then split into two competing sections, the Menshevik and the Bolshevik, five years later. In March 1918 the victorious Bolsheviks changed their name to All-Russian Communist Party (of Bolsheviks). After the establishment of the Soviet Union in December 1922, this naturally became the All-Union Communist Party (of Bolsheviks). Finally, in 1952 the organization received the name under which it is still known, and by which we shall allude to it even when referring to the pre-1952 period: the Communist Party of the Soviet Union.

The CPSU has grown rapidly in size from about 24,000 at the time of the February (1917) Revolution to about 350,000 in October of the same year. Sixty years later, in October 1977, the number of members (including the small proportion of candidates under probation) had risen to nearly sixteen million – some six per cent of the population.

The CPSU is a strictly disciplined, hierarchical body which, at the lowest level, maintains primary organizations in factories, institutions and other places of work. These elect, but are in fact subordinate and responsible to, higher organs – the committees at city and Rayon ('area') level – as are those in turn to the Oblast ('district') committee. At a higher level still, each of the Union Republics (except the RSFSR) has its own republican Central Committee, while the Central Committee of the CPSU as a whole exercises a dominating influence over those. This in turn is controlled by the Secretariat, consisting of up to a dozen Secretaries. The senior of these has been termed either Secretary-General (Stalin in 1922–34; Brezhnev since 1966); or plain Secretary at a time when the leading incumbent's position was too well established to require emphasis (Stalin in 1934–53); or First Secretary (Khrushchev and Brezhnev, 1953–66). However entitled, the leading secretaryship of the CPSU has been the most powerful position in the country since the 1920s, and that of its absolute dictator during the later decades of Stalin's tenure of the office.

The senior Secretary of the CPSU's Central Committee heads the policy-making committee, usually of some fifteen persons and several candidates, called the Politburo (but between 1952 and 1966 the Presidium), which usually contains some of the other Central Committee secretaries as well. The Politburo is the most powerful body in the Soviet Union, being rivalled only by the Secretariat, with which its membership overlaps. Both organs are nominally elected by and responsible to the Central Committee; this body has greatly increased in size over the years, to about 250 members – and with consequent loss of power, since the USSR is no exception to the tendency whereby a committee declines in effectiveness as it grows larger in size.

Since the early days of Soviet rule the composition and activities of the Central Committee have been controlled by the Politburo and the Secretariat rather than vice versa. True, Khrushchev was once able (in June 1957) to expel his rivals from the Presidium (Politburo) by successfully appealing to the Central Committee over their heads. But the episode remains exceptional, and though the Party's central organs, from the Politburo, Secretariat and Central Committee downwards, are nominally elected by and responsible to the larger, lower organizations, in accordance with Democratic Centralism, control is in practice invariably exercised from the centre downwards. The senior Secretary and his closest allies are accordingly able to ensure a majority in their favour in the lower organizations and to control their composition. But the lower bodies, including the primary organizations, do have considerable power in implementing, though far less in initiating, policies at local level.

To Party members whose chief function lies specifically in Party work, and especially to the more senior among them, the term Party Apparatus is often applied. It includes the various secretaries of Oblast Committees, and also of the inferior Rayon Committees, scattered through the country. The overwhelming majority (though not all) of powerful individuals, whether in government, administration or the professions, belong to the Party – but not necessarily to the Apparatus consisting of those primarily engaged on Party work. Apparatus men or not, Party members penetrate and pervade almost all areas of Soviet life, ensuring the implementation of CPSU policy at all levels, and instances are by no means rare of officials who are senior by virtue of their function yet subordinate in Party contexts to functional juniors who outrank them in the CPSU.

Besides convening on Party Committees at whatever level, CPSU members play a key role by forming the Communist fraction in organizations – cultural, economic, administrative and social – on which non-members are also represented. It is the fraction's function to ensure that these non-Party organizations respond to policy as laid down by and through the CPSU. That the Writers' Union of the USSR should have its own Communist fraction was laid down in the Party decree of April 1932 ordaining the establishment of that literary association.[2] The fraction is far larger and more influential than might be supposed from the fact that Party members constitute a mere six per cent of the population as a whole. At the time of the Fifth Writers' Congress in 1971 the Writers' Union numbered no less than 4,050 Communist Party members out of a total membership of 7,290. When, five years later, the Writers' Union held its Sixth Congress, 462 out of the 542 delegates were Party members.

Despite their high proportion in the membership of the Writers' Union and their preponderant influence over that body's official activities, CPSU members have not been comparably prominent in literary achievement. Their most notable writer is Sholokhov, a Party member since 1932, and a senior Communist indeed since his election to full membership of the Central Committee in 1962. Other well-known writers eminent in the CPSU have included the novelist Aleksandr Fadeyev, full member of the Central Committee from 1939 until his death in 1956; the poet, novelist and editor Konstantin Simonov, candidate member of the Central Committee in 1952–6; the poet and editor Aleksandr Tvardovsky, candidate Central Committee member under Khrushchev.

Among authors who remained in the Party's lower reaches Valery Bryusov was the only outstanding pre-revolutionary poet to join (in 1920). Other early rank-and-file writer-Communists were Fyodor Gladkov, Nikolay Ostrovsky and Aleksandr Serafimovich. A late joiner was Valentin Katayev, who took this crucial step in 1958 in his seventh decade. Women writer-members have included Marietta Shaginyan, author of *Hydrocentral*, and a trio of poetesses associated with Leningrad (Aliger, Berggolts, Inber).

It is perhaps surprising to find not a few Party members among those who, in the 1950s, ventured to infringe the requirements of Socialist Realism, as imposed under Stalin, by politically neutral writing – this being or seeming, in the context, a form of insubordination: Valentin Ovechkin, Vladimir Tendryakov, Vladimir Soloukhin. With this group may be included the poet and historical novelist Bulat Okudzhava, who was threatened with expulsion from the Party owing to the Export Only publication of some of his work. A more serious delinquent was the novelist Viktor Nekrasov: a Stalin Prize winner in his time, he was expelled for expressing liberal views in 1972, and was permitted to emigrate two years later. A still more heinous culprit was Anatoly Kuznetsov, who joined the Party in 1955, and was not suspected of dubious loyalty until he suddenly succeeded in claiming foreign asylum nine years later. Vsevolod Kochetov is a deviant in the other direction – a prolific novelist who has even been criticized in *Pravda* for adopting an excessively anti-liberal stance. His novel *The Secretary of the Oblast Committee* (1961) embodies the office of a high Party functionary in its title, and lampoons political and literary deviants from the author's ultra-loyalist position.

Literary Party members have included many more notable for their role as functionaries than for the products of their pen: for instance, the present First Secretary of the Writers' Union Georgy Markov, and his predecessors Vladimir Stavsky and Aleksey Surkov. That Chief Editors of prominent literary periodicals should be Party members is established policy, one notable early example being Aleksandr Voronsky, editor of the journal *Krasnaya nov* ('Red Virgin Soil'), which was particularly influential in the 1920s. *Novy mir*, the most prominent post-Stalin monthly, attained its greatest eminence under Tvardovsky's editorship, and was also edited for a time by Simonov. Kochetov edited both the newspaper *Literaturnaya gazeta* ('Literary Gazette', 1955–9) and the monthly *Oktyabr* (1961–71). Since 1962 *Literaturnaya gazeta* has been edited by another Party man noted as a literary functionary: Aleksandr Chakovsky.

Some prominent writers have shown such enthusiasm for Communism that one may tend, incorrectly, to conceive them as Party members of long standing. Of these non-members of the CPSU Maksim Gorky, friend and confidant of Lenin and exalter of Stalin, was most eminent. Another such figure was the novelist Fedin, long Chairman of the Writers' Union, but not a Party member – though he had been so briefly in 1919–21. Nor was Mayakovsky, for all his fervent advocacy of Bolshevism, himself a member of the Party, apart from a brief pre-revolutionary affiliation to the Social Democrats during his adolescence.

Attempts to portray Party members in fiction have been numerous indeed, the problem being closely allied with the struggle to create Positive Heroes. Such a figure must be idealized as the epitome of strength and dedication; yet he must also remain a credible human being. Hence a tendency to endow these self-sacrificing apostles of commitment to the Communist cause with some minor defect, such as a tendency to head colds and unsuccessful love affairs, or an inability to give up smoking. Their eccentricities are designed to emphasize their fallibility, and thus create human interest.

Early Communist heroes were often Jewish and leather-jacketed, thus reflecting the realities of early Bolshevism, but tended to lose these characteristics in the era of developed Stalinism. Of the Jewish Levinson, hero of Fadeyev's *Rout*, and of another Jewish hero (Marguliyes in Katayev's *Time, Forward*) we have already spoken. To them may be added many a Gentile CPSU stalwart, such as the craggy Davydov in Sholokhov's *Virgin Soil Upturned* and the still craggier Uvadyev in Leonov's *Sot*. Hagiographically speaking the most significant of fictional Communists is Pavel Korchagin, hero of the partly autobiographical novel *How the Steel was Tempered* by Nikolay Ostrovsky. Korchagin triumphs over every possible obstacle – sickness, wounds, other misfortunes – through his all-conquering will. In this he reflects comparable strength of will on the part of his blind, bed-ridden, paralysed yet indomitable creator.

That even the most exalted literary functionary might commit ideological error in depicting the Party was shown in 1947, when the great literary tycoon Aleksandr Fadeyev – full member of the CPSU's Central Committee and combined Secretary-General of the Writers' Union and Chairman of its Board – suffered official censure for underemphasizing the leading role of the Party in *The Young Guard*, his war novel about the German-occupied USSR. Fadeyev was compelled to rewrite the work (second edition, 1951), after which, owing to a contrary swing in the pendulum of policy, he was confronted with the obligation to rewrite it yet again.[3] Similarly another important war novel, *For Soviet Power* (1949) by Valentin Katayev, also incurred criticism for underestimating the Party; it was twice rewritten, and eventually emerged under a new title, *The Catacombs* (1961).

During the Second World War Party members were especially endangered at the front, since it was German practice to execute all those found in possession of a Party card. But it was also, typically of the dilemmas of Soviet life, Stalinist practice to shoot those who later – on escape, release or repatriation – turned out to have committed the crime or sin of losing their Party card. To lose one's Party card, and thereby to risk expulsion and the suspicion of treachery, is – in literature as in life – a major disaster; it becomes so, for example, in Simonov's war novel *The Living and the Dead* (1959).

Party members have the privilege of manipulating and ordering about their non-Party colleagues, but are themselves subject to still severer discipline, since expulsion from the CPSU is a potent sanction that cannot by definition be invoked against non-members. A writer-member of the CPSU may, for example, simply be ordered by the Party to sign some mass denunciation of a deviant colleague, or an endorsement of Soviet intervention in Czechoslovakia or Hungary. A non-Party member, by contrast, may more easily demur or even refuse.

For young people between the ages of fourteen and twenty-six the Party has maintained since 1918 a special youth organization, the Komsomol, this being the abbreviation for the full title of the organization: 'All-Union Leninist Communist Union of Youth'. It is more of a mass organization than the CPSU – for example, it had over thirty-five million members in 1977 – and by no means all its members go on to join the Party proper.

The Ideology

The use of the word Communist, as in 'Communist Party' or 'Communist Russia', should not blind us to the fact that Communism, in Soviet usage, by no means represents a dispensation already attained in the USSR or anywhere else. It denotes, rather, a notional and ideal system towards which the various Communist parties are claimed to be striving, but which even the Soviet Union has not attained, though it has come nearer to doing so than any other society. The features of fully realized Communism are to be the abolition of all private property and social classes, together with the disappearance of the State, which is to wither away and give place to a Utopia in which all citizens will work according to their ability and receive according to their needs. Communism has all along been the proclaimed goal of the CPSU, and in 1938 Stalin asserted that the important interim stage of Socialism had been attained with the elimination of the bourgeoisie. Thereafter the discussion of Communism, as of all other theoretical issues, remained suspended until the dictator's death. The issue was extensively debated under Khrushchev, but without any conclusive result.

Soviet Communist ideology, known as Marxism-Leninism, rests on the philosophical theory of Dialectical Materialism, based on Marx's teaching, itself a radical adaptation of propositions advanced by Hegel. According to the theory only the material world, and particularly economic production, has reality, ideas being merely the reflection of things material. The material world is in constant process of change through a pattern called dialectical. This continuing evolution arises from a series of conflicts between pairs of diametrically opposed elements, the thesis and the antithesis. Each thesis clashes with its antithesis, and forms a synthesis, which in turn becomes a new thesis or antithesis ready to take part in the next clash.

Adherents of Dialectical Materialism claim that it is a fully scientific method, and that it can be applied as a means of foreseeing the course of events and of finding 'the right orientation in any situation'.[1] Opponents of the doctrine deny this, also pointing out that any apparent ability of Dialectical Materialists to explain past events derives from their flexibility in arbitrarily choosing their theses, antitheses and syntheses from the mass of conflicting phenomena to be observed in any given historical context, and in claiming to discern a pattern where none exists.

Armed with their scientific method, Soviet ideologists believe that historical development is predetermined and that it will culminate in fully developed Communism, as defined above. However, though the ultimate goal is known the doctrine does not lay down precisely when or how it will be attained; and though history is predetermined it does not follow that Marxist-Leninists may sit back and let events take their inevitable course. Their task is to accelerate the process. The end is both infinitely desirable and ultimately inevitable, and so all means are admissible in pursuing it. Hence the militarized atmosphere of Soviet society, in which inferiors – especially within the Party – are expected to obey, blindly and faithfully, all orders handed down from above. To this process the name Democratic Centralism is given. It is called centralism because decisions are considered to be taken at the centre and to be binding on subordinates, and it is called democratic because the higher and more central bodies are deemed to be freely elected by the peripheral rank and file. The truth of the first proposition is generally conceded, but non-adherents of Soviet Marxism tend to deny the second.

The highly disciplined structure of the Party derives more from the strategy of Lenin and Stalin than it owes to their teacher Marx. Lenin also modified Marx's theories. Marx believed – though he may have deviated from the belief in later life – that a successful proletarian revolution could only take place as part of a general world revolution, and that it could only begin in one of the advanced industrial countries of the world. Agrarian Russia was not one of these, but Lenin met this difficulty by incorporating the numerically overwhelming Russian peasantry as a junior partner in his revolution. Lenin also departed from strict Marxist theory, whereby a successful proletarian revolution must be preceded by a change in the forces of economic production, since Lenin's procedure was to bring about the revolution first – and only then to set about changing the forces of production. In order to stress the primacy assigned in theory to the role of the working class Lenin gave the term Dictatorship of the Proletariat to his political system; the expression is now little used, but has never been officially abandoned. Lenin further strengthened Party discipline at the Tenth Party Congress in March 1921 by a decree outlawing fractionalism: that is, any attempt by a group of Party members to concert a policy at variance with that of the leadership. Stalin further strengthened Party discipline by liquidating anyone suspected of such urges, and many who were not. He also espoused a policy of Socialism in One Country, thereby postponing into the indefinite future the hope of a world revolution that had hitherto been a cardinal element in Marxist thinking.

Dialectical Materialism and the other major tenets of Soviet Marxist ideology are regularly inculcated at an increasingly sophisticated level at all possible stages in the education system. But they are not, so far as one can judge, generally felt to possess significance for the insights that they afford into the nature of reality. Rather are they prized for the unavoidable place that affirmation of the doctrine plays in the pursuit of almost any effective career within the system, as also in the avoidance of the serious penalties to which known unbelievers may render themselves liable. A Soviet citizen does not necessarily believe passionately in the validity of the ideology, but that will not deter him from believing with every fibre of his being in the profound influence, desirable or undesirable, that the display of a positive or negative attitude towards the doctrine may have on his personal evolution.

In general the theory is invoked as if it possessed incantational force or even occult powers. Throughout the Soviet period quotations from Lenin have been adduced, often out of context, to clinch an argument and put an opponent at a disadvantage, as have quotations from Marx and Engels, and also (during the period of his ascendancy) from Stalin. However, a knowledge of Marxist-Leninist doctrine more profound than that required for argument by quotation may prove positively dangerous, especially if tactlessly displayed by some naïve youth in the presence of an influential Party veteran less thoroughly versed in the approved texts. To study the theory in a spirit of intellectual enquiry can benefit no one; rather is it most effectively assimilated as a liturgy, its assertions being conned by rote and regurgitated in the proper contexts.

Government and Administration

Constitutionally speaking the highest organ of state power in the USSR is the country's Supreme Soviet. It is a bicameral body, and its two chambers – the Soviet of the Union and the Soviet of Nationalities – have equal status and are of approximately equal size. The first is charged with safeguarding the interests of the country as a whole, and the second with promoting the welfare of its individual peoples. The Supreme Soviet is elected every five years (before 1977 every four) on the basis of universal, equal, direct and secret suffrage, the electorate including all citizens of eighteen years of age and above except those deprived of their civil rights through criminal proceedings. There have usually been between six and seven hundred members in each chamber.

The Supreme Soviet may seem to resemble a Western parliament in some ways, and it is in fact often called the Soviet Parliament. The term is, however, misleading because Soviet elections follow the single-list principle. This means that no choice of candidates is offered on ballot papers, so that only by defacing these documents can a dissenting vote be expressed, and that without the possibility of voting for an alternative candidate. Since all candidates, whether Party members or not, enjoy the advance approval of the CPSU the election can offer no prospect of a change of government, the result being known with certainty in advance. Voting is not formally compulsory, but energetic measures are taken to ensure a full turn-out at the polling booths. Most candidates accordingly receive something approaching a hundred per cent of the votes, and from a comparably high turn-out of voters, the only element of doubt being the sequence of decimal points and not the '99' that usually precedes them. Stalin is said to have received *over* a hundred per cent of the votes on occasion,[1] but he was always a special case.

In its proceedings, no less than in its genesis, the Supreme Soviet differs significantly from Western parliaments. It meets only twice a year (but more frequently when necessary) and for sessions of a mere two to four days. It is, in fact, a ceremonial rather than a legislative institution, being convened only in order to signify assent, invariably unanimous, to the resolutions and propositions put before it. On a less public level, however, deputies are expected to represent the interests of their constituents by intervening with authority on their behalf, and some writers have performed this role. That it can be time-consuming but fascinating and valuable work I was once personally assured by Ehrenburg, who himself served for a time on the Supreme Soviet.

The Supreme Soviet also performs an important function in elect-
ing, from among its own members, two smaller organs of considerable
importance, the election being – as are all Soviet elections – a device
for proclaiming rather than deciding the outcome, and proceeding
along lines previously determined by higher authority. The first of
these bodies is the Presidium, which is largely concerned with matters
of ceremony and protocol at the highest level. The Chairman of the
Presidium of the Supreme Soviet is the Head of State. The position
was occupied by political lightweights (Kalinin, Shvernik, Voroshilov)
before 1960; it then went to Brezhnev, but this was regarded as a
setback to his career. After Podgorny had taken over as Head of State
in 1965–77, Brezhnev resumed tenure of the office, now holding it
simultaneously with the Secretary-Generalship of the Party Central
Committee.

A far more important body, also elected by the Supreme Soviet,
is the Council (Soviet) of Ministers. The Ministers have come to
number seventy or more, and their council is sometimes referred to as
a cabinet; which may once again be misleading. But the Council of
Ministers remains the supreme organ of government, for which reason
its Chairman is often called the Soviet Prime Minister or Premier.

The premiership has been held since 1917 by the following leaders:
Lenin (1917–24); Rykov (1924–30); Molotov (1930–41); Stalin
(1941–53); Malenkov (1953–5); Bulganin (1955–8); Khrushchev
(1958–64); Kosygin (from 1964).

The bodies and titles so far considered date either from 1936 (year
of the Stalin Constitution) or from 1946, when the title Minister was
introduced for the first time in the Soviet Union. Before 1946 ministers
were called People's Commissars; the pre-1946 equivalent to the
Council of Ministers was, accordingly, the Council of People's Commissars (Sovnarkom).

Though the hierarchic apparatus of the State runs parallel to that
of the Party, to which it is in practice subordinated while remaining
nominally separate, Ministers and high governmental officials are themselves of course invariably Party members. Far from having two independent hierarchies we have, in fact, something more interpenetrative
and complex; all the more so as the three most powerful figures in
Soviet history have each at certain times held office as Prime Minister but
without relinquishing their chief power base as supreme Party leader.
From 1917 onwards Lenin combined leadership of the Party, exercised

through its Politburo, with the premiership as Chairman of Sovnarkom, ceasing from 1922 to exercise these functions in practice through illness. Stalin took over the Party leadership in 1922 when he assumed the newly created secretary-generalship, but held no government office at all between relinquishing the People's Commissariat for Nationalities in 1923 and assuming the premiership (chairmanship of Sovnarkom) in 1941. He retained the premiership until his death in 1953. During the confusion immediately following Stalin's death Malenkov at first combined the senior Party secretaryship with the premiership, but for a few days only; the concurrent tenure of the two posts was presumably considered to make him dangerously powerful, and he was compelled to relinquish one of them. Choosing to retain the premiership – probably an error in tactics – he conceded the supreme Party office, now termed the first secretaryship, to Khrushchev. Khrushchev remained First Secretary until his removal from office in 1964, holding the premiership concurrently from 1958. Thus four individuals (Lenin, Stalin, Malenkov and Khrushchev) have at the times indicated simultaneously held the top posts in both Party and government. Brezhnev has never been premier. But his concurrent tenure, from 1977, of the chief Party secretaryship and the position of Head of State is, as already noted, a new departure and one clearly intended to enhance his status.

Elections to inferior Soviets – whether of Republic, Okrug, Oblast, Kray, city, Rayon, town or village – follow the same general pattern as those to the Supreme Soviet, described above. These bodies include the lowliest organs of local government, and number over 40,000 if all the village Soviets are taken into account. The lower and less significant the unit the greater is the chance that the almost invariably elected single-list candidate may not be a member of the CPSU, for though Party members predominate at all levels they tend to be less densely represented as one descends the scale to the 'grass roots'. The proportion of non-Party to Party members in the Supreme Soviet has tended to be about one to three.

Especially sensitive posts in Party and government are registered in the so-called *nomenklatura*: a secret schedule of particularly important offices to which functionaries can only be appointed after careful high-level Party scrutiny, so that this body of hyper-loyal administrators constitutes a kind of inner club within the Soviet élite.

In order to distinguish organs of the State from organs of the Party, readers of the modern literature may find it useful to remember that

Soviets and also their Executive Committees belong to the State hierarchy, whereas committees without the prefix 'executive', and in the absence of other contrary indications, tend to belong to the Party. Not only must foreign readers of Soviet fiction accustom themselves to these terms, but they must also familiarize themselves with the relevant characteristic abbreviations. For example, at Rayon ('area') level we expect to find matters under the general control of the *raykom* (*rayonny komitet*, the Party Area Committee). But the detailed management of the Rayon is, simultaneously, vested in the *raysovet* (Area Soviet), a local government organ elected by local residents and containing both members and non-members of the Party, its day-to-day operations being carried out by its Executive Committee (*rayispolkom*).

However fettered individuals may feel by committees themselves responsible to higher committees, and however helpless any individual or committee may be to initiate policy even at local level, these bureaucratic activities are not purely ornamental, and they dominate a large part of Soviet life. References to the factory committee, the town Soviet, the area executive committee, the district committee (*zavkom*, *gorsovet*, *rayispolkom*, *obkom*) and the like abound in belles-lettres. Nowhere, perhaps, are such apocopations more comically represented than in the community of plague-stricken rats described in Tsvetayeva's long poem *The Rat-Catcher* (1925–6) with their *glavkhvost*, *glavsvist*, *narkomchort* (Chief Tail, Chief Squeak, People's Commissar for Hell) and so on. How bemused individuals can become by the bureaucratic ambience is well illustrated in Aleksandr Yashin's famous story *Levers* (1956). It begins with members of a Collective Farm's administration casually discussing the wretched condition of their enterprise: the chaos, the shortages, the inanity of official verbiage. But then, when they suddenly go into session as a committee, all suddenly change their style as if by word of command, and begin employing the same meaningless official vocabulary that they had just been holding up to derision.

Owing to the proliferation of controls and controls over controls, and to the manifold custodianship of custodians, the impression is sometimes created that not a single pailful can be milked, nor yet a single lathe rotate, without the matter being multiply reported up and down the parallel hierarchies and repeatedly debated by a very army of *glavsvisty*. Yet the elections, national and local, are no empty formality – such is the effort invested in staging campaigns, in holding meetings, in seeking to ensure a hundred per cent turn-out on polling day. That it may all have been somewhat too time-consuming is suggested by the provisions of the new (1977) Constitution extending the Supreme Soviet's tenure of office from four to five years and that for local authorities from two to two and a half. But elections of one kind and another still remain an almost annual event for most citizens.

That the system is supremely democratic beyond the dreams of non-Soviet society is the official contention. Western observers are inclined to claim the opposite, pointing out that, by so intensively adopting democratic forms and terminology, the system simultaneously buttresses totalitarianism since it disarms internal opposition, while also discrediting the very democratic process as properly conceived. It is also possible that the system largely owes its evolution to the periodical doubts which, in the absence of better channels for the expression of public opinion, the rulers must feel when they ponder the degree to which the population has been rendered docile and responsive. It is through the electoral process that the general level of submissiveness can be both tested and reinforced; similarly, military authorities throughout the world are apt to check and reinforce discipline and morale through the pageantry of the drill parade, whether by platoon, company or battalion, and also through larger-scale manœuvres.

That the system excludes all forms of initiative and self-assertion would be far too extreme an assertion, and a temperate case for the existence of some degree of Soviet democracy has been made by authorities outside the Kremlin's orbit.[2] It must also be remembered that the system does at least offer considerable extra scope to those individuals, high and low, who feel cruelly frustrated in other societies – those with the kind of vision and vocation that sees their contribution to the community more in the art of marshalling and positioning others than in any direct personal creative efforts mobilized by themselves. Indeed, the recent proliferation of such persons in non-Soviet societies suggests that the future may indeed lie with the *glavkhvosty*, the *glavsvisty* and all others who operate and respond to levers such as those figuratively invoked in Yashin's story.

The Police

Since the eighteenth century Russia has possessed a succession of special organizations responsible for the security of the State and system of government. Their function distantly resembles that performed, in Britain and the USA, by the Special Branch, MI5, the CIA and the FBI, but those of the Soviet Union are larger, more powerful, have more ramifications, and are not in the least open to public scrutiny or criticism. Foreign observers allude to these bodies as the secret police, security police, political police or even thought police. As for the Russian titles, official or semi-official, they have changed repeatedly over the years, either in order to reflect modifications in structure, or to suggest the prospect of a beneficent change by supplanting a designation that had acquired particularly unsavoury repute. They have this in common, that none of them contains the word *politsiya* ('police'), which is regarded as tainted with Tsarist and capitalist associations, and which was jettisoned after the February Revolution of 1917.

After the political policing of Imperial Russia had been performed, often with anecdotal incompetence, by the Third Section (from 1826) and (in the last decades of the Empire) by the Okhrana, a Soviet security force was set up on 7 December 1917 under a Polish revolutionary, Feliks Dzerzhinsky, and was called the Cheka. The sequence of names by which it has been entitled is shown in the table opposite.

In spite of all these changes the old word 'Cheka' and its derivative 'Chekist' (an official of the Cheka), are still used colloquially to describe the Soviet security police in general. They are also employed by the Soviet publicity media as part of a recurrent drive to improve the reputation of this most dreaded of Soviet institutions. Over the years more than two thousand books have been published extolling the exploits of the Chekists, and seeking to invest them with the kind of glamour and prestige attributed to the Canadian 'Mounties'. The organization's various anniversaries are lavishly celebrated and publicly reported. For instance, on 11 September 1977 the centenary of Dzerzhinsky's birth was extensively commemorated, stress being laid on that long deceased and much feared functionary's love of children – an allegedly dominant Chekist trait.[1] But the three heads of the NKVD/NKGB and MGB during the years 1934 to 1953 – Yagoda, Yezhov and Beria – conspicuously fail to be invoked on these occasions, since all three of them were arrested and disgraced in their time, being executed or otherwise liquidated in obscurity.

Yagoda, Yezhov and Beria had been, successively, the main implementers of Stalin's purges – a reminder of the pre-eminent role assigned

Date	Abbreviated Russian title	Translation of fuller title
1917–22	Cheka	Extraordinary Commission for Combating Counter-Revolution and Sabotage
1922–3	GPU	State Political Administration
1923–34	OGPU	United State Political Administration
1934–43	NKVD	People's Commissariat for Internal Affairs
1943–6	NKGB	People's Commissariat for State Security
1946–53	MGB	Ministry for State Security
1953	MVD	Ministry for Internal Affairs
1954 to present	KGB	Committee for State Security

to the security police during the Terror, when its functions included the mass arrest and imprisonment of disgraced Party members. After Stalin's death steps were taken, the removal and execution of Beria being one of them, to bring the organization under closer Party control. The policy still remains in force, and it is significant that the present Chairman of the KGB, Yury Andropov, made his career largely in the Party's Apparatus before his elevation to be chief of security police in 1967; he became a candidate member of the Politburo in the same year and has since risen (1976) to full Politburo membership. But despite the prominence accorded to Andropov the KGB remains essentially clandestine, as we are reminded by the stipulation placing the names of all its employees, other than the head of the organization, on the secret Index of topics that may not be invoked in print; see page 210.

Reverting to the first Soviet security police force, the original Cheka as set up in December 1917, we note that its impact was not particularly severe during its first few months of existence. Only as the

Civil War gained momentum did it become notoriously ruthless, partly owing to the tendency for atrocities on each side to provoke escalating atrocities on the other. In summer 1918, after an attempt on Lenin's life and the assassination of the Petrograd Cheka chief Uritsky, the adoption of mass terror as a policy was announced by the leadership. It now became customary for the Cheka to execute batches of hostages – members of the former bourgeoisie or of rival Socialist parties. Reports of torture are also extremely prevalent. Though precise figures elude us, that of some fifty thousand for the tally of those executed by the Cheka during the Civil War is probably not an over-estimate and gives some indication of the dimensions of their operation.[2]

As for the possible psychological implications, the Export Only sketch *Hands* (1956–8) by Nikolai Arzhak (pseudonym of Yuly Daniel) represents the confession of a retired Cheka executioner whose hands have never ceased trembling since he had been compelled to shoot a number of class enemies under Dzerzhinsky's jurisdiction.

After the end of the Civil War, and the transformation of the Cheka into the GPU/OGPU, arrests and executions decreased. But this relief was to prove only temporary. From 1930 onwards the imposition of full-scale Stalinism involved the OGPU in repressions far more widespread than those imposed by the wartime Cheka. The security police now became the chief instrument for compelling the peasantry to enter Collective and State Farms; for suppressing passive or armed resistance to collectivization; and for implementing Stalin's recently announced policy of 'liquidating the kulaks as a class' by arresting or exterminating villagers offering resistance. The OGPU was also used to extract gold and jewellery from individuals by torture and intimidation, and to hound alleged saboteurs among the professional classes – engineers and technicians who had been recruited to help the industrialization drive and therefore made admirable scapegoats for the programme's many deficiencies.

The disbanding of the OGPU in 1934 and the transfer of its functions to the NKVD seemed to promise relief, but the change in fact led to repressions still more extensive. The NKVD was the main implement in mounting the Yezhovshchina, not least through the newly established subordinate authority, GULag, which took over the concentration camp network as expanded under the OGPU. Backed by this device for exterminating 'enemies of the people', the NKVD helped to stage the show trials of 1936–8, while carrying out unpublicized mass arrests of functionaries, managers, Party members and members of the professions in general. By now the security forces were heavily armed, having their own artillery, tanks and aircraft – insurance against a *coup d'état* by the army. That potential or imagined threat was also countered by using the NKVD to liquidate an overwhelming majority of the senior officers in the country's armed forces, from Marshal Tukhachevsky downwards.

The security forces themselves became a leading target for persecution in the course of the Terror. After Yezhov – a Party man by career, not a security officer – had been put in charge of the NKVD, many of that body's own officers were arrested and liquidated *en masse*. Yezhov himself went the same way in the end – as part of a predictable pattern which had already included the destruction of his predecessor, Yagoda, and was one day to engulf his successor, Beria.

The Second World War placed new responsibilities on the security forces. In addition to its more traditional functions the NKVD was also charged, in the early period of the war, with exterminating the inmates of such prisons and concentration camps as seemed certain to be overrun by the German invader. The NKVD also formed blocking battalions which lurked behind the front with orders to fire on their own combat troops if they should retreat in face of the advancing enemy. After the war another new task awaited: the screening of the millions of Soviet citizens who had found themselves behind German lines, whether as prisoners of war, partisans, forced labourers, deserters, would-be emigrants or in any other capacity; as already noted, they were consigned to concentration camps in large numbers. The Soviet security forces, now termed the MGB, were also active in directing sister security organizations in the various satellite nations that fell under the Kremlin's sway after the war. The satellite authorities were induced to stage their own show trials on the Soviet model, while many of their citizens were arrested and deported to Soviet concentration camps in the course of the accompanying repressions.

During the post-war years the MGB also implemented Stalin's onslaught on high officials in his second city – those implicated in the still obscure Leningrad Affair. It further helped to stage-manage the imaginary conspiracy, known as the Doctors' Plot, which the ageing dictator intended to make the pretext for mounting yet another wave of terror, but from which the country was saved by his death in March 1953.

The surviving security chief Beria was suspected of planning to use his office to seek dictatorial powers for himself. He accordingly disappeared, deposed in June 1953 and allegedly tried in secret and executed, after which the security forces, renamed the KGB in 1954, were brought under more stringent Party control. But though their role has inevitably declined under the relatively mild conditions of post-Stalin Russia, the organization remains extensive and active. It still maintains large militarized units independent of military control, and it still helps to organize espionage and subversion in foreign countries, besides fulfilling its prime function of monitoring political security hazards at home. And it maintains a special office in all Soviet enterprises and organizations of any size, not to mention the secret informers that it recruits within them.

In the fluctuating persecution of writers during the post-Stalin era, which has included not a few arrests, trials and camp sentences, the KGB has been active, as also in its attempts to control disaffection in general. How determinedly the organization has sought to stamp out the dissident movement we cannot tell, but a considerable measure of success seems, at the time of writing, to have been achieved in containing and reducing such activity. Political opposition has by no means been eliminated entirely, however, and one particular dissident operation still flourishes with undiminished vigour – the dissemination of disapproved literary and other documents in typed form (*samizdat*) and the spiriting of such material across the Soviet frontier. The continuance of this practice may be the outcome of calculated policy, based on the consideration that the dissidents are best kept out in the open, where they can be observed; but see also page 249.

Meanwhile the security police remains active, making widespread use of secret informers, bugging devices, clandestine and open surveillance, searches of suspected authors' residences, seizure of suspect literary archives and the like. Of these matters we may read at length in the memoirs of Solzhenitsyn, Nadezhda Mandelstam and many others. As for contact between security police and authors, history relates many such instances, of which we cull a few of the more bizarre.

Osip Mandelstam was several times publicly threatened with shooting by a flamboyant, pistol-toting Chekist, Yakov Blyumkin, who was himself to be shot as a Trotskyist in 1929 – the first Party member to suffer summary execution. Boris Pilnyak was personally assisted in retailoring his fiction to suit the current political line by the future police chief Yezhov, at the time only a minor official of the Central Committee's Secretariat. Of Yezhov it is also recorded that he 'moved in literary circles', being united with Isaak Babel by a particularly intimate tie: he met his future wife through Babel, and suspected that she had been Babel's mistress.[3] Be that as it may, Babel went out of his way to consort with the fearful Yezhov at the height of his power, whether impelled by folly, fascinated horror or insatiable curiosity; he also cultivated the company of NKVD officers in general.[4] Then again, Sergey Efron – a well-known émigré and former White officer, the husband of Marina Tsvetayeva – eventually turned out to have been acting, without his wife's knowledge, as an NKVD under-cover agent in France; he helped to organize the murder and kidnapping of several expatriate Russians inconvenient to Stalin.[5] As for more recent phenomena, Vladimir Voynovich claims that the Union of Writers is riddled with members of the KGB, active and retired; he points out that the very organizational secretary of the Union's Moscow branch has been, at least until recently, not one of the city's better known scribes but a Lieutenant-General Ilyin of the KGB.[6]

Though the security force does not figure prominently in literature, it is more to the fore in Soviet-published material than might be expected when we remember that it is, in fact if not in name, a secret police. In the 1920s fanatical Bolshevizing writers did not hesitate to glorify Cheka officers even as they signed lists of hostages destined for execution. In somewhat more subtle form the Cheka theme is invoked in three short works of fiction of 1922–3: *Chocolate* by Aleksandr Tarasov-Rodionov; *Memoirs of Terenty Zabyty* by Aleksandr Arosev; *The Life and Death of Nikolay Kurbov* by Ilya Ehrenburg. Gorky's play *Somov and Others* (1931) also introduces the security police, providing its own style of happy ending when, just before the final curtain comes down, practically the whole cast of the play is arrested by the OGPU. In the post-Stalin world investigations by both the criminal and political police, together with a remarkable analysis of their activities in terms of moral responsibility, has been contributed in short novels by Pavel Nilin: *Cruelty* and *Probationary Period* (both 1956). The theme is, however, naturally more freely treated in Export Only literature, as for example in Solzhenitsyn's *The First Circle*. This incidentally contains a detailed portrait of one of Beria's leading henchmen and potential rivals, the notorious General Viktor Abakumov, Minister for State Security.

The above is a brief survey of Soviet political security operations in their literary context. But we must not forget that the USSR also possesses a more lowly police authority, the militia. The name dates back to the February Revolution of 1917, when the Imperial police force was disbanded and the name 'police' (*politsiya*) officially abandoned; it is now used only with reference to countries outside the Soviet bloc. The militia performs such functions as controlling traffic and issuing residence permits. It also combats crimes such as murder, rape, robbery and embezzlement when these appear sufficiently trivial in their implications not to menace the foundations of the State.

Concentration Camps

Particular odium is now attached to concentration camps owing to the way in which the institution developed under Stalin and Hitler; but no such macabre associations yet existed when the first Soviet concentration camps were set up from 1918 onwards with the encouragement of Lenin and Trotsky. Until the late 1920s these establishments were preventive rather than punitive in character, and were chiefly used to isolate potential political opponents – members of the formerly dominant social classes and non-Bolshevik Socialists. During this early period inmates were not treated with the degree of severity later imposed, and they were numbered only in tens of thousands rather than in millions. The main centre of these NEP-period camps were the Solovetsky Islands, sometimes called Solovki, in the White Sea, where the number of prisoners rose from some four thousand in 1923, reaching about a hundred thousand by the end of the decade.[1]

After visiting Solovki with an OGPU escort in 1929, Maksim Gorky – by now reconciled to the Soviet system of government against which he had earlier protested, and on the point of resuming Soviet residence – wrote an article, 'Solovki', in praise of the establishment:[2] a pilot scheme, as it were, for the later, grander apologia for the use of convict labour (on the White Sea Canal) that he was to sponsor in the mid-1930s.

Under developing Stalinism the character of the camps changed significantly. There was a big increase in the intake of prisoners – chiefly 'dekulakized' peasants – in the early 1930s. The number of camps greatly increased in consequence until they formed a nationwide network with inmates soon totalling millions and administered from 1934 by GULag. By the late 1930s the social composition had again changed, owing to the new policy of arresting persons from categories relatively immune during collectivization – townspeople and members of the professions. Meanwhile a decision had been taken to exploit convict labour as a major factor in building up the economy, the claim being made by the authorities that the purpose of the operation was to re-educate the political and common criminals who formed the work force.

Among the common criminals, of whom the rank and file were colloquially termed *bytoviki* (singular: *bytovik*), a substantial number consisted of a special élite known as *blatnyye* or *urki* (singular: *blatnoy*, *urka*). These assumed the right – often with the connivance of camp authority – to terrorize, rob and murder those (including political prisoners) who did not belong to their fraternity, and whom they called *frayera* (singular: *frayer*). For camp prisoners in general the colloquial term *zeki* (singular: *zek*) was employed. The words italicized above belong to the argot of the camps, which figures prominently in literature devoted to them – especially in Export Only literature, but also in Solzhenitsyn's *One Day in the Life of Ivan Denisovich*.

Officially entitled corrective labour camps, these institutions have been rechristened 'extermination labour camps' by Solzhenitsyn, this being a pun in Russian and the title of Part Three of *The Gulag Archipelago*. As the term indicates, consignment to GULag's care proved, in the majority of cases, no prelude to re-education but rather a form of liquidation, for death in captivity usually followed sooner or later through starvation, disease, exposure, overwork or a combination of these factors. Though conditions in all concentration camps were harsh, we must note that they were graded on a scale of increasing rigour. The mildest were the ordinary camps, where survival – especially for those employed on indoor labour – was not excluded. The harshest camps were those assigned to the category *katorga* ('hard labour'), as instituted during the Second World War. The word had originally applied to the severest form of penal confinement under the Tsars; but that had been a far less lethal procedure than the Stalinist *katorga*, for which the claim is made that no prisoner ever survived it.[3]

By contrast with the pall of silence soon to be lowered over the camps by the Stalinist censorship, attempts were made in the 1930s to publicize these institutions as ideally adapted for the beneficent correction of erring humanity. This tactic was most spectacularly applied to work on the canal, about a hundred and fifty miles long, linking the Baltic to the White Sea and constructed by nearly 300,000 convicts, using wheelbarrows and with a minimum of mechanical aids, between November 1931 and August 1933.[4] The enterprise is said to have caused over a hundred thousand fatalities (though the authorities claimed that 72,000 prisoners were amnestied on completion),[5] and also contributed to the degradation of the profession of letters under Stalin. A 'brigade' of 130 writers, headed by the 'great humanist' Maksim Gorky (now Stalinism's most prominent literary apologist), visited the site, after which thirty-five of them – including Shklovsky, Aleksey Tolstoy and Zoshchenko – joined in creating a symposium (*The White Sea Canal*) that presents the grim enterprise as a triumph for progressive penology. An English version of the work (1935) appeared with illustrations showing prisoners queuing up for hot pies. Cultural amenities were also stressed, including libraries and brass bands; one caption reads 'Music Speeds the Men on the Sluice'.[6] But the book fell under a ban in its country of origin in 1937 owing to the praise lavished on the main organizer of the project, the NKVD head Genrikh Yagoda.[7] Disgraced and put on trial in 1938, Yagoda confessed to having ordered, among other infamies, the murder of the same great humanist who had so recently publicized his alleged executioner's canal-building triumphs.

While the manual workers engaged on the canal and similar enterprises were convicts, mainly of peasant origin, the technical planning too was in the hands of prisoners, for numerous engineers and technicians had been arrested with the express purpose of drafting them to this and similar projects. Such specialists figure in a remarkable play, Nikolay Pogodin's *Aristocrats* (1934), which takes construction work on the White Sea Canal as its setting, while yet contriving to turn its grim subject into material for comedy. The humour consists in this, that the highly educated prisoner-engineers are shown as slower to learn the elementary truth of life – that its purpose is to work for the benefit of the proletariat – than are the canal's true aristocrats: bandits, burglars, prostitutes and common criminals in general. With the clampdown on camp themes in literature in the late 1930s Pogodin's ingenious drama was taken out of circulation along with Gorky's collectivized documentary on the White Sea Canal.[8]

For the planning teams, composed of highly qualified imprisoned specialists, the term *sharashka* came into use, and it is such an institution that forms the setting of Solzhenitsyn's long novel *The First Circle*. Here researchers and technicians are shown pioneering new techniques for identifying individuals by their voice-prints as recorded over the telephone – a device intended to enhance the efficiency of the security police in trapping suspects, and thus incidentally to increase recruitment to the *sharashki*.

From the late 1930s until Stalin's death in 1953 the concentration camps were one of the many subjects, including the pock-marks on the dictator's face, that could not be mentioned publicly. But the institution continued to flourish in secret, more in terms of mortality figures than of economic achievement – especially as the imposition of unrealistic 'norms' (production targets) tended, in the camps no less than in life outside, to result in botched work and falsified statistics. Only a small proportion of prisoners was set free, for to serve out the term of a sentence was either to be rearrested on a newly trumped-up charge, or else to be kept in exile under conditions sometimes little better than those of incarceration. During the war and during the decade after the war the camp empire was maintained as an extensive archipelago, with clusters of camp islands spread over the entire country – especially in the far north-east of Siberia, the far north of European Russia, and Central Asia. The number of those imprisoned is likely to have exceeded ten million, remaining stable to the extent that wastage through high mortality was compensated for by the high rate of continuing arrests.

The most important literary studies of the Stalin-period camps are those of Solzhenitsyn, who himself served in three types of camp: an ordinary 'mixed' camp for both political and common prisoners, as described in his play *The Love-Girl and the Innocent* (1969); a *sharashka* near Moscow; and an *osoblag* (special camp for political prisoners only, of which many were established after the war) at Ekibastuz in Central Asia. Solzhenitsyn's play, mentioned above, his short story *One Day in the Life of Ivan Denisovich* and his long novel set in a *sharashka*, *The First Circle* – all fictional studies of forced labour camps – are overshadowed by his three-volume documentary in seven parts, *The Gulag Archipelago*. It was compiled in great secrecy on Soviet territory in the years 1958–68, and has since been published abroad. Drawing evidence from 227 witnesses whom he managed to question, as well as from his own first-hand experience, the author has constructed a monumental work that provides a detailed and authentic panorama of camp life. His picture conforms closely to that purveyed in the previously available and independently produced literature of the subject, consisting largely of the Western-published memoirs of former prisoners. The Soviet concentration camps have a bibliography more extensive than most non-specialists can realize. It is more extensive, even, than Solzhenitsyn himself was aware when he wrote his literary memoirs *The Calf and the Oak*, where he speaks of 'up to forty' books on the camps 'telling the full story' having been published in the West. The figure is considerably underestimated, but in adding that 'it all went in one ear and out of the other' Solzhenitsyn is not so far from the truth.[9]

Though we can do little more than indicate the scope of these earlier writings, mention will be made of four very different studies, all by women, all composed on Soviet territory and all published abroad before *The Gulag Archipelago*.

Among documentary accounts Yevgeniya Ginsburg's reminiscences of Kolyma, *Into the Whirlwind*, are an outstanding first-hand description by a survivor of the Dalstroy camps in far north-eastern Siberia. Galina Serebryakova's memoir *Tornado* (also 1967) portrays the experience of a dedicated Communist whose political faith survived even two decades of incarceration; the work was rejected for publication in the Soviet Union, but the loyalist author protested when informed that it had been spirited abroad and published there. Turning to imaginative works touching on the camps, as seen from outside, we note that Lidiya Chukovskaya's novel *The Deserted House* (published abroad in 1965) was written at the time of the events that it describes; it is the study of a mother's betrayal of her son, a victim of the Terror. Maternal responses of a diametrically opposite order are recorded in Anna Akhmatova's poem *Requiem*, commemorating the experience of repeatedly queuing up outside a Leningrad prison for news of her arrested son. Akhmatova's verse also includes a fragment in which she evokes the horrors of transportation as contemplated from threatened Leningrad one midnight. No longer did Russia's second city seem like 'a European capital and winner of a beauty contest'. Rather did it evoke the spectre of 'transportation to atrocious Yeniseysk; of change here for Chita, for Ishim, for waterless Irgiz, for Atbasar of evil repute; change here for Svobodny Town and the plaguey stink of rotting bunks'.[10] Only in the original Russian can the quasi-Miltonic pile-up of harsh, non-Slav, etymologically alien place names, so redolent of homelessness and despair, be fully appreciated – not least when they culminate in the crashing irony of the etymologically Russian *gorod Svobodny* ... 'Free Town'! Still more chilling are Mandelstam's superb verses anticipating his own doom, 'Should our enemies ever seize me ...' (1937).[11]

By comparison with these and other Export Only studies, Soviet-published belles-lettres and memoirs devoted to the camps are reticent, but on a fluctuating level reflecting changes in official policy. The most outspoken work is Solzhenitsyn's fictional *One Day in the Life of Ivan Denisovich*, and, among documentary reports, General A. V. Gorbatov's memoirs of Kolyma, *Years Off My Life* (1964). Others are almost ludicrously devious and oblique: for example, the sibylline description of a chance meeting with a long imprisoned and recently released old friend in Tvardovsky's poem *Beyond the Far Distance* (1950–60).

After the mass release of surviving prisoners in the immediate post-Stalin years many camps were closed down. But the institution was by no means abolished, and the number of inmates has been calculated very roughly at about 1,200,000 in 1973.[12] This figure includes all those serving sentences for civil crimes as well as those sentenced for political reasons under some such heading as anti-Soviet agitation. Since crime figures are not published, and since the status of political prisoner is not recognized by the Soviet authorities (by contrast with the Imperial period), our scope for calculating the impact of political oppression by imprisonment is limited. But it seems likely that the proportion of the population serving in camps and prisons is in the high area of five per thousand. As for conditions, most memoirs dealing with the post-Stalin period suggest considerable improvement since those days. Others, notably Anatoly Marchenko's *My Testimony* (1969), indicate that this improvement may not have gone very far. In the camps as described by Marchenko near-starvation rations were still the rule, while guards received a bonus for shooting escapers. These might also be torn in pieces by the guard dogs who were still a feature of the system and whose meat ration was nine times that of the prisoners. As this reminds us, another work of fiction (published abroad only) happens to have a guard dog as its hero: Georgy Vladimov's *Faithful Ruslan* (1975), describing the pathetic predicament of one of these canine custodians after he has been robbed of his

function in life by the abolition of the forced labour camps over which
he had hitherto faithfully kept watch.

The Military

Born in the course of a world war, Soviet Russia was almost immediately plunged into a civil war, and so we are not surprised to find that
it has evolved as a highly militarized society. Through universal con-
scription to long periods of full-time training that vary according to
the arm of the service, and through the maintenance of large regular
forces, the country has been recently (1977) estimated as having some
four million men under arms, together with a reserve of some twenty-
five million who have undergone at least two years' full-time training
followed by periodical recall to the colours.[1] Schoolchildren and
students are also required to do military training, besides which two
enormous paramilitary bodies claim a membership of fifty million
and eighty million respectively: GTO ('Ready for Toil and Defence'),
a militarized 'keep fit' organization; and DOSAAF ('Voluntary Society
for Co-operation with the Army, Air Force and Navy').

The Soviet armed forces come under the Ministry of Defence, and
are divided into five main branches: strategic missiles; land forces;
air defence; air force; navy. After exploding its first atom bomb in
1949 and its first hydrogen bomb in 1953, the USSR has developed
its nuclear missile system with particular intensiveness, threatening
to eclipse that of its only rival, the United States.

The Soviet military establishment has all along been kept under
close political control, of which a recent appointment is symptomatic:
that of the Party leader Leonid Brezhnev (as disclosed in October
1977) to the post of Supreme Commander-in-Chief of the Armed
Forces alongside his many other offices. Determination by the Party
to control the military goes back to early Soviet years, when the prospect of a 'Bonapartist' *coup* seemed particularly menacing. The figure
who most aroused this apprehension was Trotsky, Soviet Russia's outstanding war leader.

In 1918 Trotsky had been chiefly responsible for establishing the
Red Army (more officially, the Worker-Peasant Red Army) on lines
designed to emphasize a contrast between this new revolutionary force
and the old-style Tsarist military establishment. The term officer was

rejected in favour of 'commander'. Traditional designations of officers' and NCOs' ranks were also avoided; for instance, the equivalent of a major-general was *komdiv* (short for 'divisional commander').

After Lenin's death Trotsky was hampered in the struggle for power by the very prestige that his military prowess had earned. Nor did fear of a military *coup* disappear with his political eclipse in the mid-1920s. It was, presumably, partly in order to safeguard himself from such a prospect that Stalin ordained, in 1937 as part of the Great Purge, a massacre of his officer corps, liquidating the overwhelming majority of senior serving officers in the land, sea and air forces from Marshal Tukhachevsky downwards: ninety per cent of those holding general's rank, eighty per cent of those holding colonel's rank, and a total of officer victims running into five figures.[2]

After destroying most of his officers Stalin began to rebuild his military establishment along lines designed to emphasize a return to Imperial Russian tradition. The old names of ranks (general, admiral, colonel and so on) were restored; so too were epaulettes, once contemptuously discarded as a symbol of the old regime. The title of officer was restored in 1943, and the designation 'Red Army' was changed to 'Soviet Army' three years later.

Shortly after the outbreak of war with Germany, Stalin personally assumed the posts of People's Commissar of Defence and Supreme Commander-in-Chief. When the war was over he was careful to relegate his most successful commander in the field, Marshal Zhukov, to obscurity. That Zhukov may indeed have cherished political ambitions became apparent after Stalin's death, when he emerged from obscurity, was appointed Minister of Defence and helped Khrushchev to dismiss his most powerful political rivals (Malenkov, Kaganovich and Molotov: the 'Anti-Party Group') in 1957. Briefly rewarded with full membership of the Politburo (then termed Presidium) of the Party Central Committee, and the only professional soldier to have achieved such high Party rank, Zhukov was dismissed a few months later for conceiving ambitions beyond his station; but he was later permitted, under the Brezhnev regime, to publish memoirs discreetly emphasizing Khrushchev's military incompetence.

Measures to frustrate use of the armed forces in a political *coup* have not stopped short at the demotion or execution of leading generals. The military is kept under close observation by the security police (currently the KGB), which maintains a network of secret informers within the services. We must also remember that the security police has long possessed its own large and well-equipped armed forces independent of military control. Nor is this all. The structure of the armed forces is further penetrated by another organization, one directly responsible to the Party Central Committee for the ideological conformity of the military – the Chief Political Administration of the Soviet Army and Navy. The organization is represented at lower levels by officers termed *zampolity* (deputy commanders with responsibility for political affairs), who work parallel with the commanding officers of units and formations. The office of *zampolit* replaced that of Military Commissar, which was abolished in 1940, reintroduced in 1941 and again abolished in 1942. Military Commissars had originally been evolved in the Civil War as a device for controlling Red Army commanding officers, who were automatically suspect to the new regime since they so often belonged to the formerly privileged social class overthrown by the Revolution; these same 'bourgeois' military specialists were also kept in line by threats to their families, who were treated in effect as hostages. The Military Commissars' duties varied from time to time, embracing at their widest complete joint responsibility with the parallel army officer for all aspects of command.

Warfare, particularly on land, has played so prominent a part in recent Russian history, especially in 1914–20 and 1941–5, that we cannot be surprised to find it reflected very fully in imaginative literature. Some of the relevant works have already been mentioned. They include Aleksey Tolstoy's trilogy of novels *The War through Hell*, which embraces the First World War, the February and October Revolutions and the Civil War. Tolstoy also wrote a separate novel on the Civil War, *Bread*, which appeared in the peak purge year 1937 and falsified Stalin's role in the defence of Tsaritsyn (later Stalingrad) while portraying Trotsky, in the manner now obligatory, as the fount of all evil.

Perhaps because of his aristocratic origins and years spent in emigration, Tolstoy felt a need to make more concessions to political propaganda than did his younger contemporary Mikhail Sholokhov, whose *The Quiet Don* spans roughly the same historical period as *The Way through Hell*. Its hero Grigory Melekhov sees extensive military service in the First World War, and still more in the Civil War, in which he fights at various times for Reds, for Whites and for partisan bands unaffiliated to either. As we remember, the young

Sholokhov had once been a protégé of another notable portrayer of Cossacks – Aleksandr Serafimovich, whose documentary *The Iron Flood* describes the retreat of a Bolshevik army through the North Caucasus. It is a portrait of mass suffering, still regarded as a literary classic in the Soviet Union, though far less popular than Sholokhov's masterpiece. War fiction also includes Babel's laconic sketches, the reverse of panoramic in their approach, as collected together under the title *Cavalry Army*. He does not describe the Civil War proper, but a substantial foreign campaign that coincided with it in time – the Soviet-Polish War of 1920.

During the Second World War authors became more heavily involved in hostilities than in the First, as we are reminded by bald statistics: between 1941 and 1945 no less than 417 registered members of the Writers' Union fell in battle, while nearly a thousand were awarded decorations. Many served at the front, others were active as war reporters, while some of the more aged, infirm and illustrious were evacuated to the rear.

Among works of war literature published while hostilities were in progress were some outstandingly successful lyrics by Konstantin Simonov; they include the famous *Wait for Me*, addressed by a front-line soldier to his wife or mistress. Most popular of all was the long poem *Vasily Tyorkin* (1941–5) by Aleksandr Tvardovsky, describing the adventures of an ordinary soldier in humorous style and jog-trot verse. According to Solzhenitsyn, a junior officer at the time, Tvardovsky's poem was, with Lyov Tolstoy's *War and Peace*, the favourite reading of front-line soldiers.[3] During the war Pasternak too published patriotic verse in the newspapers.

One outstanding novel describing hostilities is Viktor Nekrasov's *In the Trenches of Stalingrad*; published in 1946 and awarded a Stalin Prize, it antedated the cultural oppressions of the Zhdanov period, and remains one of the most remarkable studies of the Second World War in any language. It is more effective and less propagandist than an earlier novel devoted to the same campaign, Simonov's *Days and Nights* (1943–4). Simonov, whose prose fiction is preponderantly military in theme, later wrote a tetralogy of less inhibited war novels published between 1952 and 1971, continuity between them being maintained by a tendency for the main characters to recur from work to work. These are *Comrades in Arms*, covering Russo-Japanese operations in Mongolia in 1939, and three studies of the Second World

War highly critical of Stalin's military leadership. *The Living and the Dead* describes the defeat of the Red Army in 1941; *Soldiers are Born, Not Made* revives the theme of Stalingrad from an angle less narrow than that of *Days and Nights*; *The Last Summer* portrays the Red Army's victories over the Germans in mid-1944.

Other fictional chroniclers of war and military life include Yury Bondarev, in whose novels *The Silence* (1962) and *The Two of Them* (1964) Stalin's victimization of his officer corps forms a significant theme. Vasily Bykov, who served as an army officer for about fourteen years during and after the Second World War, has published several war stories reminiscent of Viktor Nekrasov in their avoidance of pseudo-heroics. And in Bulat Okudzhava's story of the front line, *Good Luck, Schoolboy* (1961), this tendency is carried much further, the work being so devoid of conventional pseudo-heroism that it was sharply criticized as advocating pacifism.

Besides chronicling warfare contemporary to themselves, modern Russian writers have also delved into the past. Among historical novels set in the early twentieth century is Solzhenitsyn's *August 1914*, describing the rout of the Russian Second Army under General Samsonov at Tannenberg in the early weeks of the First World War. For Soviet-published historical war novels, including some by Novikov-Priboy and Sergeyev-Tsensky, see also page 78; for the Fadeyev Medal, instituted in 1974 as an award for works portraying the Soviet armed forces, see page 208.

7 The Class System

We shall consider social stratification in three parts in accordance with the official doctrine whereby the population falls into three specific categories: workers, peasants, intelligentsia. Of these only the first two are termed classes, while the third is said to constitute something inferentially inferior to a class: a mere *prosloyka* ('stratum'). The three categories are listed, in descending order of notional importance, in Article One of the new (1977) Soviet Constitution. This describes the USSR as 'a Socialist state of the whole people, expressing the will and interests of the working class, the peasantry and the intelligentsia'. We shall treat the categories in that order, while also observing that the new Constitution has promoted the intelligentsia in esteem, for in the parallel passage in the previous (1936) Constitution the USSR was baldly described as 'a Socialist state of workers and peasants'; that is, the intelligentsia was not even mentioned at this point. But though the place assigned to the intelligentsia is inferior, both in the Constitution of 1936 and (less so) in that of 1977, we must not forget that the function of Soviet – as of other – constitutions is partly liturgical. In practice, as will be stressed below, it is to the intelligentsia (workers by brain) and not to the notionally preferred manual workers and peasants, that the truly privileged sections of Soviet society belong.

Workers

The concept of the proletariat, denoting urban industrial manual workers, occupies a key place in the Communist structure of symbolism. It was workers in this sense who, according to official Soviet theory, carried out the October Revolution of 1917, though we are told that they did so under Bolshevik guidance and in alliance with the poor peasantry. To stress the primacy of the workers in overturning the previous dispensation the new order was proclaimed as constituting a Dictatorship of the Proletariat. The phrase is puzzling, since dictatorship normally denotes the exercise of authority by a single individual rather than a social category; and also because the working class, however defined, was speedily prevented from taking political initiatives except through the ruling Party. Within that neither Lenin himself nor any of his senior associates could boast professional experience of manual labour or working-class origin, though Stalin's father had been a drunken cobbler. If there was any dictator in the first years of the Soviet regime it was Lenin himself, except that his personal ascendancy exempted him from the need to adopt an excessively despotic style; moreover, he appears to have deferred in all seriousness to the mystique attributing some kind of *ex hypothesi* superiority to those who work by muscle in an urban environment, as opposed to those who toil at a desk or in a field.

Though the concept of a Dictatorship of the Proletariat has ceased to be invoked as relevant to modern times, the supremacy of the working class is still a cardinal element in official ideology, and this despite a considerable shift of balance in the numerical composition of social categories. In 1917 the workers constituted only three million, roughly, in a total population consisting largely of peasants and numbering about 140 million.[1] Sixty years later the working class had multiplied nearly thirty times, to nearly eighty million, while the overall population had not even doubled.

As for the proletariat's supremacy and alleged privileged position, attempts to assert initiative independently of the current Party line, by or on behalf of the workers, have continued to be severely repressed. These episodes include the crushing of the Kronstadt Rebellion of 1921, together with the suppression within the Party of the group called the Workers' Opposition at about the same time. They also include the occasional post-war strikes and protest demonstrations that were put down by troops – those at Temir Tau (1959), Novocherkassk (1962) and Dneprodzerzhinsk (1972); and some more recent unsuccessful small-scale attempts to establish an independent trade union movement.

Methods of ensuring workers' subservience have included the maintenance of an elaborate official trade union organization almost totally subservient to the State; the enactment, under Stalin, of severe labour legislation (since considerably relaxed) whereby minor unpunctuality could lead to prosecution and workers were not allowed to change their employment; the obligation, still imposed, to attend political meetings and register approval of propaganda campaigns periodically mounted by the Party.

By contrast with the intellectual-dominated Party of Lenin's day, many Party leaders of more recent times have sprung from the working class. Brezhnev is a case in point, and Khrushchev, though born into a peasant family, became a proletarian by working as a locksmith. Such examples could be indefinitely repeated. It must, however, also be remembered that full-time Party activity is not compatible with full-time manual work, and that any notable degree of political advancement means, in practice, leaving the working class. A member of the Party Apparatus may, indeed, boast that he is a 'worker', but it will usually be either his father or he himself in distant youth who wielded a spanner or operated a lathe. Nor does the modern proletariat, measured by the key criterion of Party membership, enjoy a degree of influence commensurate with the high value set, in Marxist theory, on industrial labour. There is a far higher proportion of Party members among mental than manual workers, though it is also true that industrial workers are considerably more strongly represented in the Party than is the peasantry.

In this context one minor linguistic difficulty may trouble students unversed in modern usage. Of the two Russian words commonly translated 'worker' (*rabochy* and *rabotnik*) the former is reserved for manual workers, while the latter tends to be applied to high officials. Visitors to the USSR may, accordingly, be informed by their guide that they are viewing workers' flats when the buildings in question in fact represent privileged housing for *rabotniki*, to which no mere *rabochy* could aspire.

Despite the occasional protests and demonstrations mentioned above the USSR has remained free from the kind of labour troubles endemic in many post-war capitalist countries. Such offences against public order are prohibited under Article 69 of the RSFSR Criminal Code as actions 'directed towards the disruption of industry, transport, agriculture, the monetary system, trade or any other branch of the economy'. Workers seeking to contravene these provisions not only render themselves liable to criminal prosecution, but also risk being harangued by activists who remind them that their factories belong to them, and that

to strike would therefore be to strike against themselves. Obliged to
signify assent to such sophistries while legally deprived of the right to
withdraw his labour, the worker finds himself considerably inhibited
by non-Soviet standards. Though he can and does have recourse to
go-slow methods such as are particularly difficult to curb through
legislation and supervision, one leading literary memoirist has well
expressed the basic situation as follows : 'This is the only country in
the world that has managed to cope with its workers' movement.'[2]
The result has been more easily achieved in the absence of any pro-
vision for unemployment relief, a deficiency obscured by the official
claim whereby the USSR, by contrast with capitalist countries, is
said to enjoy conditions of permanent full employment.

The harsh fact is, then, that those who have no pension, and who
cannot find work, must live on savings or charity; but it is also true
that local authorities, including the Rayon Executive Committees,
control funds available for disbursement at their discretion to relieve
those temporarily unable to support themselves. Since Soviet unemployment is one of those indecorous phenomena to which allusion may
not, in general, be made, we naturally find little reference to it in
Soviet-published literature. It does, however, figure in Fyodor
Panfyorov's last major work, the trilogy of novels *Mother Volga*
(1953–60), which also criticizes the officially fostered industrial campaign known as Stakhanovism.

The Stakhanovite movement was the very opposite of the unpublicized go-slow methods often unavowedly adopted by Soviet workers,
being a nationwide campaign promoted in the fullest glare of publicity
from 1935. A coal-miner, A. Stakhanov, was advertised as a prodigy
of productivity, and his phenomenal output per shift was used as a
means of spurring on others and of justifying general increases in
production targets. The use of the label Stakhanovism died out before
Stalin. But production targets, known as norms, have remained a
staple device in the drive to obtain better results from individual
workers and enterprises, both urban and agricultural. To fulfil one's
norm, or – better – to overfulfil it by a spectacular margin is, on the
pages of loyalist literature, the dearest ambition of any self-respecting
Soviet toiler, factory or farm. In practice, however, substantial over-
fulfilment is undesirable, as has been noted above, since it is likely
to result in the imposition of a new and more exacting norm.

Far from creating any regular rhythm of work, the norm system has tended to ensure that production proceeds in a series of peristaltic surges preceding the deadline for each monthly, quarterly or annual norm assessment. During the first third of each month a factory or other production enterprise tends to relax, only to speed up in the second third, and to enter a very frenzy of activity in the last ten days. To these spasms of effort the term *shturmovshchina* ('storming') is commonly applied. Since the phenomenon is inconsistent with the officially projected image of serene planning by all-wise authority, it is little reflected in Soviet-published literature. Storming is, however, a theme in the memoirs of Anatoly Zlobin, as published in 1956 (a year notorious for such startling 'revelations') and significantly entitled *The Truth That I Concealed*. Another key, unofficial institution in industrial life is that of the *tolkach* ('fixer') who specializes in supplying urgently needed materials through *blat* ('unofficial channels'), thus bypassing the endless delays imposed by bureaucratic procedure on any factory director unwise enough to attempt to manage his plant strictly in accordance with regulations.

Earlier literary works by or about proletarians include Fyodor Gladkov's novel *Cement*. Its hero is a mechanic, Gleb Chumalov, who returns from three years' fighting for the Reds in the Civil War to his home town – an unnamed port recognizable as Novorossiysk – to find both the local cement works and his own domestic life in ruins. He buckles to and overcomes all obstacles in an epic of the reconstruction period following the Civil War that long ago became a Soviet best-seller.

Among the many Five Year Plan novels commemorating Stalin's industrialization drive from the late 1920s onwards Valentin Katayev's *Time, Forward* is outstanding. Here cement is once again the theme, in the sense that the novel depicts an attempt by a building team to beat a record, hitherto held by a Kharkov collective, for the amount of concrete laid in twenty-four hours, and thus expedite the construction of a new steel plant at Magnitogorsk in the Urals. Another notable Five Year Plan novel is Leonid Leonov's *Sot*, which describes the building of a paper mill in the forests of the far north. Each novel exemplifies the staple conflicts of industrialization-oriented fiction: that between man and the elements; and that between Communist or communized heroes and 'survivals from the past' – wreckers, saboteurs, Whites, Americans and other undesirables. Both these novels are redeemed by buried humour or whimsy; they are by no means the political tracts that so brief a summary might suggest.

Far less conformist in flavour than these two works, both by authors lacking working-class associations, is the fiction of Andrey Platonov, whose father was a railway mechanic and who became a worker himself at the age of fifteen. Between the 1920s and his death in 1951 he published numerous stories in which skilled workmen figure as heroes. But much of Platonov's work did not achieve contemporary publication, for his sardonic and idiosyncratic style was out of tune with the demands of his allegedly heroic epoch. Some of his works were republished or published for the first time from surviving manuscripts in the USSR of the 1960s, while others have been exclusively brought out abroad.

An instructive study of work on a building site is to be found in Voynovich's story *I Want to be Honest* (1963), where a foreman builder can automatically gain promotion to the rank of engineer by simply signing documents confirming that a section of an apartment block, newly completed by his men, is fit for occupation. Aware that the work is in fact sadly sub-standard, he refuses to sign since he values his self-respect above his material welfare – a moral predicament of a type not uncommonly portrayed in post-Stalin literature.

A recent recruit from the proletariat to literature is Vladimir Maksimov, whose father had been purged as a Trotskyite and who was permitted to emigrate in 1974. Among several novels of his issued exclusively outside the Soviet Union is *Seven Days of Creation* (1971), which proved ineligible for Soviet publication for two reasons. First, it depicts half a century of progressive disillusionment with the Soviet system as experienced by a working-class family, the Lashkovs; and, secondly, it suggests that the remedy for these and other human ills lies less with politics than with religion.

Peasants

There is no more basic feature in Russia's evolution throughout the ages than the overwhelming numerical preponderance of the country's peasantry, together with the miseries to which this notoriously exploited class, largely enserfed until 1861, has been exposed over the centuries. Under Soviet conditions the peasantry remained by far the largest social class for a decade: three out of four citizens were still peasants as late as 1926. As for peasant sufferings, these were to be intensified under fully established Stalinism, and beyond anything experienced since the early seventeenth century, through enforced collectivization and the associated widespread famine.

The Bolsheviks naturally adopted Marx's low assessment of the peasantry as a revolutionary force. According to their doctrine the peasant was confined – by the 'idiocy of rural life', as the formula has it – to a minor role in the drama of history, being expected to defer to his revolutionary brother-in-arms, the proletarian. Since, however, an exclusively proletarian revolution seemed an impossibility in so predominantly agrarian a country as Russia, Lenin's revolutionary strategy had involved urging villagers to seize landowners' estates and conciliating the muzhik with slogans adopted from the Socialist Revolutionaries (the party of the peasantry).

As has been mentioned above, peasants played a dominant role as common soldiers in both the Red and the White Armies during the Civil War. Many, having simply been press-ganged into one or other of the competing forces, saw little to choose between them. They also joined marauding bands of anarchists and others not affiliated to either of the two main factions. But their general tendency was to support the Bolsheviks, their motives including the fear that a White victory might result in the restitution of lands that they had seized from pre-revolutionary landowners.

In due course many peasants were to consider the Bolsheviks worse exploiters than any landlord. This impression already arose during the Civil War owing to the practice of requisitioning peasants' grain stocks by armed force. Such a scene is described, with many a bucolic wisecrack, in Leonid Leonov's novel *The Badgers*. Leonov portrays a peasant revolt, possibly inspired by the anti-Bolshevik mutiny of peasants in Tambov Province in 1921. He shows the conflict between the town and the country, a common theme in literature of the early Soviet period, and also of the most recent, while displaying considerable sympathy for both sides. Other authors of the period were more partisan. In his *Naked Year* and other works Pilnyak 'interpreted the Revolution in terms of peasant anarchism, as a victory of the countryside over the city'.[1]

It would be hard to find the contrary, anti-peasant sentiment more outspokenly expressed than in Gorky's pamphlet *On the Russian*

Peasantry, published in Berlin (1922). Here the villager is accused of inhuman cruelty and an addition to torture, while also incurring blame for hoarding food while townspeople were starving. That more peasants than townsmen starved in the famine year 1921–2, as in all Russian famines, Gorky chooses to ignore; nor does he show understanding for the natural feelings of outrage experienced by a village family robbed of its entire store of grain by drunken, slogan-mumbling, armed requisitioners from the towns.

None of the writers so far mentioned in this section – Leonov, Pilnyak, Gorky – was himself of peasant origin. But the early Soviet period spawned a whole school of authentic peasant poets. For the most part their credentials as peasants were more impressive than their claims to be poets, but they included at least two outstanding artists. Of these Nikolay Klyuyev remained committed to the peasant way of life; he condemned urban civilization and Bolshevik technology, being persecuted by the authorities and eventually suffering liquidation in 1937. His more famous younger contemporary, Sergey Yesenin, was also of impeccable peasant origin, hailing from the depths of Ryazan province. He too could write as an advocate of rural simplicity: for example, in a famous poem, *Mass for the Dead* (1920). Here he describes a race between a railway train (symbol of hated modernity) and a red-maned foal, the author's sympathies being ostensibly with the latter. But Yesenin himself was, symbolically, a passenger on that train rather than an unspoilt creature of the wild. Indeed, it so happens that he was able, through some fiddle characteristic of the period, to borrow a train for his personal use in the summer of 1920 and tour southern Russia and the Caucasus.[2] He retained his idiosyncratic peasant idiom, while progressively diverting it from rustic themes to present the personal dilemmas – alcoholism, hooliganism, exhibitionism – that eventually drove him to suicide in 1925. And yet, bizarre though his evolution may seem, Yesenin was one of the finest poets writing in an age of flourishing poetry.

At the time of Yesenin's death, in the middle of NEP, peasants enjoyed conditions of relative freedom, living in a manner not strikingly different from that of the last pre-revolutionary decades. Exempted from the requisitionings of the Civil War years, they were now growing crops for the market, having largely recovered from the tribulations of war and revolution. But this was only a breathing space leading to the imposition of collectivization, with its attendant repressions and famine, in the early 1930s. These events, together with the extensive recruitment of muzhiks to industrial work under the Five Year Plans, helped to reduce the proportion of rural residents, including peasants, in the population from about eighty per cent in 1926 to fifty-two per cent in 1959 and forty-two per cent in 1972.[3]

Collectivization was an economic failure, the *per capita* productivity of agriculture being no greater – despite the widely advertised intensive mechanization – in 1953 than it had been in 1928.[4] But the process was a political success in collectivizing twenty-five million private, self-sufficient homesteads, consisting of individuals notoriously suspicious of authority and schooled over the centuries in the art of thwarting landowners, officials, legislators and other interfering outsiders. These individualists were now combined in groups averaging about seventy-five households, either in Collective Farms (*kolkhozy*), where they were paid largely in kind on the basis of the number of days worked, or else in the numerous State Farms (*sovkhozy*), which tended to be larger and where the labourers were paid wages. One justification for collectivization was the increased scope that it offered to mechanized farming such as had been beyond the reach of individual small-holders. Machine-Tractor Stations (MTS) were accordingly set up at focal points in the countryside to carry out all mechanized work in the Collective Farms; they also served as centres of political control, being rural strongholds of the Party, which was thinly represented in the villages. The Machine-Tractor Stations were phased out in the late 1950s as part of Khrushchev's agricultural reforms, their plant being sold off to the Collective Farms.

The horrors of collectivization could not be freely portrayed in Soviet-published literature, which tended rather to dilate on the exploits of idyllic norm-exceeding milkmaids. But the most famous novel of collectivization, Sholokhov's *Virgin Soil Upturned*, by no means ignores the grim side of the campaign; for example, it contains a harrowing picture of the expulsion of a peasant family from its home. As the episode reminds us, Stalin's method of destroying traditional village life depended, in accordance with his usual practice, on the adroit use of labels. He attempted to set peasants at odds with each other by placing them in three categories. Of these the kulaks ('fists') were the richest, and as such were considered to be enemies of the regime and exploiters of their neighbours. At the other end of the scale were the poor peasants (*bednyaki*), supposedly the friends and beneficiaries of the regime, who were to be loosed on their kulak neighbours, while the middle peasants (*serednyaki*) were expected to draw the correct conclusions from this spectacle and join their poorer neighbours in entering the collectives and persecuting the kulaks. As for those poor peasants – and there were many – who refused to co-operate in the campaign, they could be designated as objects of persecution by attaching to them the ingenious label *podkulachniki* ('kulak stooges').

The next most celebrated novel of collectivization is by Fyodor Panfyorov, himself the son of a peasant, who makes a more active attempt than Sholokhov to propagandize collectivization in his four-part novel *Bruski* (1928–37). As for the poetry of collectivization, we may instance *The Land of Muraviya* (1936) by Tvardovsky. He too was a peasant's son, one whose father had been repressed as a kulak. In Tvardovsky's poem the peasant hero at first refuses to be collectivized, and embarks on a journey to the land of Muraviya, a mythical Utopia. Discovering that no such paradise exists, he agrees in the end to become a model collective farmer.

Though Tvardovsky's poem is by no means as didactically Stalinist as its conclusion might suggest, it was not until the dictator's death that a more faithful portrayal of collectivization could be attempted in Soviet-published accounts of the peasantry. One of the frankest occurs in Ivan Stadnyuk's novel *People are Not Angels* (Part One, 1962); it portrays famine, imprisonment, forced labour camps and other features of the 1930s with the imputation, reinforced in the second part of the novel (1965), that these things were all ultimately justified. This was not the universal view. After witnessing the results of collectivization in the 1930s, Pasternak described conditions as unimaginably catastrophic: 'I fell ill. For a whole year I couldn't sleep.'[5] Nor can it be doubted that the following view, put into the mouth of a character in *Doctor Zhivago*, was the author's own: 'I think that collectivization was both a mistake and a failure, and because that couldn't be admitted, every means of intimidation had to be used to make people . . . maintain the contrary of what their eyes told them.'[6] What Pasternak seems to be suggesting is that the general oppressions of the late 1930s, as instituted after the imposition of collectivization, were to some extent a gigantic cover-up for that disastrous transformation of peasant life.

Events since Stalin's death have wrought a slow but impressive change in the position of the peasantry. The class has continued to dwindle numerically, totalling only 19·3 per cent of the population in 1972 (and even forming a minority within the overall rural population, then constituting forty-two per cent of the country's population as a whole).[7] But it has been considerably relieved from various disabilities imposed on it under Stalin, who sought to finance his ambitious industrialization projects by exploiting the peasants even more harshly than other sections of the community. The change began under Khrushchev, who at least paid lip service to the importance of the peasantry, even if he tended to confine himself to exhortations, to agricultural pseudo-panaceas including a misplaced emphasis on maize, and to being photographed chatting to norm-exceeding pigmen. But he also pioneered provisions for collective farmers to receive pensions – admittedly small – to which they had not previously been entitled. Under his successors agricultural wages, no longer paid in kind, rose substantially by comparison with those of the rest of the community. Moreover, peasants are now to receive domestic passports, like members of other social classes. When this reform is implemented the Soviet peasantry will have shed yet another attribute of second-class citizenship.

Meanwhile agricultural productivity has steadily risen, having maintained an average annual growth rate of 3·4 per cent in 1951–75.[8] But this general improvement has been accompanied by violent fluctuations and crises, whether effected by climatic conditions, lack of incentives or bureaucratic paralysis. For whatever reason, the USSR has been compelled to import grain from North America in years of shortfall. Though these shortages emphasize the failure of Soviet agriculture to keep pace with the rapidly expanding population, they are also due to the fact that the population now expects and receives a better diet.

Post-war improvements in diet and food production were the more easily achieved since they began from such a low base in 1945, when agriculture had been devastated by four years of war and occupation. Output, yields, productivity, labourers' living conditions have all improved since then. Yet the average output of grain per farmer in the USSR was still, in 1975, only one tenth of that of the farmer in the USA, while the yield per acre was only half as much. Hence the disparity between the number directly employed in agriculture in the countries: some 25·4 per cent of the labour force in the USSR, but only 4·6 per cent in the USA.[9]

One notable feature of the Soviet agricultural system is the peasant's private plot. On this rent-free land, averaging three quarters of an acre, he is free to grow whatever he likes for the use of his own family or for sale – at prices regulated by supply and demand – at one of the many Collective Farm markets in the towns. Owing to the absence of effective incentives for working on collectively farmed land, peasants tend to invest their major efforts in their private plots. They amounted to a mere 1·6 per cent of the total cultivated land in 1975, yet they were producing nearly one third of the country's meat and milk; fifty-nine per cent of potatoes; thirty-four per cent of other vegetables; and thirty-nine per cent of eggs.[10] Since similar allotments are also culti-vated by many non-peasants, they are extremely numerous – as may be observed from almost any train window on the outskirts of a town – and are even said to total about fifty million in all. They are also said to absorb one third of the total man hours devoted to agriculture.[11]

The most remarkable corpus of modern Russian peasant literature is that which arose in the early 1950s and is known as *derevenskaya proza* ('Village Prose'). It includes novels, short stories and docu-mentary sketches, and it first attracted attention by what it lacked: idealized milkmaids and blissful bumpkins all gladly co-operating in a vast collectivized agricultural idyll in the spirit of Socialist Realism. An early pioneer of Village Prose was Valentin Ovechkin, whose sketches were highly critical of Party bureaucracy as imposed on the countryside. He was followed by another influential author of bucolic sketches, Yefim Dorosh, and a whole school of successors. They include Fyodor Abramov, who attacked traditional idealization in a critical essay of 1954 ('Collective Farm Villages in Post-War Prose'), and has since written numerous stories and novels conveying a grimly comic picture of rural conditions. One of these, the short sketch *Around and About* (1963), takes a day in the life of a squalid, run-down collective farm where everyone is out picking mushrooms, saunaing or lying around dead drunk instead of heaving eagerly away at their pitch-forks, while the only surplus is of marriageable girls. Mud, rain, toothache, general hopelessness dominate the scene.

In making his theme a typical day in the life of a collective farm, Abramov was adopting a technique similar to that of Solzhenitsyn in *One Day in the Life of Ivan Denisovich*; which reminds us that Solzhenitsyn's hero, Ivan Denisovich Shukhov, is a peasant. So too is the heroine of his story *Matryona's House* (1963). The non-peasant

Solzhenitsyn records a correction made to the draft of this story by his editor Tvardovsky, a peasant born and bred – though one divorced from his native clod by many years as a metropolitan literary tycoon. Solzhenitsyn had used the phrase 'the village carpenters', but Tvardovsky pointed out that this betrayed ignorance of Russian rural life. So universal a rustic skill was carpentry that every muzhik was an adept, and so there was no scope in the Russian village – Tvardovsky claimed (unconvincingly) – for specialists in the craft.[12]

Some Village Prose is remarkable for its political neutrality. But much of it conveys outspoken criticism of Party policy as imposed on the villages, and this despite the fact that several of the authors concerned (including Abramov, Ovechkin, Soloukhin, Tendryakov and Yashin) wrote as members of the Party. Village Prose authors are above all hostile to the all-pervading bureaucracy that has filled the countryside with town-bred officials liable, for example, to corral the muzhiks for conferences on artificial insemination or the drafting of a new constitution at a time when harvesting is in full swing. This anti-urban stance reminds us of earlier writers, including Pilnyak, and is well illustrated in Vladimir Voynovich's story *We Live Here* (1961): a young poet goes to a village 'looking for experience of life', but is abruptly told to clear out by one of the locals, speaking on behalf of those who are compelled to reside in the place and prefer to do so in the absence of muzhik-fancying intellectuals.[13]

These authors of Village Prose do not, as a group, confine themselves to negative criticism, for some go out of their way to portray Russian rural life as a worthwhile cultural milieu wholly distinct from that of the towns.

To influential examples of Village Prose already mentioned may be added Vladimir Soloukhin's *Vladimir By-Ways* (1957), Vladimir Tendryakov's *Pot-Holes* (1961) and Aleksandr Yashin's *Vologda Wedding* (1962). But these are only a few among the many products of a school that also includes Vasily Belov, Yury Kazakov, Boris Mozhayev, Valentin Rasputin, Vasily Shukshin, Sergey Zalygin and others. Despite much hostile criticism incurred over the years, Village Prose now seems to be well established with the award, in 1975, of a State Prize for Literature to the leading exponent Fyodor Abramov for a sequence of three rural novels, *The Pryaslins*, issued as a whole in the previous year.[14] Of the second novel in this series, *Two Winters and Three Summers* (1968), a leading American specialist has remarked that if it 'had been written by Aleksandr Solzhenitsyn it would have immediately been translated in the West and proclaimed a masterpiece'.[15] Abramov enjoyed the distinction of delivering an address on Village Prose to the Sixth Congress of Soviet Writers in June 1976 – a further sign that the genre is fully accepted by authority despite its politically neutral or seemingly aberrant features. Here are further confirmations of a claim made by another Western authority, who calls village and peasant life *the* dominant fictional theme between the mid-1950s and the present, 'certainly in quantity and arguably in quality too'.[16]

The Intelligentsia

Since the 1860s a key role has been played in Russian social history by the so-called intelligentsia. On the importance of this concept there is general agreement, but there is less consensus on its scope, for the word varies considerably in use from one speaker to another. At its broadest the intelligentsia embraces a wealth of overlapping categories: the professional classes, the middle classes, educated society, intellectuals, white-collar workers other than the most lowly, and in general all who toil with brain, desk, pen, typewriter, telephone and pocket calculator rather than with hoe, tractor, screwdriver, spanner or lathe. More important still, 'intelligentsia' traditionally tends to embrace a voluble section among those who do not toil at all.

'Intelligentsia' may also have a narrower bracket according to the extent to which an individual user confines it to those educated or semi-educated persons who do not accept, or who violently seek to overthrow, their society. Thus 'intelligentsia' was sometimes used in Imperial times as an equivalent for the political radical movement, and was sometimes said to constitute the 'general staff of the Russian revolution'. Nor has this narrower use of the word disappeared in Soviet times. Officially disapproved authors, including Solzhenitsyn and Nadezhda Mandelstam, still employ it to denote what are termed in the West members of the Russian dissident movement – those educated persons who, while not necessarily advocating the violent overthrow of the Soviet system, are either indifferent to its aims or would welcome its radical modification.

While noting the continuance of this latter usage, we are here more concerned with the Soviet intelligentsia as the term is officially used in the USSR. It has been succinctly defined by one Western authority as comprising all those who have received and are receiving higher education, together with others who hold posts normally occupied by persons holding higher educational qualifications. Here is a conveniently precise definition enabling us to count the numbers of the intelligentsia; on this computation they totalled 10,676,000 persons in December 1967, for instance.[1] They represent the most rapidly increasing sector of Soviet society, one which more than doubled in size in the course of the 1960s, and which has since continued to expand. The expansion reflects a sizeable increase in the figures of those attending institutes of higher education: from about 30,000 a year in the 1920s they swelled to over 400,000 a year in the 1960s.[2]

Higher education is vocationally oriented, with considerable emphasis on technology and scientific subjects. Among institutes of higher education universities form only a minority (65 out of 856 in 1975), the largest and most prestigious being that of the capital, Moscow State University. The most eminent of all institutions of higher learning is the Academy of Sciences of the USSR, now located (since 1934) in Moscow, and originally opened in St Petersburg as the Imperial Academy of Sciences in 1725. The Academy's chief activity is scientific and technological research; but its comparatively small arts departments, which include that of literature and language, also have a certain significance. The number of academicians has tended to be small (for example, 231 full members and 414 corresponding members in 1969). Individual Union Republics also possess their own Academies; these too are prestigious, though naturally junior in status to that of the USSR as a whole. Academicians, wherever located, belong to the country's élite, enjoying valuable perquisites that include large salaries for what is not necessarily a full-time job.

At the other end of the educational scale the USSR has virtually solved the problem of illiteracy that confronted it in the immediate post-revolutionary years. In 1917 some sixty per cent of the population, aged ten and above, was illiterate. The proportion was reduced to about twenty per cent by 1939 through the campaign to liquidate illiteracy (*likbez*) carried out in 1920–35; and by 1959 illiteracy could be claimed as virtually liquidated.

During the NEP period there was comparatively little interference with scholarly activity at the highest level, the Academy of Sciences and universities remaining relatively immune from Party control as it was to be imposed in later years. Meanwhile the schools were going through a phase of experiment with advanced methods involving minimal emphasis on intellectual and behavioural discipline. This gave way during the Stalin period to its opposite, a phase of severe educational regimentation. The Academy and the universities were brought under the strictest Party control. So too were children, teachers' and parents' authority being restored throughout the community as a whole. Despite some relaxation in the post-Stalin period the educational system leaves little scope for variety, textbooks, syllabuses and curricula being virtually identical within the individual republics or throughout the country. Schools are free, and are attended by children wearing uniform dress. To the system of standardized education certain establishments for linguistically, mathematically and musically gifted pupils form an exception.

Political indoctrination plays a prominent role throughout the educational system, not least in universities and institutes, where Dialectical Materialism and other fundamentals of Marxism-Leninism form a mandatory part of all courses. That the subject is studied in a rigidly ritualistic spirit is the universal testimony of witnesses who are not themselves committed to affirming the doctrine. As already indicated, periods of military or paramilitary training are also obligatory for schoolchildren and students.

With certain exceptions at certain periods education has been provided free by the State, in return for which those passing out from higher educational institutes are required to work for three years after graduation in a post assigned to them by the authorities.

The result of this system has been to create an extensive section of the community consisting largely of graduates and sometimes called the toiling intelligentsia: it is officially termed a stratum (*prosloyka*) of society, as we have noted – not a 'class', such as only the manual workers and peasantry form. The stratum includes all the country's most highly paid and prestigious individuals: academicians, professors, university administrators, high functionaries of Party and State and senior industrial managers, together with outstanding exponents of the creative and performing arts. Among them are those writers who have enjoyed the greatest success as measured in material terms – whose works have gone into many large editions, and who have won their Stalin, Lenin or State Prizes. The top intelligentsia enjoys salaries and other privileges vastly in excess of those available to average citizens, and it wields far more power and influence than do members of other social groups. But it must be strongly emphasized that excessive privilege is enjoyed only by a small favoured minority within the intelligentsia, and certainly not by the group as a whole: a high proportion consists of doctors and teachers, whose earnings tend not to exceed the average industrial wage, and who incidentally consist preponderantly of women.

An index of the intelligentsia's influential role in society is the high percentage of Party members who are graduates (24·3 per cent); so too is the distribution of Party membership (including candidate membership) between the three main sections of Soviet society, as follows (1976 figures): workers 41·6 per cent; peasants 13·9 per cent; white-collar workers 44·5 per cent.[3]

The intelligentsia is to some extent a self-perpetuating caste, since its offspring are far more likely to enter it themselves, through higher education, than are those born into worker and peasant families; in 1972, for instance, 'workers' children accounted for only 36·2 per cent of students enrolled in higher education', according to the Soviet Minister of Higher Education as reported in *The Times* (London).[4] The intelligentsia's access to higher education has sometimes been improved by the exercise of parental influence on admission boards, not excluding the use of bribes. Against such abuses the Soviet authorities have vigorously campaigned, and not without success; for though it may be hard for a worker's or peasant's son to enter the intelligentsia, it is very far from impossible. Indeed, it is largely through the higher educational system that the USSR has achieved a measure of social mobility not necessarily less than that to be found in other countries.

Since the pre-revolutionary professional classes were not on the whole sympathetic to Bolshevism, Lenin's government was faced, immediately after the October Revolution of 1917, with a dearth of managers, technologists, engineers, administrators and specialists in general. The most immediate lack, as the Civil War spread, was of experienced army officers, a need met by Trotsky's policy of drafting ex-officers of the Tsarist forces into the newly formed Red Army. Similarly, engineers, industrial administrators and managers were recruited, in the years immediately following the Civil War, from among those who had performed these functions in pre-revolutionary Russia, and were therefore politically suspect. Meanwhile urgent attempts were also being made to train new cadres of such specialists among those whose social origin might be expected to make them more amenable to Bolshevism. By the time of Stalin's emergence as dictator the older specialists, largely of bourgeois origin, were falling under increasing suspicion. A number of them were arraigned at show trials from 1928 onwards, while the group as a whole was subjected to widespread repressions which abated somewhat in 1931.

These developments in the handling of specialists are reflected in the work of Leonid Leonov. One theme in his Five Year Plan novel *Sot* is provided by the veteran engineer Renne, who commits suicide under suspicion of sabotage. As this episode reminds us, the *spets* ('specialist') with the non-Russian surname is a staple figure in Five Year Plan novels. But these foreigners or russified foreigners are rarely the main heroes of the works in which they appear – by contrast with Professor Skutarevsky in Leonov's next novel, *Skutarevsky*. A senior loyalist scientist with roots in the previous regime, the Professor faithfully serves the new dispensation as head of an important scientific institution, and conducts experiments designed to effect the transmission of energy by radio. But Skutarevsky turns out to be surrounded by traitors in his own family; they include his son and his brother-in-law. In the end the plotters are unmasked, and Skutarevsky too falls under suspicion when his great experiment fails – but in an atmosphere indicating that it may yet succeed at some time in the glorious future.

Among other leading members of the intelligentsia in Leonov's work are Professors Vikhrov and Gratsiansky, both experts in forestry and both prominent in the author's last and longest novel, *The Russian Forest*. Once again, as in *Skutarevsky*, Good and Evil clash, Good being naturally equated with loyal supporters and Evil with covert opponents of the Soviet system; the former are headed by the ultimately vindicated hero Vikhrov, and the latter by the plausible villain Gratsiansky, who eventually commits suicide.

No other post-Stalin work depicting the specialist intelligentsia has created more stir than Vladimir Dudintsev's *Not by Bread Alone*. It describes the tribulations of a physics schoolteacher and inventor, Lopatkin, who has evolved a technique for the mass production of centrifugally-cast large-diameter piping, a typical theme of technological belles-lettres. However, Dudintsev went too far when he pitted the blatantly honest Lopatkin against a clique of wicked careerists, headed by the factory director and later high official Drozdov. The trouble was that the author seemed to be denouncing the smugness and complacency of this neo-bourgeois, self-seeking 'establishment' as a *typical* feature of Soviet society; it was not, he implied, merely an exceptional streak of villainy as personified by the innumerable traitors and saboteurs who had infested officially approved Russian fiction for some thirty years. For this reason the novel set off a chain of politico-literary scandals, even provoking public comments (including both praise and abuse) from Khrushchev himself. But Dudintsev had not been the first to ventilate the theme. For instance, Daniil Granin had also castigated the stagnation and complacency of the Soviet technical and managerial establishment in his novel *Seekers* (1954).

Works such as these help to emphasize what Lenin himself regarded as a major evil of emerging Soviet society – proliferating bureaucracy. For this he openly blamed Stalin, not without reason, but the bureaucratic current was to prove stronger than all who have sought to control it, even the most powerful. It was little affected by Mayakovsky's devastating short poem of 1922, *The Overcommitted Committeemen* (*Prozasedavshiyesya*). Sarcastically proposing the creation of a Committee for the Extirpation of Committees, Mayakovsky in effect admits the impossibility of suspending the operation in the Soviet Union of what has later come to be called Parkinson's Law.[5]

That excessive committee work, together with bureaucratic formalities and delays, constitutes an endemic source of inefficiency and distress in the USSR has been common ground between the system's spokesmen and opponents from 1917 onwards. But the evil has only increased despite the frequency with which it has been denounced at home and abroad by journalists and authors of belles-lettres. These still cling to the Russian tradition, long antedating the Revolution, whereby the upper reaches of the administration are immune from attack by Russia-published satirists. It is low-grade officials who still constitute the traditional target, having been so ever since the days of Gogol.

8 Private Life

Women

The emancipation of women is claimed as one of modern Russia's major achievements, having been a prime concern of the country's revolutionaries, many of whom were themselves female, since long before 1917. Enjoying equal rights in law, receiving equal pay for equal work, women play a larger part in economic life than do those of any other advanced country of the modern world. In the medical and educational areas they are particularly prominent, furnishing two thirds or more of the country's doctors, teachers, librarians and other cultural workers.

Despite these achievements there are aspects in which Soviet practice falls short of the feminist's ideal. In the highest administrative, managerial and educational posts women are not prominently represented, and they account for under a quarter of the membership of the country's key power-channelling institution, the CPSU: 24·3 per cent on 1 January 1976.[1] As for that organization's upper reaches, only one woman (Yekaterina Furtseva) has ever attained – and that only briefly, in 1957–61 – membership of the supreme policy-making body, then called the Presidium.

Most wives are employed outside the home, and so suffer an additional disadvantage, since housekeeping chores tend to engulf their after-work hours, whereas a man may claim his as sacrosanct to dominoes, vodka-drinking or dozing in a chair. The strain of child-bearing is mitigated by paid leave and maternity grants, but it remains a fundamental cause, in the USSR as elsewhere, of disparity between the sexes that no social system has yet contrived to eliminate. As Pilnyak remarks in one of his novels, 'Women, made equal to men in civil rights, were not rendered equal in everyday life and were

certainly not made equal by biology.'[2] Nor, for many years, have
women been equal to men in the search for a marriage partner, since
(as stated above) they suffer from a preponderance of numbers owing
to the greater incidence of political and war casualties among males
in the years 1930 to 1953. Though the imbalance is decreasing, there
were in 1973 still fifteen per cent more females than males in the
overall population.[3]

On the martyrdom of the overworked wife and mother, through
excess of combined domestic and professional responsibilities, the
modern literature has little to say since the reality conflicts with the
official image of the emancipated Soviet woman as man's free and
equal partner. That she may in practice be very far from man's
equal is illustrated in a story by a little-known author, Natalaya
Baranskaya, published in *Novy mir* of 1969: *All in the Week's Work.*
It describes a typical week's ordeal endured by a Moscow professional
woman – ordeal by shopping, cooking, mending, cleaning and looking
after husband and children while discharging full-time duties as the
employee of a scientific institute.

By contrast with the nineteenth century, when not a single authoress
attained prominence, woman writers have made a major contribution
to modern Russian literature. This is particularly true of three outstanding poets: the home-based Anna Akhmatova; Zinaida Gippius,
who emigrated in 1919; Marina Tsvetayeva, who lived abroad between
1922 and 1939. All these were established authors before the Revolution and their achievements have not yet been rivalled by any later
poetess; but the feminine tradition in verse has been maintained by
Aliger, Akhmadulina, Berggolts, Gorbanevskaya, Inber, Matveyeva
and others. Women have also been active as authors of prose fiction.
They have chronicled the sexual laxity of the 1920s (Aleksandra
Kollontay); celebrated the early 1930s with Five Year Plan novels
(Marietta Shaginyan), or by practising the 'genre of silence' (Lidiya
Seyfullina); won their Stalin Prizes (Vera Panova); contributed to the
literature of the Thaw (Galina Nikolayeva). Among woman memoirists
Nadezhda Mandelstam is, as stated above, exceptionally informative
on the modern period as a whole. But the most celebrated autobio-
graphizing lady is Svetlana Alliluyeva, Stalin's daughter, whose writings
owe their vogue chiefly to the author's parentage. She transferred her
residence to the West in 1967 and wrote two volumes of reminiscences

casting a few shafts of light on the great dictator's well-concealed domestic life.

Despite their importance women authors are, as a whole, by no means as prominent as men, and they accounted (to put the matter statistically) for only 1,097 of the Union of Writers' total membership of 7,833 in 1976.

Turning from female writers to female characters in fiction, we find literature of the 1920s dominated by the theme of sexual promiscuity and by obtrusive pornographic motifs that stand in sharp contrast with the compulsory prudery of the later period. Kollontay's story *The Love of Three Generations* (1923) depicts a heroine, Zhenya, who changes her lovers according to her mood; becoming pregnant, she remains indifferent to her child's paternity even when it turns out that her mother's lover is one possible candidate. In Sergey Malashkin's *The Moon on the Right Side* (1926) another dissolute heroine, Tanya, indulges in alcoholic and narcotic orgies, but can at least remember the precise number of 'husbands' (twenty-two) with whom she has cohabited; as she explains, she dislikes saying 'no' to any of the comrades for fear of being considered a *petite bourgeoise*. Then there is Nikolay Bogdanov's *The First Girl* (1928), in which a Komsomol member, having spread venereal disease 'in the performance of her obligation to the comrades', is murdered by her best friend in order to save the Party's youth organization from scandal.

These and many other works treating of rape, venereal disease and promiscuity reflect the atmosphere of Bolshevism's first decade of power, during which an officially sponsored attempt was made to overthrow the family as an institution. In pursuit of this aim abortion was made available on demand, while marriage was considered equally valid in law whether it was registered or not. It was an era when many a high official casually jettisoned the homely wife who had been his companion for years, and took a more decorative younger mate, often a former member of the upper classes.

Not all female characters in literature of the 1920s were insubstantial and fickle, for many were dedicated to the political ideals of the period, among which sexual licence was only one. Perhaps the best known of these combined Amazons, idealists and dedicated self-emancipators is Dasha Chumalova, heroine of Gladkov's *Cement*. Jettisoning her pre-revolutionary husband Gleb, she abandons the role of housewife and tolerates the lecherous embraces of a local Party tycoon. Dasha even carries Party-mindedness to the extent of consigning her small daughter to an orphanage, where the child dies from neglect. For all these feats Dasha was enthusiastically acclaimed at the time, but such indifference to the role of mother and housewife was later to become a matter for censure; indeed, Gladkov himself systematically modified and expurgated this material in the course of prolonged and radical revisions of this, his most famous work. Another proletarian Amazon, by no means wholly unfeminine, is the female sniper Maryutka, heroine of Boris Lavrenyov's story *The Forty-First* (1924). Having shot forty White officers in the course of the Civil War, she fires at her forty-first, but misses, only to embark on a passionate love affair with him after the two have become stranded on a deserted coast while she is conveying him by boat as her prisoner to Red headquarters. But then a boatful of Whites approaches the lovers' retreat. Remembering her proletarian class loyalties, Maryutka shoots her prisoner-lover before he can be rescued, and collapses on the corpse in an orgy of grief.

Turning to the two chief epic novels covering the revolutionary years and published in the 1920s and 1930s, we find Sholokhov devoting much of *The Quiet Don* to a tempestuous extra-marital love affair, that of his Grigory and Aksinya. Here is full-blooded writing in which, despite the many atrocities with which the novel is littered, the characteristic atmosphere, bordering on sadism and pornography, of the 1920s is yet largely avoided. That the same novel also portrays the profound love affair of a nineteen-year-old female Jewish machine-gunner we have also noted. Then again, in his trilogy of novels *The Way through Hell*, Aleksey Tolstoy traces the evolution of two idle, attractive sisters, members of the pre-revolutionary privileged classes, through the Civil War in which their husbands fight on opposite sides, up to their transformation into a socially useful schoolteacher and nurse.

With the onset of fully-fledged Stalinism, and the beginning of the first Five Year Plan at the end of the 1920s, literature begins to throw up more and more jolly milkmaids and boiler-suited factory girls wielding pickaxes and pushing wheelbarrows. Such is the cement-mixing Olga in Katayev's *Time, Forward*. 'The palms of her hands were on fire. She strained, pushed, turned deep red to the roots of her hair, and, with a crash and a clang, rolled the heavily jumping barrow across the rails between the two uncoupled freight cars.'[4] Or Five Year Plan women may operate on a more professional level, as does Suzanna Renne in Leonov's *Sot* – a chemical engineer and a Party member so dedicated to the cause that she casually brushes aside the suicide of her father as of little moment.

By the late 1930s official policy towards marriage and the family had almost been inverted. A decree of 27 June 1936 prohibited abortion and placed obstacles in the way of divorce, while making State aid and alimony more easily available to mothers. A further decree issued in the last year of the war, on 8 July 1944, withdrew the legal recognition that unregistered marriages had hitherto enjoyed, made divorce prohibitively difficult and expensive, and established a subsidy for unmarried mothers. The measures were aimed at increasing the birthrate and encouraging large families. They have since been substantially relaxed, abortion again becoming freely available in 1955.

In the immediate post-war period the female characters of Soviet literature entered, in common with the male, a phase of unnatural docility owing to the particularly harsh restraints imposed on imaginative literature during this era when the internal conflicts of Soviet society had become virtually taboo to writers. Under such circumstances premarital and extramarital love affairs, the very stuff of imaginative fiction in so many countries and eras, came under a virtual ban. Vsevolod Kochetov was therefore being somewhat adventurous when, in his novel *The Zhurbins* (1952), he drew 'the first full-length portrait of a promiscuous villain'.[5]

For more daring excursions into sexual adventure readers had to wait for the thaws that followed Stalin's death. It then became possible not merely to recognize the existence of love affairs outside marriage, but even to portray non-condemned characters participating in them. During this period the love of young unmarried women for older married men became a staple theme, often ending in a noble gesture of renunciation in the interests of preserving the family. Meanwhile the public, 'starved for books on love',[6] was nurtured on such studies as Galina Nikolayeva's novel *A Running Battle* (1957). It describes the liaison between a married, middle-aged engineer (Bakhirev) and a young married woman engineer, Tina, whose husband is an invalid. By stressing one particularly realistic detail – the unavailability of privacy in suitable premises – the author incidentally points out a major obstacle in the path of those pursuing illicit (or even licit) love in the USSR. Forced to meet his Tina in a squalid, cockroach-infested suburban room, Bakhirev remarks all too accurately that 'the era of Socialism is ill-equipped for adultery'.[7] The adventure ends in suitably decorous fashion when Bakhirev decides to stay with his wife and to eschew further infidelity. Both he and Tina, who accepts a post in the distant provinces, have decided, like many another victim of sexual temptation in the literature, to seek solace in work. However, not all Soviet-published post-Stalin writings are as sexually timid as Niko-layeva's; witness the lusty sensuousness into which not a few writers, including Simonov and Panfyorov, have occasionally deviated.

That such self-sacrificial solutions were by no means always adopted in real life the marital and extramarital history of many a writer demonstrates. Partly estranged from his wife Zinaida, Pasternak never-theless did not abandon her, but simultaneously maintained two house-holds in Peredelkino – the second with Olga Ivinskaya, whom he first met in 1946; and he drew on both women for the characteristics of the two main heroines of *Doctor Zhivago*, 'Lara' and 'Tanya'. A less comfortable arrangement was created when Anna Akhmatova became the common-law wife of the art historian Nikolay Punin in Leningrad in about 1926, since accommodation shortage dictated that Punin's previous wife, also an Anna, must continue to be part of the *ménage*.[8]

Despite the various grotesque evolutions through which female characters have passed in the literature, they tend to be more artistically convincing and better equipped with strength and self-confidence than the men. Here is a tradition long antedating the Revolution and pioneered by Turgenev among other nineteenth-century authors: that which opposes a courageous, well-integrated, strong, self-confident young woman to a spineless, dithering ninny of a man. Where men are prone to figure as lonely, ill-adjusted weaklings or demoniac, sexless, production-obsessed fanatics, the women tend to possess more *tselnost* ('wholesomeness, integrity'). As has been well said of the early Stalin period, and as is true of the literature in general, 'The male hero, harrassed by external pressures and by internal self-doubt, [is] seldom a match for the buxom heroine.'[9]

The Home

Chronic shortage of living-space is one of the basic and, it seems, ineradicable features of modern Russian life. In theory each individual is officially entitled to a norm of nine square metres' floor area, but the *de facto* allotment has tended to fall below even this modest level, though varying from town to town. A *samizdat* source dated December

1971 has calculated the average living-space in the USSR at one third to one half of that available in the West.[1] Against this disadvantage may be set the low level of rents, which rarely bulk large in a family budget. Most urban dwellings are State-owned, but there is a sizeable minority of private and co-operatively owned properties in the towns, while most rural housing is privately owned.

Intense overcrowding has led to the characteristic institution of the communal flat: a dwelling originally designed for a single family, but now housing a family in each room, with collective use of kitchen and ablutions. Such were, in the mid-1970s, the conditions of 'more than 25 per cent' of the urban population,[2] but since they are considered damaging to the Soviet image they are imperfectly reflected in USSR-published literature from the 1930s onwards. For an unforgettable picture of a communal flat readers may turn to Panteleymon Romanov's novel *Comrade Kislyakov* (1930), which describes such a warren; it contains ten families – twenty-seven persons, all huddled into rooms which give on to a common corridor, and perpetually quarrelling over the toilet and culinary facilities. A more recent example of the macabre implications of the housing shortage will be found in Yury Trifonov's *The Exchange* (1969). It describes a state-owned flat occupied by an elderly woman who is dying of cancer and whose son and daughter-in-law conspire to expel her from her home in order to gain possession of her accommodation. Such is the context in which a recent foreign-published memoirist claims that future generations will never understand the dominant role played in Soviet psychology by the housing shortage. 'Husbands and wives who hate each other, mothers-in-law and sons-in-law, grown-up sons and daughters, ex-charwomen who have attached themselves to the room next to the kitchen – all are eternally bonded to their floor-space and can't be parted from it.'[3] Sometimes, however, they were forced to leave when arrested during the Stalin terror on the denunciation of sub-tenants desiring to increase their own living-space.

As this reminds us, accommodation is one of the perquisites dispensed by authority, and may thus be used as a lever for keeping the citizenry in order. It can be all the more effective as a control medium through the practice of grouping members of a single profession in a single tenement or dacha colony. An early example of such swarming was provided by the House of the Arts, the former residence of a rich Petrograd businessman, where Mandelstam and other writers lived and held a non-stop literary seminar in the early 1920s.[4] Such too are the writers' dacha colonies in the villages of Peredelkino and Komarovo, near Moscow and Leningrad respectively, and such is the housing co-operative 'The Moscow Writer', amusingly described in Vladimir Voynovich's foreign-published *Ivankiada* (1976). From unofficial literature, and from other sources, we learn that to attain a modest flat or cottage may represent the summit of an individual's ambitions in life, the general keynote of the whole period being what Nadezhda Mandelstam calls 'fantastic homelessness'.[5] Akhmatova never felt that she had a home at all until she was assigned a dacha at Komarovo towards the end of her life.[6] When, in old age, the critic Shklovsky was granted a new flat 'he turned to his companions in good fortune who were moving into the same block and said: "Now we must pray that there won't be a revolution." '[7]

As is illustrated in Voynovich's Ivankiada, a documentary account of his own accommodation problems, members of the Union of Writers enjoy preferential housing conditions. They are entitled, as are journalists and members of certain other professions, to an additional twenty square metres' living-space over and above the basic entitlement of nine. When Voynovich's wife became pregnant he calculated that their small family should, after the child's birth, be able to move out of their existing one-room flat (24·41 square metres) and claim a larger flat containing fifty square metres in all. Their entitlement worked out as follows:[8]

Three members of family	=	27
Additional allotment to family with child	=	3
Writers' Union allotment	=	20
Total	=	50

However, as was to emerge, to possess an entitlement in theory is by no means the same as making good a claim to it in practice. Voynovich was to find his ambitions contested by a rival candidate for the same extra space – a certain Ivanko, who had powerful connections in the Party and KGB, and was able to conduct a long feud by committee and clandestine pressure before being eventually forced to yield.

Scarcity of housing is far from the only hardship imposed by residence conditions. To it must be added the registration system. According to this no citizen may change his place of domicile until he has obtained a residence permit (*propiska*) from the militia. But the *propiska* may be denied unless the applicant can show that he already has a place to live; and, by an arrangement that will surprise no student of bureaucracy, he tends to be unable to obtain accommodation unless he can produce the necessary *propiska*. As a third complication, employers are often unwilling to take on applicants who lack a residence permit, and yet registration may be denied to an individual unless he is already in employment. Thus each of the three requisites for town life (residence permit, housing accommodation and employment) tend to be interdependent and unavailable to anyone who cannot show that he has already acquired the other two!

By such means the authorities have resisted the constant pressure on living-space in the large towns, particularly Moscow – a pressure so intense that it has led to a spate of 'fictitious' marriages. A young Muscovite man may, for instance, be prepared for a suitable consideration to marry a woman from outside, and thus to bestow on her the coveted metropolitan *propiska* that she could never have obtained as an out-of-town spinster.

With the *propiska* system is allied the internal passport system. The passport in this sense is an identity document required for travel inside the country, and it is in the passport that the *propiska* is registered. The passport must also be presented before a train ticket can be issued. Passports were introduced in 1932 as a means of regimenting the citizenry, and though they have always represented a major inconvenience, it can be still more inconvenient to be denied one. Such has been for many decades the peculiar misfortune of the peasants, who have thus been prevented from leaving their Collective Farms, except for short visits or with official permission. As is noted above, peasant passportlessness has been one among several provisions imposing the status of second-class citizen on the muzhik; however, under the new system now in process of implementation, peasants too will receive passports – and with them, presumably, a greater degree of freedom to travel or change their residence.

Turning from housing, registration and travelling problems to income and its purchasing power, we remember that the average industrial wage stood at just under 150 roubles a month in 1976. This – for what little it may be worth as an indication of living standards – works out at about £1,400 or $2,400 a year at the rate of exchange then obtaining of about 1·30 roubles to the pound and

0·75 roubles to the dollar. The minimum wage was seventy roubles.[9] As for the highly privileged section of society, including the most successful writers together with other exceptionally favoured individuals, their earnings, especially those of Party and State officials, remain a closely guarded secret, but there is reason to believe that they may rise to 2,000 roubles a month.[10] The differential between privilege and lack of privilege is, however, even greater than this figure might suggest, owing to the fact that income tax plays only a minor role in the Soviet fiscal system, not being imposed on a progressively escalating scale comparable to that levied in some Western countries. To this Soviet peculiarity must also be added the access enjoyed by favoured individuals to preferential housing, shopping and travel facilities. The USSR does not, therefore, constitute an egalitarian society. True, its official spokesmen may in certain contexts seek to imply that it does, but the fact remains that egalitarianism ceased, after some years of hesitation, to represent official policy back in 1932. It was then that the Seventeenth Party Conference condemned the levelling out (*uravnilovka*) of wages and benefits as economic and political heresy. Since then the Soviet system has based itself firmly on the use of financial and other material incentives so substantial as to create a wide gap between those who receive them and the unfavoured rank and file.

To express Soviet incomes in terms of dollars, pounds or other foreign currencies (as was briefly done above) can be most misleading. A clearer idea of the standard of living may be obtained by considering how many hours' work are required to pay for necessities. Such a comparison has been made, for May 1976, between the cost of food and clothing in Moscow, Washington, Munich, London and Paris, as expressed by the number of hours' work, at an average rate of pay, required to purchase given commodities. Calculating on this basis, we find that to pay a typical family's weekly food bill would then have involved the following number of hours' work in the five cities mentioned:

Washington	17·2
Munich	22·4
Paris	25·7
London	28·2
Moscow	64·6

This suggests that the Muscovite of 1976 had to labour more than twice as long to buy his food; but it must be added that with certain common foods – bread, beef and fish – he was nearer to enjoying parity, as assessed on this basis, while with potatoes he was actually better off than any of his rivals. However, an increased need to queue, the more limited availability of foods and their generally poor quality must also be taken into account as Muscovite disadvantages in any survey of comparability. As for clothing, the cost and availability of that were even more to the disadvantage of the average Muscovite of 1976 when his situation was compared with that in the other four cities. Footwear, requiring an outlay of roughly five times as many hours in Moscow as in Washington, was a particularly labour-expensive Soviet item.[11]

Against these handicaps may be set a progressive rise in Soviet living standards from the very low level of the immediate post-war years. We also note that the USSR has remained immune from inflation in a degree comparable to that recently experienced in the West; for though Soviet prices have risen substantially during the period, they have done so far less drastically. The greatest increase, perhaps, has been in the level of the average Soviet citizen's expectations in terms of a rising standard of living. Considerably better-off materially than he was thirty years ago, he is far more liable to compare his conditions with what little he may know of 'capitalist' countries, the affluence of which he may tend to exaggerate. He may therefore experience a much greater degree of dissatisfaction than he had dared to feel under the harrow of Stalinism.

To counteract dissatisfaction with the low average standard of living, official propaganda has long been accustomed to pillory those citizens who err by attaching excessive importance to material objects; for though Communist ideology is avowedly materialistic, it is so only with regard to the possessions of the State, not to those of individuals. Persons excessively addicted to food and drink, to amassing comfortable furniture, to acquiring their own dacha in which to spend country holidays, accordingly tend to be denounced for exhibiting *poshlost*. The word denotes complacency, vulgarity and the acceptance of the second-rate, characteristics all decried as bourgeois, and as revealing a mentality inherited from Tsarist times and unworthy of Soviet Man. Here once again an old tradition has been maintained, since Russians have been denouncing *poshlost* for at least a hundred and fifty years. This has sometimes been done at a high level of artistic achievement,

as by Gogol and Chekhov. Modern writers and literary critics continue to expose it, those who do so most effectively being enabled to
pay for a surplus of these same deplored creature comforts through
money earned by the very process of deploring them.

Religion

Religion is rejected by the official ideology as incompatible with
Marxism, a militantly atheist creed, and believers and priests have
accordingly been persecuted since the Revolution. Repression has
varied in intensity from phase to phase, and was especially intense
during the Great Purge of the late 1930s; priests were then fed into
the camps in large numbers, but so too were members of all other
professions. During the Second World War persecution of the churches
was relaxed as part of the general lowering of ideological pressure.
But the faithful were again repressed with especial severity during
Khrushchev's ascendancy, when the closure of churches was imposed
on an increased scale, numerous believers being arrested and prosecuted.
Repression of religion continued under Brezhnev, but not with the
degree of severity that Khrushchev's policies seemed destined to impose
at the time of his fall in 1964.

The result of these campaigns, and of persistent official attempts
to inculcate atheism, has been disappointing to the authorities. So far
is religion from having been eliminated that the USSR still remains,
as Imperial Russia had been before it, an outstandingly multi-religious
state. True, there has been a general decline in religious practices and
activities. But such a decline is common to the world at large, and
the Soviet fall-off may therefore be more explicable as part of the
world-wide trend towards greater secularization than as a testimony
to the success of official anti-religious measures.

The most important denomination is that of the Russian Orthodox
Church, the country's traditional and formerly established religion. As
with all branches of religion, the number of adherents is difficult to
compute, but is commonly believed to total twenty or thirty millions,
and thus to be far in excess of what the casual observer might assume.[1]
The Orthodox communion is very largely controlled by the Soviet
State, through the Council for the Affairs of the Orthodox Church, and
it represents an autocephalous church within world-wide Orthodoxy.

The Russian Orthodox Church possesses an elaborate hierarchy: a patriarch as the head, followed in descending order of grandeur by metropolitans, archbishops and bishops.

The Old Believers – members of various groups deriving from a seventeenth-century breakaway movement from Orthodoxy – also continue to practise their faith, while two Caucasian republics are associated with their own Christian communions. Of these the Orthodox Church of Georgia can boast special distinction. Autocephalous before 1811, and also after 1917, it was annexed to the Russian Orthodox Church during the interim, but took what has proved a particularly effective form of revenge for this period of colonial subordination: it was responsible for the whole of Stalin's formal education, at a provincial church school and at the Tiflis (Tbilisi) Orthodox Seminary. Armenia's Gregorian Church has spawned no comparably illustrious son. Of other Christian churches the Roman Catholic flourishes in Lithuania and among citizens of Polish origin, while Lutheran Protestantism is common among the Soviet Union's Estonians, Latvians and Germans. Another Protestant denomination, the Baptist, is spread widely throughout the country, and is perhaps, of all branches of religion, that which has most impressively expanded under Soviet rule.

Moving outside the confines of Christianity, we find the Muslims to be a particularly numerous group, chiefly based in Central Asia. They are followed by the Buddhists (largely in Asia) and the Jews (widely scattered). The Jewish religion, and also the Buddhist, have been repressed with particular severity. But they have not been prohibited outright, as have (to return to the Christian area) the Uniates of the Ukraine; these followers of Orthodox ritual, who yet acknowledge the Pope, came under an official ban on being forcibly incorporated in the Orthodox Church in 1946. Other non-approved creeds such as Jehovah's Witnesses have also been legally prohibited but without necessarily being eliminated in practice. For the regulation of all non-Orthodox religious affairs the State maintains a Council for the Affairs of Religious Cults.

The more widely professed denominations, with Russian Orthodoxy as the most important, have come to terms with Soviet authority. Granted, at least in theory, freedom to worship (though a place of worship may not be easily available), they are also at liberty to determine their own liturgy and doctrine. But they are expressly forbidden to proselytize, also being frequently recruited for the political campaigns which the Party periodically mounts in the international arena. One of these was the Peace Campaign vigorously promoted under Stalin, whereby the world was invited to identify hatred of war with the blanket approval of Soviet foreign policy. Prominent members of the clergy have been enlisted in support of this and of other international ideological promotions, and have travelled abroad to attend conferences at which they have spoken in support of current Soviet policies. This practice has not been confined to Christian apologists, for Muslim clerics too have been used to exercise influence on their Asian or African co-religionists.

Each of the main denominations has, accordingly, evolved a leadership which has in effect accepted a concordat with the State, but without necessarily becoming subservient in the ultimate degree. If religious leaders have been prepared to support the government's public relations campaigns, and to co-operate in restraining their flock, they have done so in order to preserve freedom to worship, in so far as this is still conceded in the USSR in a degree varying from phase to phase and from creed to creed. Justifiable or not, such concessions by the hierarchies' top leadership have naturally bred dissatisfaction among humbler believers, who tend to feel that too much has been rendered to Caesar. Consequently they have sometimes formed breakaway groups less amenable to official manipulation, but far more exposed to official persecution. From this the breakaway Baptists in particular have greatly suffered. As we are reminded, religious issues affecting the Baptists and all other major denominations have loomed prominently in the protests of the dissident movement active since Khrushchev's fall.

Since religion is officially deplored we cannot expect to find religious themes sympathetically treated in works published with official approval. In these believers are apt to figure, if at all, in somewhat caricatured form as pathetic 'survivors from the past'. Such is the community of monks which, in Leonov's *Sot*, shares the primeval forest background of northern Russia with an army of construction workers. When the monks' chief holy man, the aged Eusebius, is on the point of expiring, considerable suspense is created by the expectation, widespread among the faithful, that he is about to pronounce some deathbed spiritual message of shattering profundity. But when the old man at last croaks out his final words they are excruciatingly comic in a manner reminiscent of Dostoyevsky's blasphemous passages: 'There is no God.' Here is one of the great anti-climaxes of literature. Yet the author of the novel is reputedly a religious believer like Dostoyevsky before him.

Other authors have been more atheistically inclined, among them Mayakovsky. After the Revolution he was able to restore the many blasphemous passages excluded by the Tsarist censors from his poem of 1914–15, *A Cloud in Trousers*. Here he addresses the Almighty in familiar fashion, offering to act as a celestial pimp, and to restock paradise with Eves ('this very night I'll bring you the most luscious little floozies of the boulevards'); but he then performs a typically Russian volte-face by threatening to eviscerate the deity 'from here to Alaska' with a cobbler's knife.[2] Mayakovsky's rival Yesenin, apostle and practitioner of hooliganism, was given to smashing icons, another Dostoyevskian theme. He was known to scrawl his verse in the form of enormous graffiti on monastery walls, though he was also periodically subject to nostalgia for the simple Orthodox faith of his childhood. Pilnyak, too, evokes conflicting images – very much *à la russe* – of religion. In his story *Mahogany* (1929), for example, he laments the fate of the church bells in the provincial town which forms the scene of the action. They are to be melted down and thus contribute to the output of the metallurgical industry, but this project is not portrayed as a triumph for modern technology. Rather does it figure as a symbolic tragedy that creates nervous disorders among the townspeople.[3] In his *The Naked Year*, by contrast, Pilnyak depicts a deranged monk calling from his ruined monastery for oceans of blood and a return to pre-Petrine (pristine, nobly savage, un-Westernized) Russia.

Among writers who held or retained their religious faith Nadezhda Mandelstam lists two Orthodox believers: Gumilyov and his divorced wife Akhmatova, who was to make extensive use of religious motifs in her poetical lamentation for the Great Purge: *Requiem*.[4] Less conventionally pious, Mandelstam too was sympathetically inclined towards religion at certain phases of his life, and this tradition has been maintained among officially disapproved authors active in a later age and partly dependent for the dissemination of their work on foreign publication. Pasternak, in *Doctor Zhivago*, 'makes it quite clear that in his view there has been only one revolution in human history, namely the coming of Christ'.[5] Nor is the religious content of Maksimov's fiction confined to the title of his best-known and exclusively foreign-published novel, *Seven Days of Creation*.

Religious motifs are not obtrusive in Solzhenitsyn's writings, but he has increasingly turned to the Russian Orthodox Church in the course of his evolution, his fictional work most concentratedly devoted to a religious theme being the Export Only sketch *The Easter Procession* (1968). In 1971 he formalized his affiliation to the Church by receiving his first communion, and he has since outspokenly defended Orthodoxy and its traditions. His publicistic writings include an open letter of 1972 to Patriarch Pimen, head of the Moscow-based Russian Orthodox Church. Here Solzhenitsyn laments that Russia has lost 'the radiant ethical atmosphere of Christianity in which for a millennium our morals were grounded . . . We are losing the last features and marks of a Christian people.'[6] This contention contradicts the impression of other witnesses, who feel that prolonged martyrdom has only strengthened the religious faith of the USSR's believers. True, frequent religious observance is most prevalent among the very old and very young (grandmothers and their infant charges); but it is by no means confined to such, even though church attendance can prove a stumbling-block to those who hope to pursue a successful career within the system. Nor are religious themes and strivings by any means forbidden territory for officially acceptable authors, as is illustrated by Tendryakov's Soviet-published story of a man's search for faith, *On Apostolic Business* (1969).

Part Three
THE LITERARY PROFESSION

9 Movements and Theories

Pre-1932 Currents

The evolution of literary movements falls into sharply differentiated phases separated by the Party decree on literature of 23 April 1932. It abolished all existing groups and set up a new, comprehensive literary association, the Union of Writers of the USSR, which flourishes to this day and will be discussed separately in due course. By contrast, the previous fifteen years, and especially the 1920s, had witnessed the proliferation of competing literary movements and theories so numerous that their detailed workings can be of interest only to the specialist. Some of them did not throw up a single writer of note, while others are now remembered, if at all, chiefly for the achievements of a single prominent individual. The relative insignificance of two poetical movements of the period, Imaginism and Futurism, as opposed to the great significance of their leading representatives, has been expressed as follows by Zamyatin: 'Yesenin ... had as much right to say "Imaginism – is I!" as Mayakovsky had the right to say "Futurism – is I!" '[1]

One reason for the uncontrolled – and therefore arguably healthy – condition of early post-revolutionary literature was the lack of any officially accepted Bolshevik literary theory, for the pronouncements on aesthetics of the major prophets Marx and Lenin are sparse and open to diverse interpretations. Moreover, what with fighting and winning the Civil War, and then attempting to reconstruct their shattered empire, the early Bolsheviks were too busy with urgent non-literary problems to bother with imaginative writers. It was in these circumstances that so many different literary groups were able to compete with each other, some being principally active in seeking government subsidies and power over other writers, others chiefly aiming to be left to work in peace, while authors of all persuasions commonly believed themselves to be pioneering the new and wonderful art of an indescribably splendid future.

The many literary groups of the period 1917–32 fall into two main classes according to whether they claimed to give the new political dispensation active support or tended to ignore it: that is, to put the same point differently, according to whether they were or were not self-consciously 'proletarian'. Proletarian status could be claimed on grounds of working-class origin; but it might also be asserted, by those sprung from a more genteel milieu, on the basis of membership of the Communist Party. To the Proletarians may be tentatively assigned Mayakovsky, who could boast neither of these distinctions, but compensated for his middle-class origins and lapsed membership of the Party with norm-exceeding zeal on behalf of Bolshevism's purportedly proletariat-favouring policies. He was, however, violently hostile towards the more militant proletarian literary associations, even though he did join one of them (RAPP) shortly before his death.

The other main current of the period, and the more significant from a literary point of view, is covered by the general label popularized by Trotsky: Fellow Travellers. Fellow-travelling writers were not, of course, overtly anti-Bolshevik, for even in the relatively permissive 1920s the expression of counter-revolutionary views was not allowed. But they did enjoy official tolerance and the freedom to publish, while assuming a considerable degree of political neutrality, or even openly proclaiming their neutral status with impunity.

We shall consider the Proletarians first. Their earliest noteworthy movement was Proletkult, which had been born before the October Revolution, and was greatly expanded immediately afterwards, its programme being the development of a specifically working-class culture. Numerous literary studios were set up for apprentice worker-writers, whose numbers are said to have reached 80,000 (1920).[2] Not one of them has left a lasting name in literature, however, besides which Proletkult soon fell out of favour with the political leadership since it seemed to challenge the Party's monopoly of the right to speak in the name of the working class. In 1920 Proletkult was accordingly subordinated to the People's Commissariat for Enlightenment (Ministry of Education). Some leading Proletkult writers, mainly poets, then broke away and founded new groups: *Kuznitsa* ('the Smithy') in Moscow and *Kosmist* ('the Cosmicist') in Petrograd. Obsessed with such themes as blast furnaces, pig iron, basic slag and the colour red, they tended to celebrate industrial work in exalted, rhetorical and even religious or mystical language. Factories are compared to the churches that they have supposedly supplanted; a million toilers grasp a million hammers at precisely the same instant; hooters hoot out anthems to proletarian unity; machines screech at each other through the echoing vaults of outer space; blood turns to molten steel. There are also occasional descents to a more prosaic level with such lines of verse as: 'My father is an ordinary smelter', or: 'She was only a pipe-welder's daughter'.

The above is an impressionistic description of a movement that has left no lasting legacy. But one temporary member of *Kuznitsa*, Fyodor Gladkov, is still remembered for his novel with the characteristic title *Cement*, a work that foreshadows the Five Year Plan fiction of the 1930s. On the whole, however, the attempt to evolve a specifically proletariat-based culture, and thus to out-Bolshevize the very Bolsheviks, found disfavour on high, as we have said; both Lenin and Trotsky were against it.

Nor did Lenin and the leadership endorse another notion widely mooted in proletarian and over-Bolshevizing artistic and literary circles of the period: that the accumulated culture of the pre-revolutionary past was no more than a load of junk; that Raphael's paintings and Pushkin's poems should be burnt; and that museums and monuments should be dynamited to make way for the glorious new art of the future. These ideas were advanced by some of the Futurists, a group that dates back to 1910, and of which we have already mentioned Khlebnikov and Mayakovsky as the best-known representatives. To contempt for the past the Futurists added a passion for *avant-garde* experimentalism. This tendency too aroused the antipathy of Lenin, who heartily disliked Mayakovsky's verse and questioned the propriety of publishing it; he believed, indeed, that it would be quite enough to bring out the poet's *One Hundred and Fifty Million* in a mere 1,500 copies, 'for libraries and eccentrics'.[3] But the Futurists were not to be quelled, and they proceeded to found two groups of some importance: the Left Front (LEF), and later the Revolutionary Front (REF).

More congenial to the leadership among the Proletarian groups was that which began life under the name *Oktyabr* ('October') in Moscow in 1922. In the following year the Octobrists founded a literary journal with a military-sounding title characteristic of the epoch (*Na postu*, 'On Guard'), and in the year after that they gave the name of their group to another journal, *Oktyabr*, which still flourishes. The *Oktyabr* group was concerned to support governmental policies – by contrast with *Kuznitsa*, which wanted to improve on them, and which strongly disapproved of the retreat from revolutionary fervour signalized by the adoption of the New Economic Policy (NEP) in 1921. The adherents of *Oktyabr* tended to be disciplined Party members, and as such they were obliged to accept NEP without demur. Far from cultivating an exclusively working-class culture, as had the Proletkultists, and even further from rejecting the art of the past, as did the Futurists, the Octobrists sought to learn from earlier artistic models. They avoided technical experiment and *avant-garde* pyrotechnics in favour of imitating the nineteenth-century classics, especially Lyov Tolstoy. Of these Tolstoyizers the most successful and influential was to be Aleksandr Fadeyev.

From 1924 onwards the *Oktyabr* group went from strength to strength. It helped to found, or succeeded in obtaining control of, the many 'proletarian' groups calling themselves Associations of Proletarian Writers (APP preceded by a variety of prefixes). They included MAPP (Moscow), LAPP (Leningrad) and the united organization termed VAPP (All-Union Association of Proletarian Writers). In 1928 VAPP was renamed VOAPP through the insertion of the Russian word for 'united' between the first two terms of the title, and an all-Russian branch – RAPP – was also constituted. RAPP became the most dominant and notorious of all the APPs, being permitted from its foundation in 1928, and for a period of four years, to exercise a near-monopoly in dictating literary policy and in dragooning writers. Abusing and denouncing all other groups in the militant style of the period, RAPP cowed its rivals and absorbed them until it had acquired a general hegemony over letters. Though we should beware of exaggerating the degree of despotism that it developed,[4] the sudden and unexpected liquidation of the unpopular RAPP, in 1932, seemed like a move towards greater freedom at the time, even though it was accompanied by the abolition of all other surviving groups and the incorporation of all authors in a single, newly-founded Union of Writers. The general reaction was one of relief: evidently the raging dictatorial fanatics of RAPP had been superseded by a benevolent new dispensation under which all writers would unite in mutual harmony and stop abusing each other. But this impression soon subsided when the Union of Writers began to be used as a quieter, but far more effective, literary control mechanism than anything that had preceded it.

We must now turn back to the non-proletarian writers of 1917–32, particularly to the Fellow Travellers. This is a vague term, principally used in the 1920s to describe most of the important authors who were neither of proletarian origin nor closely identified with official policies. Though constantly abused by the Proletarians for lack of political zeal, the Fellow Travellers remained free to choose their own literary manner and matter, provided that their work did not display overt counter-revolutionary tendencies. On 18 June 1925 this freedom was formally confirmed by a Party decree officially permitting the continued co-existence of competing movements in literature.

By rejecting for the time being the Proletarians' claim to a dictatorship over letters the decree of 1925 at first seemed to mark a defeat for *Oktyabr* and the various APPs. And yet the liberal-sounding decree can also be seen, with hindsight, as an earnest of increased literary regimentation, containing as it did the first clear indication that the Party regarded the arts as entirely subordinated to its authority. In other words, though the Party had for the moment legislated in favour of artistic freedom, the crucial point was that it had decided to legislate for the arts at all. There was no guarantee that what had been graciously bestowed might not be ungraciously removed.

The Fellow Travellers included a high proportion of the major literary talents of the 1920s and beyond. Among them were Babel, Ehrenburg, Leonov, Pilnyak, Mikhail Prishvin and Aleksey Tolstoy, besides which even Gorky and Mayakovsky were sometimes assigned to the group. It also included the Petrograd/Leningrad association calling itself 'The Serapion Brothers'. These were authors, mostly young, who met weekly from 1 February 1921 onwards, and who were under the literary tutelage of Shklovsky and Zamyatin. The title of their group was taken from a work dated 1819–21 by the German writer E. T. A. Hoffmann and consisting of short stories narrated by six authors who meet regularly for the purpose. In keeping with this the new Serapion Brothers each proposed to write as an individual, being united only in disclaiming any ideological or propagandist purpose. According to the movement's manifesto, contained in an article of 1922 by the Serapions' leading theoretician, the playwright Lyov Lunts, 'We demand only one thing: a work of literature must be organic, real, live its own special life.'[5] The Serapions were, accord-

ingly, not merely neutral in politics, but militantly so. The association
included the leading humorous writer Mikhail Zoshchenko; the novelist
Venyamin Kaverin; two writers, young in the 1920s, who later became
pillars of political conformism: the poet Nikolay Tikhonov and the
novelist Konstantin Fedin.

Though the latitude extended during the 1920s to non-Bolshevizing
authors was considerable, it had its limits, and some prominent figures
retained too much individualism to qualify for the main concession
allowed to the Fellow Travellers: permission to continue publishing
original work. From 1923 Mandelstam and Akhmatova – the two survivors after Gumilyov's execution of the leading trio in the Acmeist
movement – were virtually silenced as creative artists. Though they
could continue to bring out translations and occasional articles, they
were officially regarded less as reluctantly tolerated Fellow Travellers
than as internal émigrés, an opprobrious term implying serious ideological disaffection.

A position intermediate between the Fellow Travellers and the
Proletarians was occupied by *Pereval* ('The Mountain-Pass'), founded
in Moscow in late 1923. Its affiliates consisted largely of Party members
who accepted the social command – that is, the obligation to put their
art at the service of the community – yet believed that they should
retain freedom to choose their own themes. Nor did they adopt the
attitude of militant hostility towards the Fellow Travellers of the main
Proletarian associations. Far from it, for *Pereval* authors – who included
the poet Eduard Bagritsky and the short story writer Andrey Platonov –
made a practice of publishing alongside the Fellow Travellers in
Krasnaya nov.

Brief mention must also be made of a fascinating but short-lived
Leningrad literary group, Oberiu, which was active in 1926–30, its
most prominent representatives being Daniil Kharms, Aleksandr
Vvedensky and Nikolay Zabolotsky. Though the name of the group
stands for 'Union of Realist Art' in Russian, its members made a cult
of absurd, irrational and chaotic themes and narrative techniques – of
everything, in fact, that was the very opposite of realism as normally
conceived. After publishing a manifesto in 1928 Oberiu succumbed
to political persecution two years later.

The two main currents in literary criticism of the 1920s, the
Formalist and the Marxist, have been briefly discussed in an earlier
section (see page 90 ff.). The point is there made that the Marxist critics

of the decade exhibited a wide range of variety from proletariat-obsessed fanaticism to considerable tolerance for competing theories, and that they were later exposed to particularly severe persecution during the Great Purge. As is also noted above, the label 'Formalism' came to be adopted as a term of abuse applied indiscriminately to literary deviants lacking any connection with Formalism in the stricter sense.

By the end of the 1920s all the fellow-travelling and kindred groups were wilting under the attacks of the Proletarians of VAPP and, from 1928, of RAPP. The non-Proletarians were progressively silenced, or converted by argument and intimidation to propagandizing intensive industrialization and collectivization. But then, in 1932, the Party decree of 23 April took both RAPP's missionaries and their converts by surprise. Fellow Travellers, Serapion Brothers, Perevalists, Futurists, Acmeists, Imaginists, Constructivists, Young Guardists, On-Guardists, Octobrists, adherents of *Kuznitsa* and *Kosmist*, remnants of LEF, REF, LAPP, MAPP, VAPP, VOAPP and of the feared RAPP itself – all were suddenly deprived of these affiliations and merged into a single Writers' Union which was soon to acquire its own mandatory literary technique: that of Socialist Realism.

The Union of Writers

Established by the Party decree of 23 April 1932, the Union of Writers of the USSR held its First Congress in August–September 1934, having already replaced such literary groupings as had survived into the 1930s. It remains to this day the only officially tolerated authors' organization, having expanded from a membership of 1,500 in 1934 to the 7,942 members recorded at the Sixth Congress in June 1976. This is the total for the Soviet Union as a whole, and it embraces authors writing in no less than seventy-six languages. We are of course concerned only with the most common of them – Russian, which is the vehicle for about one half of the membership.

The Writers' Union has branches in all fifteen Union Republics, except that the RSFSR lacked a branch of its own until 1958. Besides many provincial ramifications of little moment there are also important branches in Moscow and Leningrad, of which the former developed particularly liberal and near-dissident tendencies in the mid-1950s. It was in response to these that an RSFSR Writers' Union, nominally senior to the Moscow branch and staffed with obedient provincials, was called into being as a loyalist counterweight in 1958. As already indicated, the Writers' Union is a highly bureaucratized organization. It is nominally controlled by its all-Union Congress, of which six have so far been held: in 1934, 1954, 1959, 1967, 1971 and 1976. The delegates tend to include a weighty proportion of Party members: 462 out of 542 at the 1976 Congress, as already noted. One function of the Congress is to elect a Board consisting, in recent years, of over two hundred members, and this elects a Chairman and a Secretariat of about fifty members, including a First Secretary. The Secretariat in turn elects a small Bureau of about a dozen to conduct current business. In this Bureau the main power and influence of the Union resides; for the Writers' Union operates, like all Soviet organizations, on the principle of Democratic Centralism whereby the rank and file control the leadership *de jure*, while the leadership controls the rank and file *de facto*. Meanwhile the Writers' Union leadership is, of course, itself subordinated to still more powerful non-literary governmental and Party agencies: to the Ministry of Culture, and also to the CPSU Central Committee's Departments of Culture and of Propaganda.

The Union wields a large array of inducements and deterrents designed to facilitate the manipulation of its members. It can influence the acceptance or non-acceptance of a manuscript by a periodical or publishing house, as also the scale of fees and the size of editions. Its Literary Fund, which levies a percentage on all literary earnings, grants subsidies or loans to needy members. The Union also controls a sanatorium, clinics and other medical services specifically for the use of writers. It disposes of living accommodation such as the twelve-storey apartment block, including a bank and a barber's shop, built in the 1930s especially for writers in Lavrushensky Street, a desirable residential area of Moscow. The Union also controls dacha (country cottage) colonies, for example at Peredelkino, about fifteen miles south-west of Moscow; at Komarovo, near Leningrad; at Planyorskoye (formerly Koktebel) in the Crimea. It maintains the Gorky Institute of Literature in Moscow, where courses in 'creative writing' are offered, and it also maintains the Central House of Writers in Moscow with its lavish premises, large lecture hall and private restaurant. The Union further controls a large number of periodicals, the most influential being the newspaper *Literaturnaya gazeta* together with the monthlies

Novy mir and *Oktyabr*. It has its own substantial book-publishing house, Sovetsky pisatel.

So much for the facilities and inducements that the Writers' Union can offer. As for disincentives, the withdrawal of the above publishing, residential, medical and other perquisites rates high among them. Moreover, so bureaucratized – indeed, almost militarized – is the organization that it has the power to punish lack of political responsibility, or conduct prejudicial to the honour and dignity of a writer, with a carefully calibrated array of rebukes, reprimands, severe reprimands, warnings, severe warnings and the like, as has been mentioned above. These strictures might seem more appropriate to the findings of a court martial than to the context of cultural activity, but are paralleled in other Soviet professional organizations, for example in the Union of Journalists. The supreme sanction that can be imposed by the Union of Writers is expulsion from membership. This has been visited over the years on many an illustrious deviant, including Akhmatova and Zoshchenko (1946), Pasternak (1958), Chukovskaya and Voynovich (1974), as well as on authors who have undergone criminal prosecution in the USSR for literary offences and/or have since left the country: Sinyavsky, Daniel, Solzhenitsyn, Nekrasov, Maksimov. Precisely what disadvantages expulsion carries is not clear. It does not seem to involve any automatic ban on publication; nor does it necessarily involve exclusion from the Literary Fund designed to help authors who fall on evil days. In any case there are many ways of silencing a writer who is under a cloud, whether he has been expelled from the Union or not.

One of the system's features, which has been publicly castigated by writers during periods of liberalism, is the latitude given to minor, failed or mediocre authors. These, if endowed with a flair for bureaucratic manipulation, may contrive to be put in charge of colleagues more gifted, and empowered to decide such matters as where these envied and superior talents may or may not live, publish, eat and breathe. Of this the persecution of the major poet and non-functionary Boris Pasternak by the minor poet and major functionary Aleksey Surkov has been a notorious instance. To such literary custodians, as we shall term them, we shall return later in greater detail, as also to the elaborate system of incentives and disincentives offered to authors both through their own professional union and through other agencies.

Socialist Realism

Socialist Realism was evolved as the mandatory literary method for Soviet-published authors, and its emergence coincided with the establishment of the Union of Writers in 1932-4. Since then doctrine and Union have supported each other, successfully resisting during more than four decades not a few attempts to challenge and discredit them.

The earliest traced mention of Socialist Realism is in a speech of 20 May 1932 by Ivan Gronsky, Chairman of the Organizing Committee of the Union of Writers, then in process of formation.[1] As defined in the Union's first statutes, of 1934, Socialist Realism is 'the basic method of Soviet imaginative literature and literary criticism', and 'demands from the artist a truthful, historically concrete depiction of reality in its revolutionary development.' According to official theory, Socialist Realism is the basic method of all the arts, not merely of literature. Nor are its operations confined to Soviet territory, for certain foreign authors – Bertolt Brecht, Louis Aragon, Pablo Neruda – are also claimed as practitioners. But the core and essence of Socialist Realism is claimed to be Russian.

Gorky is considered to have pioneered the method with his play *Enemies* (1906) and his revolutionary novel *Mother* (1907), while he in turn allegedly derived inspiration from Critical Realism (as opposed to the Socialist variety), which was now proclaimed *ex post facto* as the principle guiding the major Russian nineteenth-century novelists. Among others officially accepted as practitioners of Socialist Realism are several more who are claimed to have followed the method before it had been formally enunciated: Mayakovsky, Serafimovich, Sholokhov, Fadeyev. To them were added, among writers who began publishing in the 1930s, Nikolay Ostrovsky (author of *How the Steel was Tempered*) and the poet of peasant life Aleksandr Tvardovsky. Practitioners acclaimed outside the literary field include the theatre producers Stanislavsky and Nemirovich-Danchenko; the film directors Eisenstein and Pudovkin; the composers Shostakovich and Prokofyev. Also included are various comparatively obscure representatives of the visual arts.[2]

As the above list shows, it would be a grave error to deny the presence of formidable talent among those acclaimed as following the new method. The theory of Socialist Realism is enshrined in many thousands of books and articles, and though we may doubt whether a single word of this has contributed an iota of inspiration to any creative artist, we must yet take note of certain ancillary concepts commonly associated with it. They include *partiynost*, which may be translated 'Party-mindedness' or 'conformity with the Party line'; and *narodnost*: devotion to the common people combined with patriotism (both Soviet and Russian). From these principles may be elucidated certain features in the practice of Socialist Realist literature.

Out of deference to the common man and under the rubric of *narodnost*, literature must be written in simple, comprehensible language without stylistic experiment or *avant-garde* devices such as were prevalent in Soviet-published writings of the 1920s, including the work of some Proletarians. *Narodnost* also dictates a degree – under late Stalinism an extreme degree – of political and national chauvinism, whereby foreign characters have tended to be depicted as skulking, self-seeking, *poshlost*-bemused villains, whereas Soviet characters, excluding the small quota of untypical traitors, are healthy, well-integrated, strong, self-confident and positive.

As for *partiynost*, that obligation – to write in conformity with the Party's teaching – has imposed no little distortion on the concurrent obligation to give a truthful depiction of reality. It soon became clear that vulgar, empirically perceived truth might on no account be depicted in the numerous areas where it contravened the higher truth, as enunciated by the Party and often easily equatable by non-converts with the opposite of the truth. For example, it is abundantly evident from a mass of contemporary evidence that the peasants of the 1930s detested collectivization, and that they did so almost unanimously. But to depict them in literature as irrevocably opposed to so cardinal a Party policy would be untruthful in the higher sense, since it would conflict with the Party-sponsored revealed truth whereby the muzhiks (always excepting the evil kulaks) accepted collectivization enthusiastically. Indeed, any peasant fundamentally opposed to collectivization, like any worker lacking enthusiasm for the Five Year Plan, would automatically qualify as *untypical* (even though he might represent the overwhelming majority), and therefore as unsuitable for depiction in literature except in a context emphasizing the exceptional and deplorable nature of his outlook. Such sophistries have led cynics to think of Socialist Realism as imposing not so much a truthful, historically concrete depiction of reality as a fraudulent, historically inaccurate depiction of unreality. It all depends, really, which set of symbols you choose to employ.

Some writers of the early 1930s, slow to absorb these lessons, were reprimanded by the loyalist philosopher P. Yudin for drawing attention to the great famine of 1932–3. This was only a food shortage in certain villages, he claimed, being caused by class enemies who hoarded grain and slaughtered cattle. It was the struggle against the kulaks, not the miseries of a few insignificant peasants, that the Socialist Realist writer of the era must depict.[3]

As Yudin's intervention suggests, compulsory optimism has tended to be the most basic of all ingredients in Socialist Realist writing. Miseries, doubts and failures should either not be presented at all, or should be heavily outweighed by positive elements. Heroes whiter than white and villains blacker than night; obligatory happy endings; the suggestion that the Stalinist world was the best of all possible worlds, while the non-Stalinist world was the worst; the relegation of famines, concentration camps and mass executions to the limbo of that which may not be discussed, or which may be invoked only distantly; the consignment of the victims, both individually and collectively, to the status of unpersons – such were some of the results, under fully developed Stalinism, of offering truthful, historically concrete depictions of reality in its revolutionary development.

The same point is made in a different way in Vasily Grossman's foreign-published novel *For Ever Flowing* (1970). He claims that Socialist Realist literature is as artificial as the bucolic novels of the Russian eighteenth century. Its collective farmers, workers and village women resemble, according to him, 'those graceful rustics and curly-headed shepherds who played their pipes and danced in the meadows, surrounded by dear little white lambs wearing dear little blue ribbons'.[4] The same point is also made in one of the most acute studies of the topic: Andrey Sinyavsky's Export Only essay, published under the pseudonym Abram Tertz: 'What is Socialist Realism?'

Imposed with maximum harshness, as it was in Stalin's post-war years, Socialist Realism in effect converted authors into advertising copywriters on behalf of the regime, but copywriters whose bucolic eclogues and industrial idylls were ineffectual by the standards of Madison Avenue, since this cumbrous material was self-defeatingly repetitious, exaggerated and falsified. The trend reached its culmination in the No Conflict theory, also mentioned above, according to which Stalinist society provided no scope for struggle, having attained a condition of universal harmony in which the Good might occasionally have to yield to the Better, while Evil was represented only by American spies and duped traitors.

Fortunately Socialist Realism has been imposed with less severity at other periods. The three authors generally claimed as its foremost Russian practitioners were each major artists; and none of them conformed fully with the demands of the doctrine as most rigorously enforced. Since Gorky's post-revolutionary creative writings, as opposed to his essays in political propaganda, were largely devoted to pre-revolutionary themes, they enjoyed some of the immunity from Socialist Realist discipline extended to historical fiction. Mayakovsky, though one of the regime's most enthusiastic propagandists, remained ambivalent and was always a potential rebel at heart. Like Gorky, he remained outside the Party, and he detested bureaucratic regimentation. Nor was Mayakovsky immediately recruited as an exemplar of Socialist Realism, for only after Stalin had endorsed his canonization in 1935 was he suddenly rescued from limbo to become one of the method's patron saints. Even Sholokhov, Party member from 1932 though he was, retained far more individuality as a writer than the imposition of Socialist Realism normally permitted. Indeed, he flagrantly infringed the spirit of the doctrine in his novel *The Quiet Don*, for this not only lacks the mandatory happy ending, but also maintains an even balance of sympathy between Whites and Reds in the Civil War. Above all Sholokhov deviated in portraying his hero, Grigory Melekhov, as one whose personal experiences were self-evidently more important than his political significance. In asserting the primacy of personal over political life – as also does Pasternak's officially condemned *Doctor Zhivago* – Sholokhov offended against the most basic canon of Socialist Realism. However, adverse criticism of him naturally expired once he had been fully accepted as an officially licensed champion of the new method. The simple fact is, of course, that the literary policy-makers needed *some* writers of repute who could be promoted as exemplars of Socialist Realism. For the sake of claiming Gorky, Mayakovsky and Sholokhov as adherents of the method it was well worth overlooking their many deviations from strict practice as imposed on lesser, non-canonized scribes.

Sholokhov himself once defined Socialist Realism with admirable clarity, in a discussion with Czech writers in 1958. 'Socialist realism is that which is written for the Soviet government in simple, comprehensible, artistic language.' Sholokhov added that he himself had once been denounced as a kulak writer and a counter-revolutionary, only to be later proclaimed a lifelong Socialist Realist. No less helpfully, he also quoted a comment on Socialist Realism that remains astonishing, coming as it did from the Stalinist literary tycoon Fadeyev. 'If anyone should ask me what socialist realism is [Fadeyev told Sholokhov] I should have to answer that the devil alone knows.'[5]

Though Socialist Realists were indeed expected to use simple language comprehensible to the common man, they were not permitted full latitude to incorporate the common man's language, in so far as it consisted of slang, obscenities and the equivalent of 'four-letter words' – to which usages the Russian *hoi polloi* are no less given than are those outside the Soviet orbit. Such crudities did indeed bespatter the original published texts of Sholokhov's own work, but were later toned down as part of a general movement to impose a featureless, flat, homogeneous style on all authors. Of all the ingredients in Socialist Realism this attempt to create a uniform style was probably the most inimical to creativity. But Sholokhov himself succumbed to it far less than obscurer scribes, not only in his original writings, but also in his public speeches. At post-Stalin Writers' Congresses and elsewhere he has been known to deride top literary functionaries in a casual, insolent, off-the-cuff style, the opposite of the kind of officialese otherwise obligatory on these occasions. In assuming such licence Sholokhov was unique among writers of the Khrushchev era, as was the earthy Khrushchev himself among the Soviet politicians of his heyday.

After Stalin's death the pressure to write in decorous, featureless, homogenized Russian was relaxed slightly, while other obligations associated with Socialist Realism were relaxed considerably. Extreme xenophobia ceased to be mandatory, while the insistence on maximum optimism tended to be quietly forgotten. It also became possible to publish material politically neutral in that the Soviet dispensation could be portrayed as a fact of life without being constantly held up for admiration. As for the extent to which Soviet institutions and practices could be ridiculed, condemned or criticized, though such indiscipline was by no means totally excluded, this has remained a sensitive area within which writers have operated at their peril, enjoying only a limited and varying degree of licence to mock. They have always enjoyed, at least in theory, latitude to take part in self-criticism –

an officially approved activity involving the exposure of minor abuses and petty officials in areas demarcated as legitimate targets, provided always that all indecorous phenomena are presented in a manner implying that they are untypical of Soviet life as a whole. These conditions have precluded the emergence of Soviet-published Swifts or Orwells, and have placed all the more responsibility on witnesses who have eluded the censorship system by bringing out their work abroad as Export Only or *émigré* writers. The most important recent representative of these, Solzhenitsyn, has added to the theory of Socialist Realism the following illuminating comment with reference to his Soviet-published contemporaries: 'All have agreed, whatever their subject and material may be, to leave unspoken the main truth, the truth that stares you in the eye even without literature. It is this vow to abstain from the truth that is called Socialist Realism.[6] So much for the truthful, historically concrete depiction of reality in its revolutionary development.

How fortunate, then, that the doctrine of Socialist Realism is essentially fluid, and has of late been enforced somewhat laxly, so that it no longer tyrannizes over imaginative literature, as in the immediate post-war years. Among recent writers who have published worthwhile material in their own country, despite the notional continued supremacy of Socialist Realism, Solzhenitsyn lists Tvardovsky, Vasily Shukshin, Boris Mozhayev, Vladimir Tendryakov, Vasily Belov and Vladimir Soloukhin (all chroniclers of rural life), together with certain unspecified 'bold young poets'.[7]

Nor has the doctrine of Socialist Realism remained immune from attack in the Soviet press and at Writers' Congresses, though such discussions usually proceed, as is the Soviet manner, in a kind of code. Precluded from denouncing the creed in so many words, its opponents have tended to call for more 'sincerity' and for an improvement in 'artistic quality'. Such have been the slogans of liberals opposed to traditional Socialist Realism, but not permitted to say so openly. Almost equally coy, their loyalist opponents tend, in support of the *status quo*, to clamour for more 'contemporaneity', but without necessarily leaping to the defence of Socialist Realism in so many words, since to do so would imply that the sacrosanct doctrine is sufficiently controversial to become a subject for debate. Meanwhile Socialist Realism still remains notionally mandatory, its inhibiting effects being greatly mitigated by the vagueness of its purport and by continued failure to impose it with former rigour. We may say if we wish that Socialist Realism has been tacitly abandoned; or we may choose to express the same idea in different form by saying that the doctrine has come to be applied more flexibly. But the terminology and concepts of Socialist Realism are still sacrosanct, and they are still frequently used as a stick with which to beat the ideologically recalcitrant.

10 Control Mechanisms

Incentives

That authors, especially those enjoying official approval and large sales, enjoy many perquisites through their Union of Writers – privileged shopping, housing, travel and medical facilities – has already been noted. We now consider the writer's economic position more directly in an attempt to answer, in the Soviet context, a crucial question that has obsessed men of letters throughout the ages: how is the writer paid, and what sort of economic and financial entity does he constitute?

In the highly collective Soviet community, where almost everyone works for some enterprise with its own hierarchy and pay structure, writers and other creative artists are an anomaly. However much they may be notionally dedicated to the public weal, they tend to operate as individuals, not as members of a team. They work for their own and their families' upkeep and profit. They work where they wish and when they wish, negotiating their own contracts with periodicals and publishing houses. They thus belong to what is, even in the Soviet Union, a profession by its very nature resistant to institutionalization, and represent a kind of cottage industry that has survived into an age of mass production. But their position is not unique, as has already been indicated. Not only is it shared with other creative artists, but it resembles that of fur-trappers and prospectors for precious metals, since they too are permitted to exercise their skills on an individual basis at times and places of their own choosing. So too, in their spare time, do the country's countless allotment-holders, as also those doctors and dentists who engage in private practice, together with teachers who give private tuition for a fee (all activities permitted in law), not to mention such officially disapproved groups as prostitutes and *shabashniki* (illicit building workers; 'the lump'). All these belong, in effect, wholly or partly to what has been called the USSR's Second Economy. It represents a sizeable shadow organization operating parallel with the highly centralized and elaborately regulated command economy within which the majority of the population is employed. As a Western expert on the Soviet publishing business has written, the author-publisher relationship is 'the only example we have of an entire Soviet industry (with an 800-million-rouble annual turnover) drawing upon forty thousand or more individuals each year to create, compile or edit the material which it must place on the market'.[1]

The channels through which a work achieves publication are not radically different from those employed in the West. An author may send in his completed typescript, unsolicited, to a suitable periodical or publishing house for consideration or he may submit a digest; or a work may be commissioned by the publisher. In any event the author will, if successful, be offered a contract. But he will not be paid a royalty consisting of a percentage of the published price, as is usual with book publication in the West. The basic principle for calculating authors' fees in the USSR is, by contrast, that of a manuscript's length. They receive so much a line for poetry; and, for prose, so much per Author's Sheet. The Author's Sheet, sometimes called a Printer's Sheet, consists of forty thousand typographical signs, including spaces between letters, this being equivalent to about sixteen pages of a normal book. For each genre a scale of fees is fixed by a decree of the Council of Ministers in the relevant republic (in our case usually the RSFSR). The rate for prose fiction is normally between 150 and 400 roubles, depending on the category of the manuscript in terms of excellence as determined by the publisher; but the rate is open to negotiation with the author, who is free to seek another contract elsewhere if the proposed terms do not suit him. For especially large printings, as for reprintings and new editions, additional fees become payable on a comparable basis.

Though precise comparisons are difficult to draw the profession of letters is clearly somewhat more remunerative, on its lower and middle levels, in the USSR than it is in Europe and America. As for the handful of best-selling authors, these are richly rewarded both in Western and in Soviet society, with the general balance in favour of the West, but with the obvious exception of authors resident in such depressed and fiscally confiscatory countries as Britain of the 1970s.

Turning to individual instances, Sholokhov may well be the highest-

paid Soviet-domiciled author. He is said to command a special rate of
500 roubles an Author's Sheet, and to have maintained a private
aeroplane on the proceeds of works that have appeared in dozens of
editions and in many tens of millions of copies.[2] Earlier in our period
we find Mayakovsky punctuating the output of lyrics denouncing the
sin of acquisitiveness with the purchase of a four-cylinder Renault car,
then the height of luxury, in Paris of the 1920s.[3] In the following decade
Valentin Katayev became the first Soviet-based author to acquire an
American refrigerator, and that at the peak of the Great Purge.[4] Even
a new author may find himself suddenly affluent, judged by the lot
of the common salary-earner: when *Novy mir* accepted Solzhenitsyn's
first published work, *One Day in the Life of Ivan Denisovich*, he was
paid an advance equivalent to two years of the earnings on which he
had hitherto been living as a part-time schoolmaster.[5]

The emoluments of successful authors are sporadically boosted by
literary prizes. The most important has been the Stalin Prize, awarded
between 1941 and 1952 and superseded (since 1956) by the no less
important Lenin Prize, as also (since 1966) by the State Prize of the
USSR. These are bestowed either for recently published work, or
for literary activity spread over a period, and have been graded into
First Class, Second Class and so on. The number of individual awards
has varied from year to year. As an indication of their number a
total of about 220 Stalin Prizes was conferred on Russian authors in
the relevant period.[6]

Literary prizes can be very lucrative: for example, 100,000 (old)
roubles for the First Class Stalin Prize, 10,000 (new) roubles for the
First Class Lenin Prize. Indeed, they are even more remunerative than
these figures may suggest, since the award of a prize is also a guarantee
of further publication in large editions, paid for at top rates, as also of
translation into major languages of the USSR and into those of the
Soviet bloc – and hence of further substantial increases in fees.

Stalin Prize winners have included Ehrenburg, Simonov and Aleksey
Tolstoy, who each received the award more than once; Kaverin,
Nekrasov and Tvardovsky; also authors less widely esteemed such as
Semyon Babayevsky, a scribe more subservient to the Party line than
the above. Among Lenin Prize winners have been Leonov, Simonov,
Tvardovsky and the present First Secretary of the Writers' Union,
Georgy Markov.

That literary merit can be a major factor in the award of prizes some of the above names suggest. But it is even more obvious, as is inevitable in Soviet conditions, that the Prize Committees, sometimes consisting of more than a hundred influential individuals, have been guided principally by political considerations. These came to the surface during the campaign, openly waged in the Soviet press, to have Solzhenitsyn awarded a Lenin Prize in 1964. Unfortunately his candidature chanced to coincide with a swing of the Party line against the liberal movement that he represented; he was eventually unsuccessful, the prize going to an inoffensive, comparatively unknown writer, Oles Gonchar.[7]

Another success for the conservative or re-Stalinizing camp was the establishment in 1974 of silver and gold medals (for works portraying the Soviet armed forces) named after the Stalinist literary tycoon Aleksandr Fadeyev; gold Fadeyev Medals have been awarded to the two loyalist stalwarts Sholokhov and Surkov. In contrast with this arguably reactionary step may be quoted a recent liberalizing move: the bestowal in 1975 of a State Prize on Fyodor Abramov. He has been invoked above as a leading exponent of Village Prose, and as the author of descriptions of rural life that faithfully record the more unedifying aspects of the Collective Farm.

Censorship

Official spokesmen will always inform the inquiring foreigner that there is no literary or other censorship in the USSR – as, for example, was stated to an American publishers' delegation in 1970: 'Everywhere we were told there was no actual censorship of books.'[1] This is true only in the sense that the terms for 'censorship' and 'censor' (*tsenzura* and *tsenzor*), formerly applied to institutions and officials of the Imperial period, have not been carried over into official usage in the Soviet period; compare also the abandoning of the word *politsiya* ('police'). Moreover, the cuts and alterations imposed by the Tsarist censorship on pre-1917 authors have been restored in Soviet-published editions. As examination of the relevant texts shows, the censoring of pre-1917 belles-lettres was restricted in its impact by comparison with the modifications imposed on post-revolutionary work under the successor regime by persons and institutions of which none bears the official name of censor or censorship.

Since the present study does not seek the imprimatur of Soviet publishing authority we shall not hesitate to use the term Soviet censorship – as, indeed, is the common practice of Soviet citizens or ex-citizens publishing Export Only writings and works written in emigration.

The brief history of the Soviet literary censorship is as follows. From 1917 to about 1930 it was largely negative, being concerned to purge belles-lettres of material tending to undermine the Soviet system of government. This left authors a fair degree of freedom, which was eroded with the introduction of intensive Stalinization. To negative censorship of the severest order was then added what may be called positive censorship: writers were no longer told only what they must *not* write, but were given detailed indications of how and what they *must* write: they were to show unfailing optimism, display the victorious onward march of Stalinist industrial and agricultural policies, and so on. By contrast with other societies, in which censorship tends to be intensified in wartime, the USSR enjoyed comparative relief in the years 1941–5. It was in 1946–53 that combined negative and positive censorship reached its most extreme degree of intensity, virtually restricting authors (as we have seen) to composing political advertising copy barely recognizable as literature and ineffective even as propaganda. After Stalin's death penal sanctions for the evasion of literary controls were substantially relaxed, and censorship under Khrushchev became mild by previous standards, but erratic and unpredictable in its impact. Under Brezhnev eccentric impulses have been eliminated, while the censorship has become more sophisticated, efficient and severe, especially in its effect on works and periodicals enjoying a large circulation. But there has been no return to the stringencies of rampant Stalinism, and there has even been an increased tendency to pass potentially suspect material provided that it appears in publications with a restricted circulation.

Censorship being, like the security police, a highly sensitive institution, we shall not be surprised to find it subject to those periodical changes of name that serve to cast a decent pall of obscurity over operations deemed inadvisable subjects for publicity. After the Revolution censorship was at first exercised by the State Publishing House. Then, on 6 June 1922, a special censoring body was set up, the Chief Administration for Literary Affairs and Publishing. This is commonly known, from the short form of its Russian title, as Glavlit.

Like *tsenzor* and *tsenzura*, Glavlit has become an officially discouraged
term, but it too continues in use colloquially (and will be used here),
even though the body that it designates has since been re-entitled the
Chief Administration for Safeguarding State Secrets in Print. The
new and still more cumbrously termed body certainly regards itself as
the lineal successor of Glavlit, as is shown by the fact that the fiftieth
anniversary of the institution's foundation was celebrated by members
of the rechristened Chief Administration – in Moscow's October Hall,
the scene of Stalin's chief show trials, on 6 June 1972.[2] This feast of
censors was even attended by representatives of the Union of Writers;
as if, one is tempted to add, rabbits had been trained to sup from
the same dish as stoats.

Despite this publicly reported orgy the institution – whether we
term it censorship or Glavlit, or call it by its most recent title – is
shrouded in secrecy that only the revelations of recent émigrés have
enabled us to penetrate. From a former Soviet newspaper editor resident in the West, Leonid Finkelstein, we learn of a 300-page Index
of banned subjects, known informally as the Talmud, on which Glavlit
officials base their scrutiny of material submitted for publication. The
most fascinating of these taboo subjects is naturally censorship itself,
and we learn from Finkelstein that the disappearance from circulation
of the terms Glavlit, and (except with reference to the Tsarist period)
of *tsenzura* and *tsenzor*, is no accident, since there is a formal ban on
employing the words in correspondence or over the telephone. How
many censors are there? That too comes under a censorship ban, but
Finkelstein's own estimate which (he says) 'may well be inaccurate',
is seventy thousand.[3] If he is right the censorship apparatus must out-
number the membership of the Writers' Union by nearly ten to one,
though we must also remember that Glavlit's operations extend well
outside imaginative literature to embrace all manifestations of the
printed word together with radio and television.

The Talmud's list of banned subjects includes the following: natural
disasters such as earthquakes and landslides; fires; aeroplane and train
crashes; the price of goods and price increases; improvement in the
living standards of countries outside the Socialist Camp (the USSR
and approved Communist countries); deterioration in the living standards of countries inside the Socialist Camp; food shortages; the names
of KGB operatives other than that of the Chairman. Also banned
from mention are disgraced politicians – Trotsky, Zinovyev and

Kamenev among earlier figures, and Khrushchev. To this category of unpersons further belong anathematized writers such as Solzhenitsyn, Kuznetsov and many others; also Gumilyov and the other unrehabilitated dead. Nor may reference be made to the existence of the special shopping, residential and other privileges enjoyed by the élite. Crime statistics are outside the pale too.[4]

What of Glavlit's *modus operandi*? In keeping with the official fiction that the organization does not exist (though its number was to be found in the Moscow telephone directory for 1966),[5] its representatives never come face to face with the authors whose work they scrutinize, but deal only with Chief Editors or their immediate deputies in the periodicals and publishing houses. Censors first see material in proof, and they see it twice: first to identify any non-approved material that may be present; a second time, in corrected proof, to ensure that any of their *suggestions* made for removing improper material have been carried out. I stress 'suggestions' since the censors do not give orders, their style of work tending to the tactfully courteous, as is pleasantly characteristic of not a few areas in the *mœurs* of the Soviet élite. And that censors indeed do belong to the élite we are reminded by their salary scale; it begins at about 280 roubles a month, nearly twice the average industrial wage, and rises to impressive heights at the top.[6]

In keeping with the general atmosphere of secrecy, censorship-imposed alterations to a text are commonly called author's corrections, and the unfortunate author may even find that he has to pay for them. But what of the author who is not prepared to accept such corrections of his work, still less to pretend that they are his own? He is free to withdraw his text from publication, but may be deterred from doing so by having to return the sizeable advance which will already have been paid, and which may constitute his main or sole source of income.

By no means is the censoring process confined to the organization colloquially and illicitly termed Glavlit. In cricketing terms that is merely a long-stop, or even an extra long-stop, rather than a wicket-keeper. Before any manuscript reaches a censor's desk it has already been subjected to a variety of controlling pressures that begin – as is characteristic of any rigorous censoring system – inside the author's head. If he wishes to see his work in print there is no point in him conceiving of it, at any stage, in a form that would render it unsuitable for publication. Hence Kuznetsov's claim, that everything issued in the USSR bears the stigma of two censors – the external official censor and the internal self-censor. 'Usually only half of what I submitted for publication was printed, and that was only a third or less of what I would have put to paper if there had been freedom of speech and the press.'[7] The same author has made it possible to trace the operations of the censorship in detail by publishing, in 1970 and in English translation, a new and revised version of his documentary novel *Baby Yar*. He here incorporates passages excluded by the censor from the original Soviet-published Russian-language version of the work (1966), distinguishing them by the use of a different type fount. The reinstated passages include material suggesting that the policies of Lenin and Stalin were no less pernicious than those of Hitler; and also numerous references to such indecorous phenomena as looting, spitting and copulating. Kuznetsov has further distinguished material newly added (in 1967-9) by the use of square brackets, but these insertions presumably cannot reconstitute the work as it would have developed had it not been distorted at its very genesis by the self-censoring process.

In suggesting that censorship takes place at only two levels, that of self-censorship and Glavlit, Kuznetsov is misleading since he omits the vital intermediate screening performed by the editors of the periodicals in which most works of belles-lettres receive their first publication. Editors are more familiar with current publishing policy than most authors. Anxious to avoid unnecessary trouble at a later stage, they are liable to demand extensive cuts and rewriting long before the question of submitting proofs to Glavlit could arise. The sketch *A Soviet Robinson Crusoe* (1932) is a minor masterpiece devoted to this theme as it presented itself to the combined fantasies of Ilf and Petrov. An editor commissions an adventure story with this title from a zealous author who quickly submits a stirring account of a shipwrecked Soviet citizen taming a desert island and triumphing single-handedly over the elements before eventually being rescued. But the editor at once raises a series of fundamental objections. Where, for example, is the island's Party Committee? What of the 'guiding role of the trade unions'? Where are the female activists, the broad masses of the toilers? When the unfortunate author protests that his assignment had been to describe life on a desert island his representations are swept aside; and he eventually retires, promising a revised version on the morrow. In this the original island will have been downgraded, on the editor's insistence, to the status of peninsula. Far from being deserted, it is to be infested with every possible kind of bureaucrat, and the action is to culminate in a mass meeting of workers, activists, trade unionists and the like. As for the hapless hero – the original Crusoe – he has long ago been summarily ejected from the tale as a whining individualist.

Such is the imagined impact of a Soviet editor as described by the country's leading humorists. No doubt few real-life editors have gone as far as this, but there is abundant evidence that their interventions may be persistent and far-reaching. Nor are editors the only problem, for figures far more exalted may – however exceptionally – become closely involved in the details of publishing policy. The best-documented of such episodes must be the pre-publication history of Solzhenitsyn's *One Day in the Life of Ivan Denisovich*. Its eventual appearance, in *Novy mir* for November 1962, was preceded by eleven months of intense wrangling behind the scenes.[8] As has since been revealed, the work could only be published at all through the direct intervention of the country's supreme political leader of the period, Nikita Khrushchev. Extra copies had to be produced at short notice for pre-publication consideration by influential members of the Central Committee. Even then the affair may well have damaged Khrushchev's standing, conceivably contributing to his fall from power two years later. 'We got into such awful hot water over Solzhenitsyn', the leader's wife once told a retired general, according to gossip picked up by the author of their embarrassment.[9]

Evasions of censorship have been by no means uncommon. One striking example is given by the literary critic Arkady Belinkov, who has explained in emigration how he contrived to introduce no less than two hundred pages of uncensored extra material into the second edition (1965) of his study of the historical novelist Yury Tynyanov. He submitted for the censor's consideration a false title page so made up as to suggest that the text was an exact reprint of the first edition, and not a new recension – which, being new, should most certainly have been recensored.[10] The effect of this trick was to smuggle into print a work vastly expanded by the insertion of material savagely criticizing Soviet practices under the thin disguise of a denunciation of Nicholas I's Russia (1825–55). Ingenuity can also be shown in the opposite direction. Censors have been known to pass a work for publication, despite its patent unsuitability, simply because higher authority wants to make an example of a particular author and use his case as a general deterrent. Only thus could Mikhail Zoshchenko explain the imprimatur given to his *Adventures of a Monkey*, which became a basis for the savage attack launched on him by the cultural satrap Zhdanov in 1946.[11]

Another device for avoiding controls has been to publish in the provinces material likely to be blocked if submitted at the ever-watchful centre. In August 1959, for example, two young poets, Kharabarov and Pankratov, who were in trouble in Moscow for too close an association with the disgraced Pasternak, suddenly erupted into print two thousand miles away in a Tashkent newspaper, *Kazakhstanskaya pravda* ('Kazakhstan Truth').[12] Khrushchev himself complained of this practice in a speech of 1963, pointing out that the motives of such far-flung organs were suspect: 'It flatters them to put out a book by a writer from the capital.'[13]

The most notorious of such publications was the collection of articles, poems and stories called *Tarusa Pages* and brought out in Kaluga (about 120 miles south-west of Moscow) in 1961 under Paustovsky's editorship. Containing articles praising the liquidated theatre producer Meyerhold and the émigré author Bunin, as well as verse by such politically compromised poets as Tsvetayeva and Zabolotsky, *Tarusa Pages* even 'became a nation-wide event, a challenge to "socialist realism", and a manifesto of "revisionism".'[14]

More recently, in the Brezhnev period, literary critics and scholars have been able to publish, in small quantities and in Tartu (Estonia), neo-Formalist material that could not conceivably hope for large-scale issue by a metropolitan house.[15] Alma Ata (in the Kazakh SSR) and Samarkand (in the Uzbek SSR) have also given their imprint to such sensitive material, as have Kemerovo, Saratov, Tula, Vladimir and Voronezh in the RSFSR, besides which Soviet literary scholars are also known to contribute to foreign journals outside the Communist orbit.[16]

Though the main impact of censorship controls has naturally tended to fall on dissidents or liberals, opposed in however small degree to the regime, loyalists have not been immune. Brief reference has already been made to the sequence of radical surgical interventions to which the text of Gladkov's industrial novel *Cement* – originally published in 1925, and a by-word for political acceptability – was subjected by its author over the years, so that it has possibly become the most extensively and multiply remodelled of all leading Soviet-published works. Sholokhov's *The Quiet Don* has also passed through a sequence of radical modifications. Nor has its author's pre-eminent position among Soviet-published writers saved even a relatively minor work of his from the censor. From his uncompleted war novel *They Fought for their Country* he was forced to remove a chapter describing the persecutions of 1937–40; he tried to appeal against this ruling directly to Brezhnev, but was refused an interview.[17] The rewriting of the novel *The Young Guard* by another ultra-loyalist, Fadeyev, has already been mentioned, and was an example of the retrospective censoring of an item already published, as was the obligation imposed on the dramatist Nikolay Pogodin to rewrite his drama *Kremlin Chimes* (1941) in no less than four versions. The first text of the play had given prominence to Stalin and the second to Lenin, while the third sought to hold an even balance between the two. By the fourth time round the unfortunate Pogodin had no idea what was expected of him, but was rescued from the dilemma by his death in 1962.[18]

To the keen vigilance of Khrushchevite censors must be credited the removal from S. I. Ozhegov's one-volume dictionary (1960 edition) of a sentence that appears in the 1952 edition to illustrate the use of the word from which their master's surname derives: *khrushch – vreditel selskogo khozyaystva* ('the *khrushch* [cockchafer] is an agricultural pest'). Nor has the offending sentence been restored in the Brezhnev period (e.g. in the 11th, 1977, edition of Ozhegov), for despite the anti-Khrushchev bias of the new dispensation, the tendency is to consign the ousted leader to oblivion rather than to take opportunities to disparage him.

From dictionaries we turn to libraries. Yet another form of censorship is that whereby they maintain *spetskhrany* ('special depositories') of works unavailable except to categories of readers cleared for access. In Soviet libraries, including the Lenin Library in Moscow, this dispensation involves an elaborate dual cataloguing system: there is the emasculated catalogue for the ordinary reader and the full catalogue available only to those with security clearance. That the Lenin Library is 'probably the only great library in the world with two entire sets of catalogues' has been claimed by a Western journalist.[19] Access to the secret stacks was one of the privileges conferred on Solzhenitsyn when, in 1962, he was suddenly inducted into the Union of Writers. 'I received permission to work in the Public Library's *spetskhran* and pounced lecherously on the illicit tomes.'[20]

Disincentives

In the system of pressures to which writers have been subjected over
the decades censorship – whether exercised by the author himself, by
his editor, by Glavlit, or by some other authority – has been only one
item among many. Others have included attacks on individuals' livelihood and material welfare; psychological warfare; criminal proceedings. We shall consider these three main types of pressure in turn.

An author's livelihood can most easily be threatened by a ban on
publication such as has frequently been unavowedly applied. From
about 1923 both Akhmatova and Mandelstam began to find the placing
of their original work at first difficult and, after a few years, downright
impossible. Thus hampered in their main literary activities, they could
nevertheless earn money from the pen in humbler fashion. Mandelstam,
for instance, dabbled in journalism, even publishing an interview with
an obscure Indo-Chinese who was later to become famous as the
North Vietnamese Communist leader Ho Chi Minh.[1] But the main
refuge of otherwise unpublishable writers was translation. For example,
Akhmatova was able to earn a fee for the first time in several years
from a translation of Rubens's letters that appeared in 1937.[2] However,
neither she nor Mandelstam nor Pasternak took kindly to translation
as a process, since it seemed to sterilize their creative powers. It could
involve other dangers too. From 1928 Mandelstam was plagued
through the vicious exploitation of a misunderstanding, the point at
issue being his revision of two translations into Russian of a French
novel by Charles de Coster, *La Légende de Thyl Ulenspiegel et de
Lamme Goedzak*. Whether by accident or design, Mandelstam's revised
version was published without acknowledgement to the original translators. One of them was a certain A. G. Gornfeld, who made charges
of plagiarism that led to a sequence of court cases and interrogations
extending over some eighteen months. This campaign could not
have developed so malevolently except as part of an officially sponsored
persecution.[3]

Other excursions into translation have been less disastrous. They
have included Mikhail Lozinsky's version (1936–43) of Dante's
Divine Comedy and Pasternak's admired renderings of several of
Shakespeare's plays, as also of Goethe's *Faust* and Schiller's *Maria
Stuart*. There is also the practice of translating from a language un-

known to the poet; such work, based on a literal line-by-line version, has included Pasternak's renderings of Georgian verse, as noted above. Though officially disapproved creative authors might make a living from journalism and translation, or sometimes by writing for children when no longer permitted to write for adults, these lower forms of activity too depended on official sanction and access to such earnings might also be withdrawn in due course. This happened to the Mandelstams in the mid-1930s, when they were left without means and thus dependent on the charity of friends to save them from starvation. Reduced to begging, they benefited from the generosity that is an acknowledged Russian trait and formed one of the brighter aspects of the years of Terror. Even servants or beneficiaries of the regime, including the literary functionaries Fadeyev and Surkov, made discreet subventions to the destitute poet, thus helping to alleviate his years of martyrdom.

Not only writers' earnings but also their other material resources are ultimately controlled by the State, usually operating through a section of their own profession in accordance with the tradition whereby politically conforming 'activists' are used within a given group to supervise and manipulate politically lax or suspect colleagues. Reverting again to Mandelstam, on whose case we are particularly closely informed, we find him the recipient from the early 1920s of an almost comic series of favours and disfavours. The Great Humanist Maksim Gorky sanctions the issue of a sweater to the poet, but withholds a pair of trousers; the Symbolist poet Valery Bryusov capriciously ordains that he shall receive food rations on a lower scale than could equally well have been sanctioned; the Leningrad poet and literary tycoon Nikolay Tikhonov rules that the rival poet Mandelstam shall not be permitted to reside in that city.[4]

We now turn to the practice of disciplining deviants by verbal assault. This may take place privately at a specially convened, Party-rigged meeting of colleagues, where an errant writer will be subjected to a verbal working-over (*prorabotka*) for infringing some taboo or simulating insufficient civic zeal. The working-over may or may not remain secret from the population at large, but in either case it can be a painful experience for the victim.

Nor is there any lack of scope for public obloquy, such as may be conveyed on the most humble level, in factories and institutions, by the omnipresent wall newspaper. Where writers are concerned the press is the natural vehicle for such disciplining. It may take the form of hostile critical articles, Russian literary criticism having a particularly strong censorious and inquisitorial tradition long antedating the Revolution. On a more farcical level the press frequently prints letters of protest from an 'average Soviet worker', an 'ordinary collective farmer', or from a group of such 'honest toilers' writing from the depths of the provinces to express their spontaneous righteous indignation at some non-approved author's breach of current taboo.

Naturally these nuisances were particularly prevalent during the Stalin era, when psychological warfare against non-approved writers also made widespread use of *provokatsiya* ('provocation'). This might involve tricking the victim into associating with foreigners, and thus into risking the charge of espionage. Alternatively it might be possible to stage some form of public fracas that could later be made the basis for criminal charges or at least for persistent minor harassment. Spied upon *ex officio* by doorkeepers, lift attendants, charwomen, chauffeurs and the like, authors were also exposed to intrusion by acquaintances recruited as informants of the security police. These snoopers were liable to enter a suspect's apartment without notice, and to begin ferreting among his papers without even a word of apology. Nor was it, in the context, always safe to resist such impertinent prying. A friend of Solzhenitsyn's once visited the author's dacha in his absence, chancing to stumble in just when the place was being ransacked by a team of nine KGB operatives; only by pretending to be a foreigner did the visitor escape with his life, since the security police 'was not permitted to kill foreigners without authority'.[5] Nerve warfare might further include being watched and followed by emissaries of the security police who were intended to be recognized as such, and whose deliberately obtruded surveillance could, after a while, develop into a major irritation. Then again, there was also the common security police practice of installing concealed microphones in the homes of important suspects. These naturally included writers, not all of whom were as bold as Pasternak in wishing the instrument a 'Good day to you, microphone', and in addressing orations to it in the intervals between carrying on normal conversation wholly uninhibited by the thought of any unseen ear.[6]

Turning now to more sinister methods of control, and again with the accent largely but not exclusively on the Stalin period (when these abuses were at their most formidable), a writer might be disciplined through pressures against someone with whom he or she was bound by ties of intimate relationship. Akhmatova was rendered miserable, apprehensive and comparatively docile for many years by action taken against Lyov Gumilyov, her son by her first marriage. When the young man was arrested, and not for the first time, in November 1949, the poet immediately burnt the text of her play, *The Prologue*, which has consequently not survived.[7] In the same year an attempt was made to curb the intransigence of Pasternak by arresting and consigning to a concentration camp his intimate associate Olga Ivinskaya. She was released in 1953, but was to be rearrested and subjected to further imprisonment and harassment after the poet's death in 1960. As this reminds us, though the worst abuses are associated with the period of the Stalin dictatorship, they by no means died out with Stalin.

No method of controlling writers has been more characteristic than the orchestration of concerted attacks on carefully pre-selected scape-goats. This was first applied on any notable scale with the great press campaign already mentioned as having been mounted in 1929 against Pilnyak and Zamyatin. It was, we remember, based on the foreign publication of the former's novel *Mahogany* and of the latter's novel *We*, objection being taken to the content of these works, which it was not difficult to interpret as anti-Soviet, and also to the fact of their publication abroad. Though foreign publication contravened neither Soviet law nor common usage, it was now retrospectively denounced as a crime. But the culpability or innocence of Pilnyak and Zamyatin was neither here nor there, the purpose of the operation being to proclaim to the writing fraternity as a whole that a new era of inten-sified political regimentation had dawned. To do this through two carefully chosen scapegoats was more eloquent, dramatic and effective than merely to issue some impersonal decree. The method also had the advantage that other writers could be intimidated into joining the chorus of denunciation. It was a means of dragooning the un-decided, of involving them in complicity with the witch-hunt, while simultaneously isolating the independent few who refused to take part. In the end the affair gathered such momentum that the very authorities called a halt, whereupon the witch-hunters found themselves under attack for excess of zeal. Here was a characteristic device by which the Stalin government could claim credit for its broad-minded tolerance in calling off the very persecutions that it had instituted in the first place.

Among other prominent scapegoats of the Stalin era we also remember Akhmatova and Zoshchenko, suddenly singled out for attack as a means of proclaiming the end of wartime ideological relaxations. The main promoter of this campaign was Stalin's chief controller of culture, Andrey Zhdanov, whose assault came out of the blue and took the form of the Central Committee decree, dated 14 August 1946, that censured the journals *Zvezda* ('Star') and *Leningrad* for publishing the ideologically harmful and apolitical works of the two pilloried authors. Zoshchenko was accused of *bezydeynost* (operating in an ideological vacuum), and of slandering Soviet life with his short story *Adventures of a Monkey*, while Akhmatova was pilloried for bourgeois-aristocratic aestheticism, pessimism, decadence and adherence to the condemned doctrine of Art for Art's sake. Shortly afterwards Zhdanov issued a report in which he described the poet in a famous phrase: 'part nun and part harlot, or rather both harlot and nun, in whom harlotry is mingled with prayer'.[8] Here was an indelicate reference to the sensual and religious elements in Akhmatova's verse. Once again, though, the purpose of the attack was independent of the personalities and writings of its overt targets. Rather had they been carefully selected as a means of announcing to the Soviet cultural world that easy times were over and that a period of harsh regimentation had been reinstituted. As for the personal fates of the two victims-in-chief, despite the prevalence of arrest in this period, and of consignment to the camps, they suffered no severer fate than virulent public abuse and expulsion (later rescinded) from the Writers' Union. Akhmatova and Zoshchenko were accordingly far less severely treated than literary colleagues and countless other fellow citizens who were consigned to the camps under Stalin.

The Stalinist punitive system recognized many grades of severity. One of the milder forms was exile, which might either be positive – to a specific designated location – or else negative: the victim might, for example, be forbidden to live within 105 versts (about seventy miles) of Moscow. So common was this form of banishment, especially as imposed on women, that the sufferers received a special name: *stopyatnitsy* ('hundred-and-fivers'). Victims of the process might find themselves suddenly ordered, as by the sheriff in a Western film, to 'get out of town within twenty-four hours'. At one time the periphery of Moscow was teeming with hundred-and-fivers, who were thus conveniently placed for mass arrest when the decision was taken to step up the quota of concentration camp inmates in 1937.[9] The camps too had their grades, we remember: some were 'ordinary', and others were placed under a particularly severe regimen; but in all human life was cheap. Very probably not a few authors were executed outright by shooting, a common practice during the Terror. But we cannot fully document such a fate in the case of any prominent literary figure, by contrast with the openly admitted shooting of Gumilyov back in 1921. For the most part, indeed, there are no reliable details on the manner, place and date of the deaths of writers, as of non-writers, liquidated during and after the Yezhovshchina. Moreover, as we shall see, the post-Stalin authorities appear to have made a practice of fabricating dates of death for certain victims of the Purge.

Since 1953 writers' lives and liberty have remained in jeopardy, though to a reduced extent. From the post-Stalin scapegoats we select two *causes célèbres* to which brief reference has already been made. Iosif Brodsky was tried in Leningrad in 1964 on a charge of 'parasitism' before a court that was not prepared to recognize the writing of verse as a serious occupation and sentenced him to forced labour. Two years later the old Stalinist tradition of arraigning scapegoats in pairs was revived when Andrey Sinyavsky and Yuly Daniel, authors of pseudonymous and foreign-published works deemed derogatory to the Soviet system, also received forced labour sentences. The case aroused international indignation – far more than it deserved, according to Solzhenitsyn, who claims that there had been a million other, unpublicized cases a hundred times worse during the previous half century of Soviet rule.[10] Be that as it may, the Sinyavsky and Daniel affair was not to prove an effective deterrent. On the contrary, the year of their trial (1966) was the very point at which Export Only literature, such as they had pioneered, began to develop from a trickle into a torrent.

Concentration camp sentences imposed on writers, among whom Brodsky, Sinyavsky and Daniel are only three, have been by no means unknown in the post-Stalin period. But their incidence has been drastically reduced. They have, moreover, at least been confined to those turbulent and stubborn spirits who have challenged or resisted the regime over a long period – a far less oppressive policy than that of the Stalin era, when arrests were widespread and embraced many citizens who had never dreamt of opposing the system.

Despite the marked relaxation of punitive procedures after Stalin's death, writers are still potentially menaced with long periods of

imprisonment for activities that would not incur punishment in other
societies regarding themselves as civilized. Moreover, the post-Stalin
period has witnessed the widespread application of a new control
device: the compulsory consignment of authors, and of other dissidents,
to psychiatric wards where they are at the mercy of doctors and
keepers operating in secret and responsible only to the Soviet authorities. An early account of the procedure is Valery Tarsis's Export Only
documentary study *Ward Number Seven* (1965), the author being
one among many who have suffered this form of persecution; for a
fuller and more systematic analysis of the phenomenon of psychiatric
detention, Bloch and Reddaway (see Bibliography) may also be consulted.

Rehabilitation

Rehabilitation was most actively developed in the middle and late
1950s. It consisted of removing the stigma from the names of individual
victims of the Stalin Terror; and, in the case of such as had physically
survived, of restoring to them such civil rights as were enjoyed by the
population at large. The formal basis for rehabilitation was a Party
decree of 1956, 'On Overcoming the Personality Cult and its Consequences'. In this document the repressions of the Terror were un-
emotionally described as 'serious infringements of Soviet legality';[1]
writers who had suffered from them now became eligible for reinstate-
ment, posthumously in many cases.

   With literary victims two stages were involved, of which the first
was rehabilitation as a citizen and the second rehabilitation as a writer.
In the case of Mandelstam the former occurred when, in August 1956,
his widow received 'a flimsy slip of mimeographed paper', emanating
from the Supreme Court of the USSR and indicating that his sufferings
and death had been due to a regrettable oversight.[2] In February of
the following year the long process of the poet's literary rehabilitation
began with the appointment by the Union of Writers, in accordance
with normal routine after an author's death, of a commission of literary
executors to process his archive and arrange such publication of his
work as might seem appropriate. By tradition the commission included
the closest surviving relative (the poet's widow); literary colleagues
(Akhmatova and Ehrenburg); a leading literary functionary (Surkov)

and others. Plans were made to publish a selection of the deceased's verse, but these were – again by tradition – repeatedly shelved, partly because no one was prepared to take the political risk of writing the mandatory introduction instructing readers in the correct political attitude to be adopted towards the rehabilitated author and his writings. Not until 1973 did the selection at last appear, with an introduction by A. L. Dymshits. On the poet's terrible – but still obscure – fate the following information only was given, and that incorrect in its second particular: 'Mandelstam's creative activity was cut short in 1937. The poet died at the beginning of 1938.'[3] In fact the most probable date of his death was December of that year. Like other editions of rehabilitated authors, the Mandelstam volume has been issued with a print run substantially below the potential demand, and has been extensively exported, few copies having been made available for purchase by Soviet readers.

Though Pilnyak too was rehabilitated in 1956, a commission of his literary executors being duly appointed in the same year, he had to wait even longer than Mandelstam for posthumous publication, since not a word of his works was published for twenty years: a selection at last appeared in 1976. V. Novikov's introduction deals with the author's fate in characteristically cryptic terms: 'B. Pilnyak's literary life was cut short in 1937. He died on 9 September 1941.'[4] According to other information Pilnyak was shot by the NKVD while serving a twenty-five-year sentence for treason, espionage, Trotskyism, sabotage and terrorism.[5]

Babel was fortunate enough to receive speedier rehabilitation in 1954, and a selection of his work, with an introduction by Ehrenburg, was published as early as 1957. Babel had been arrested in May 1939, and his death is given in Soviet sources as 17 March 1941, but characteristically without indication of cause or place. As this reminds us, the collation of dates of death in Soviet reference works sometimes throws up conflicting evidence suggesting that the same person died more than once.[6] There is also reason to believe that dates may have been deliberately falsified: carried over, that is, into a bracket including the war years in order to divert attention from the particularly high rate of casualties in 1937–8, the peak period for arrests and executions. 'It was statistically convenient to merge the camp deaths with military casualties. Thus was the picture of the repressions blurred and what really happened was no one's business. In the period of the rehabilitations 1942 and 1943 were almost automatically given as the years of death.'[7] In this unobtrusive fashion was the impact of the Yezhov-shchina unobtrusively reduced.

So much for three outstanding rehabilitated writers out of the many who perished in the purges. Rehabilitation could also be earned by those who returned from the concentration camps to the land of the living. An example is the poet Nikolay Zabolotsky, who was in camps and exile from 1938 to 1946. Publication of his verse had of course been suspended during those years, but was resumed in 1948. Another notable returner was the novelist and senior Party member Galina Serebryakova, who had committed an unusual double indiscretion: that of marrying, in succession, two politically prominent husbands (Sokolnikov and Serebryakov) destined for extermination as victims of Stalin's show trials. She was arrested in 1936 and rehabilitated twenty years later, after which she completed her trilogy of novels based on the life of Karl Marx. Undeterred by two decades of repression, Serebryakova was mobilizing undiminished fervour to condemn literary nonconformists at writers' meetings of 1962–3.[8] For example, she earned Khrushchev's approval for an attack launched, at a writers' reception of December 1963, on Ehrenburg, who was then temporarily in disgrace for over-liberalizing.[9] Serebryakova had been rehabilitated with, as it were, a vengeance.

How careful and individually 'personalized' rehabilitation may be we can judge from the continuing failure to bring the poet Gumilyov, shot in 1921 for counter-revolutionary activity, out of unperson status. His work continued to be published in the Soviet Union for a few years after his death, by contrast with the practice of a later age, when to be arrested was to become an unperson on the spot. But none of Gumilyov's works have appeared on his native soil since the 1920s, except for a small edition published in Leningrad in 1962.[10] Meanwhile a four-volume edition, published extra-territorially in Washington DC, has admirably rescued the poet's heritage.

Other writers have been rehabilitated without ever suffering trial or prolonged imprisonment. Thus Akhmatova, disgraced in 1946, was granted dacha status in 1955 and slowly restored to esteem, her son being released from the camps in the following year. The first of several post-Stalin selections of her work appeared in 1958; in 1961 a fuller selection appeared, preceded by a slanted account of her experiences from Surkov. Further samples of her work have continued to appear after her death in 1966.

In other cases a form of rehabilitation has been accorded to writers, who, without ever being subjected to extreme public obloquy or to the severer forms of oppression, had fallen into unofficial disfavour in the sense that publication of their works had been unavowedly discontinued. Among authors thus denied to the Soviet reader for many years and rediscovered, as it were, in the post-Stalin era have been Bulgakov, Khlebnikov, Olesha, Platonov and Tsvetayeva. In each case selections of a given writer's work have been published – posthumously, except for Olesha – after careful consideration has been given to the political implications of the operation and to the choice of contents. Introductions and commentaries have been angled so as to relieve readers from the need to form an unguided opinion on this long-buried material. Such aids to the formulation of opinion are particularly helpful in cases where extended unperson status long ago cut off the usual evolution of a political line indicating the proper attitude to be adopted to a given author by his readership.

11 Conformists and Nonconformists

The inducements and penalties described in the previous chapter have tended to polarize writers, especially from the early 1930s onwards, into conformists who avail themselves of the inducements, and nonconformists who incur or risk the penalties. We now consider representatives of these opposed attitudes in turn – the instruments and the opponents of literary processing – under the headings Custodians, Liberals and Dissidents.

Custodians

By Custodians we understand those leading literary figures who, having rejected exclusively literary careers and obtained advancement in the administrative hierarchies, have used their influence to support official policies and bolster the *status quo*.

Promotion within the Writers' Union includes the following grades, in ascending order of exclusiveness: election as a delegate to one of the all-USSR Writers' Congresses held roughly every five years; election to the Union of Writers' Board, Secretariat, Bureau; election to the office of Chairman, Secretary-General or First Secretary, the titles and functions having varied somewhat over the years. Similar offices exist within the Union's subsidiary branches, from those of the RSFSR, Moscow and Leningrad down to those of minor provincial centres.

Outside the literary sphere writers may, as we have seen, obtain a foothold in the State hierarchy by becoming delegates to the Supreme Soviet, a position conferring no political power. Far more influential is, of course, membership of the CPSU, and especially of its Central Committee, to which (as noted above) Fadeyev, Sholokhov, Simonov,

Surkov, Tvardovsky and other senior literary figures have belonged, as candidates or full members, over the years.

It is under these conditions that the USSR has spawned a class of writers or ex-writers such as are not found outside the Soviet bloc; those substantially or principally engaged in manipulating, supervising and determining the activities, privileges and emoluments of subordinate scribes. Solzhenitsyn calls such members of the administrative élite *velmozhi*,[1] an old-fashioned word with eighteenth-century associations, for which 'potentates' is a possible rendering; so too are 'tycoons' and 'nabobs', since such functionaries tend to be affluent as well as influential. Alternatively they might be termed trusties, prefects or monitors; but since these terms are perhaps too closely associated with school or prison life, we prefer here the more neutral Custodians.

Many Custodians have made no mark as writers, and are remembered if at all only for their administrative fervour. There was Ivan Gronsky who originally helped to establish the Union of Writers. There was Vladimir Stavsky, who became the Union's Secretary-General in 1936 and survived the Yezhovshchina to perish in the war. And there was Vsevolod Vishnevsky, appointed Deputy Secretary-General of the Union of Writers after the Zhdanov crackdown of 1946, and author of a Stalin Prize-winning play falsifying the dictator's role in 1919; he is credited with having been as dedicated an alcoholic as his superior officer in the Union, Secretary-General Fadeyev – a reminder of the close correlation to be observed in general between spectacular drinking feats and the attainment of high rank in the literary hierarchy.[2] To author-functionaries of later years belong still others whose administrative record is more impressive than their literary achievement. They include Aleksey Surkov, composer of war poetry and prominent in the persecution of Pasternak; Georgy Markov, author of novels about Siberia and of policy-making speeches at all Writers' Congresses from 1954 to 1976, who became First Secretary of the Writers' Union in 1971.

All the above were or still are Party members of some standing and their main literary function has been the implementation of Party control over writers. Among those mentioned Fadeyev alone has attained high stature as an author, contriving to combine extreme loyalist sentiment with no little force of utterance and best-seller status. Both as a writer and as an official Fadeyev had a chequered career. He had been a leading figure on RAPP before the dissolution of that organization in 1932, after which he was lucky enough to escape liquidation as meted out to other leading RAPPists. In 1934 he was elected to the Board of the newly formed Union of Writers, becoming one of its Secretaries five years later.

A macabre episode marks Fadeyev's dossier for early 1938, when Mandelstam chanced to let slip in his presence that he had been lucky enough to receive an official invitation to spend a two-month holiday at Samatikha – a mysterious rest home in the depths of the provinces, and one to which authors were not normally assigned. What the politically sophisticated Fadeyev at once correctly concluded – but the more innocent Mandelstam did not yet suspect – was that this particular invitation could, in its context, only have been issued in order to isolate the poet as a prelude to his arrest and liquidation. As this was borne in, the warm-hearted Fadeyev was moved by compassion, and he refrained from informing Mandelstam of the impending disaster, while staging a demonstrative farewell embrace complete with kisses.[3] Was he modelling himself on the practices of such as Alphonse Capone in contemporary Chicago? Or reviving the older tradition of Judas Iscariot? We cannot tell; but at all events Fadeyev continued to rise in the hierarchy of literature's potentates while Mandelstam's bones rotted in some unknown resting place in the Soviet far-eastern camp archipelago.

Fadeyev became a member of the CPSU Central Committee in 1939, and he was appointed joint Secretary-General and Chairman of the Board seven years later, as one of the tough measures taken under the Zhdanov crackdown of 1946. However, as we remember, the promotion did not save him from the obligation to rewrite his novel *The Young Guard* and later to embark on a second rewriting, almost as if he were a rank and file member of the Union of Writers and not its supreme overlord. The episode naturally rendered humbler authors still more amenable to discipline: if the great Fadeyev could be called to order in this way, how could any lesser scribe resist regimentation?

When Stalin died and the process of de-Stalinization began, Fadeyev's position as the deceased dictator's premier literary hatchet-man became an embarrassment to himself and others. Compromised by his past, he stepped down from the secretary-generalship of the Writers' Union in 1954. Fate had not yet finished with him, however. Widely held responsible for the consignment of so many authors to concentration camps under Stalin, he is said to have suffered acute pangs of conscience when confronted by released survivors. One of these, the minor writer Ivan Makaryev, administered to the ex-Secretary-General a form of reproof classic in the annals of Russian literary quarrels: a slap on the face.[4] Fadeyev also enjoyed the distinction of being singled out for abuse by Sholokhov, a fellow member of the Central Committee who, at the Twentieth Party Congress of February 1956, was unkind enough to sneer at the ex-Secretary-General of the Writers' Union as 'power-mad'.[5]

Whether stung by Sholokhov's taunt, weary of endlessly revising his work, hounded by feelings of guilt, or – the official version – tormented by chronic alcoholism, Fadeyev shot himself through the heart at his Peredelkino dacha on 13 May 1956. He was one of modern Russian literature's many 'Shakespearian' figures, with more than a touch of Richard III, Macbeth and Iago in his make-up. Pasternak wrote that Fadeyev was well disposed to him personally, and we also know that Fadeyev could recite Pasternak's verse by heart. And yet, had Fadeyev received orders to have Pasternak hung, drawn and quartered, he would (the poet claimed) have carried them out faithfully and made his report without a flicker of remorse, 'though the next time he got drunk he would say how sorry he was for me and what a splendid fellow I had been'. Pasternak also pronounced over Fadeyev's body, as it lay in state with a guard of honour, a superb epitaph: 'Aleksandr Aleksandrovich has rehabilitated himself.'[6]

Mention has already been made of another important Custodian – the minor poet Aleksey Surkov, First Secretary of the Writers' Union from 1953 to 1959. A literary official such as Surkov, or his successor Markov, may well be consulted – and on a level more exalted than that of mere literature – about politically sensitive publication problems by some potentate of the CPSU Central Committee. But it is the writer, not the high Party functionary, whose word is apt to be decisive on these occasions. 'The proceedings are quite informal and intimate; everyone concerned sits around in the office . . . in the Central Committee building, and it is Surkov, for example, who advises Demichev [a Secretary of the Central Committee] what to do, not vice versa, because Surkov knows more about it.'[7]

A fascinating account of the co-operation between Surkov and another exalted non-literary Party functionary, D. Polikarpov (head of the Central Committee's Cultural Department), will be found in Olga Ivinskaya's memoirs of Pasternak. Not that Surkov's relations with authority were always a model of propriety and smooth co-operation, at least on the highest level. Khrushchev is said to have once grabbed him by the collar, shaken him ferociously and abused him for failing to point out at the time of the *Doctor Zhivago* scandal that Pasternak was an internationally famous author. Surkov had thus, in Khrushchev's view, betrayed the Soviet authorities into mounting a campaign against Pasternak of greater virulence than would have been sanctioned had it been realized that the poet's fate was a matter of concern to the world at large.[8]

Another writer-functionary, of comparable eminence to Fadeyev, was Konstantin Fedin: prolific novelist, First Secretary of the Union of Writers from 1959 in succession to Surkov and Chairman of that organization from 1971. Since Fedin was not even a member of the Party and was thought to be milder than Surkov, his appointment as First Secretary was initially regarded as a liberal triumph. But Fedin's tenure of office did not bear out this prognosis. As later emerged, it had been he who initiated the hounding of Pasternak;[9] and he pursued this feud to the grave by ostentatiously failing to attend Pasternak's funeral at Peredelkino, even though the two authors had been next-door neighbours and the coffin was borne past Fedin's window.[10] It was Fedin too who originally suggested putting Sinyavsky on trial, according to Solzhenitsyn. Fedin also appears to have been the individual chiefly responsible for the rejection of Solzhenitsyn's novel *Cancer Ward* for publication in the Soviet Union: a stance that provoked letters of protest from the liberals Tvardovsky and Kaverin.[11] Solzhenitsyn's intense dislike of Fedin is therefore understandable. He speaks of the Chairman's face as that of a corrupted wolf, adding that it bore 'layers of imprints left by his compromises, betrayals and foul deeds of many years'.[12]

Another notable loyalist of recent times, again a combined novelist and literary Custodian, was Vsevolod Kochetov. Both as an author of fiction and as a Chief Editor (of *Literaturnaya gazeta* in 1955-9 and of *Oktyabr* in 1961-73) he consistently opposed all the liberalizing tendencies of post-Stalin literature. In novels ascribing a monopoly of virtues to Stalinists, and of vices to liberals, he abused literary victims of the Terror (Babel, Mandelstam, Tsvetayeva) and caricatured contemporary nonconformists (Yevtushenko). At times of political relaxation Kochetov accordingly functioned as a dissident of a type less familiar to the West than are those who advocate further relaxation.

Where he seemed to deviate from the Party line was in calling for greater restrictions and even, apparently, for a return to Stalinism. Among other author-functionaries who represent the same diehard tendency has been Nikolay Gribachov – candidate member of the CPSU Central Committee from 1961, poet and author of works idealizing Collective Farm life.

Sholokhov is an ultra-loyalist far more celebrated than Kochetov or Gribachov. Nor can we deny him the status of Custodian or functionary, for he has been a member of the CPSU Central Committee since 1961. However, it is hard to see Sholokhov as a typical bureaucrat. In a society where public utterance, even of vicious denunciations, is traditionally couched in conventionalized and liturgical speech, and where individuals tend 'to be actuated by', 'to envisage' or 'to visualize' various 'factors', 'eventualities' and the like, Sholokhov has often – especially under Khrushchev – assumed the licence to give tongue in plain, even scurrilous, Russian. Far from seeing himself as an official, despite his high Party rank, he has made a practice of venomously denouncing more orthodox Custodians, including not only Fadeyev, as mentioned above, but also Surkov and Simonov. Nor have his denunciations been confined to fellow conformists. Indeed, whom has Sholokhov not denounced? Described by Solzhenitsyn as the *palach* ('hangman, executioner, flogger') of literature, the author of *The Quiet Don* has criticized as inadequate the camp sentences imposed in 1966 on Sinyavsky and Daniel, even suggesting that these two errant writers should have been executed.[13] He has also suggested that they, and others whose works have been published in the West without official sanction, should be exterminated like the Colorado beetle.[14] He was prominent, too, in attacking Pasternak during the *Doctor Zhivago* scandal, though he once frankly admitted (in answer to a direct question put to him by myself) that he had never read the novel which he so contemptuously disparaged.

Liberals

To ultra-loyalists such as Kochetov and Gribachov various labels have been applied by their enemies: conservatives, reactionaries, Stalinists, dogmatists, diehards, orthodoxists, hawks or Hards. They have been opposed by others advocating a more permissive policy –

figures who, without necessarily being so hostile to the system as to rate as dissidents, are sometimes termed liberals, doves or Softs. The liberal camp has included some Party members, among whom Tvardovsky has been the most prominent.

A running controversy between the two sides, however labelled, was a persistent feature of the Khrushchev era, spilling over into the early years of the Brezhnev regime. It began in 1954, when the division into opposed literary camps first became evident at the Second Writers' Congress of that year. Speeches at Writers' Congresses, all-USSR, republican, metropolitan and provincial; even speeches at Party Congresses; articles in the non-literary press; original works; critical studies and reviews in the two opposed literary monthlies (the conservative *Oktyabr* and the liberal *Novy mir*) – these were some of the vehicles in which the two sides attacked each other. While doing so they preserved the usual decorous ritual of Soviet public utterance, their accusations (Sholokhov's always excepted) being veiled rather than open and couched in a code easily read by those initiated into the conventions. As we remember (see page 203), the Softs called for more 'sincerity' when they were really asking for more latitude to express individual opinions; clamouring for 'contemporaneity', the Hards were asking for yet more happy milkmaids and lathe-operators.

Far from arbitrating this dispute, the leadership appeared content during much of the time to permit the two camps to settle their differences without guidance from above – as had happened to a far greater extent in the 1920s. However, given Khrushchev's volatile character and penchant for public buffoonery, it was inevitable that sudden and unpredictable corrections of course should be sporadically ordained from on high. Now a group of errant Softs would be harangued from a Hard point of view by the leader at a dacha or in the Kremlin, now Khrushchev would personally proclaim a policy of official tolerance, as at the Third Writers' Congress of 1959. One notable move towards intolerance was the establishment, in 1958 and for the first time, of an RSFSR branch of the Union of Writers; it became, as was intended, a dogmatist stronghold and a counterweight to the liberalizing Moscow branch of the Union. A notable move in the opposite direction was the appointment (mentioned above, page 102) of a new Board of the Moscow branch in April 1962 through an election that expressed the unmanipulated will of the majority of members, bypassing normal Soviet electoral procedures whereby the result inevitably reflects the wishes of superior authority. The episode has no close parallel in post-1932 literary or non-literary history. It represented a triumph for the liberals, and incidentally involved the failure of the conservatives Gribachov and Kochetov to secure election. These Hards were rejected in favour of such Softs as the poets Yevtushenko and Voznesensky.[1] The holding of an election seemingly free, in the Western sense, has been described as 'a precedent of momentous importance'.[2] But the most momentous aspect of the precedent was that it was never, so far as we know, to be repeated. Nor, under the more decorous regime of Brezhnev, has the Hard-Soft controversy been permitted to rage, as it could within its modest limits under Khrushchev. 'Only about 1 per cent of the members of the Writers' Union can be clearly identified with one or the other group.' Such is a recent (1978) appraisal of the liberals and conservatives from which it is difficult to dissent. Nor can it be denied that 'The overwhelming majority of Soviet writers have a vested interest in the security provided by the *status quo*.'[3]

A prominent feature of the post-Stalin era has been the skilful exploitation by the authorities of certain literary figures of carefully obtruded liberal complexion. Permitted to travel widely and frequently in the non-Communist world, and to give public lectures or recitals of their work, they have freely expressed libertarian sentiments such as they could not publicize unchecked at home – and have thus created in the minds of foreign audiences the misleading impression that the USSR is in process of liberalization in excess of that confirmed by other evidence. We term these touring littérateurs 'licensed liberals': not to suggest that their liberal sentiments are necessarily simulated, but rather to indicate that they have permitted these sentiments, however sincerely held, to be used for a political purpose arguably the reverse of liberal.

The classic example is Ehrenburg, the theme of whose whole life has been described as an 'attempt simultaneously to-be-and-not-to-be a communist writer'.[4] We remember him as a pioneer of literary de-Stalinization, and as author of a novel, *The Thaw*, that gave its name to the early de-Stalinizing period. He went on to publish critical essays, on Chekhov and Stendhal, containing thinly disguised appeals for a further relaxation of cultural policy, while also promoting the rehabilitation and republication of deceased victims of the Terror. However, in order for Ehrenburg to be permitted to advertise his

reformist views at all he had to make widespread running concessions
to the official point of view, so that he can neither be summed up as
a champion of reform nor yet as an apologist for the system. He was,
perhaps, usually the former rather than the latter. For example, when
summoned to writers' conclaves called in order to pronounce anathema
on Pasternak, Ehrenburg would brazenly announce over the telephone,
and without troubling to disguise his voice, that 'Ilya Grigoryevich
[himself] has gone away and will not be back for some time'.[5]

Similar use has been made of a younger writer, the poet Yevtushenko,
who has created not a few literary scandals in his time. They include
his poem of 1962, *Stalin's Heirs*, where it is suggested that henchmen
and admirers of the late dictator are waiting to resurrect their hero
and engineer a return to the Terror. By arranging to publish his
Precocious Autobiography abroad Yevtushenko precluded its appearance in the Soviet Union and struck out as a fashionably dissident
Export Only author, at no small political risk. He has, however, also
published propaganda on behalf of the system, after first rising to
prominence by seeming to defy it, and is not regarded within the
dissident movement as a powerful force leading to reform. Rather does
he tend to be interpreted as one exploited by the regime that he flouts
with ever-decreasing fervour.

Justified or unjustified, such accusations have been frequently made.
Other, perhaps more authentic, liberals have tended to escape them.
Among them was Konstantin Paustovsky; he survived to become a
benevolent grand old man of literature, a champion of liberal causes
whose consistency of outlook has seldom been challenged. Liberal
figures from the older generation have also included Venyamin
Kaverin and – to some extent – Konstantin Simonov. The latter has
passed through many alternating conservative and liberal phases, each
seeming more integral while it lasted than the mentality of the many
ambiguous figures who have apparently combined simultaneous liberal
and conservative promptings within the same psyche.

Much ambivalence is to be detected in the dossier of another figure –
Aleksandr Tvardovsky, on whose spiritual evolution we are now
minutely informed in Solzhenitsyn's memoirs. Tvardovsky is remarkable as a leading liberal who was both an outstanding literary functionary and an original writer. Not only did he enjoy great vogue as a
poet of peasant life, but he was also renowned as Chief Editor of the
liberal monthly *Novy mir*, and sat on countless committees and boards,

including the CPSU's Central Committee, of which he was a candidate member under Khrushchev.

Showered with the usual cars, chauffeurs, domestic servants, dachas, preferential medical care, foreign travel facilities and other luxuries, Tvardovsky was as devoted as any conservative to maintaining the elaborate 'pecking order' that has naturally established itself in the Soviet literary milieu, as in all other Soviet contexts. He much prized his status as, by definition, the country's premier living poet, jealously guarding his many offices and the marks of respect that surrounded him in his main stronghold, *Novy mir*. 'During these years of the denigration of the cult of [Stalin's] personality this freedom-loving and most liberal of editorial staffs in the USSR functioned on the basis of a cult of [Tvardovsky's] personality.' Such is Solzhenitsyn's verdict. So it is in every Soviet institution, he continues, for this was a natural, organic development, not something instituted by Tvardovsky himself, who was in any case very popular with his subordinates.[6] Condescending to his employees and authors, yet correspondingly deferential to those who outranked him in the Party, Tvardovsky could not tolerate equals, and he always tended to treat his original 'discovery' Solzhenitsyn as his personal property.

So authoritarian was the world of letters, still, that even the most liberal editor in the country thought nothing of requiring one of 'his' authors to report to the office on demand, like an errant subaltern called before his Commanding Officer. Tvardovsky also made repeated demands that Solzhenitsyn, who was mildly Bohemian in his personal style, should shave off his beard, stop wearing unbuttoned open-necked shirts, and adopt a dark suit and a tie together with the whole depersonalized image and uniform of the literary Apparatus.[7] That Solzhenitsyn could, with some difficulty, successfully resist these well-meant and persistent recommendations, designed to groom him for membership of the literary establishment, shows that there is at least a limit to the degree to which the Soviet literary world has been institutionalized.

How, we are tempted to ask, would a Mayakovsky or a Yesenin have responded to such pressures to conform? Their possible reactions may best be left to the imagination of those initiated into the arcana of Russian obscene usage and creative hooliganism, as so often mobilized in the early days to *épater les bourgeois*. Not that Tvardovsky's own life style was a model of bourgeois decorum. As Solzhenitsyn has described, the Chief Editor was given to drinking bouts impressive even by the formidable standards of the Soviet literary bureaucracy, and he has been described to me by a foreign observer of these as a 'distillery in trousers'. But this hobby was, in the present context, rather a manifestation of conformism than an assertion of individuality.

One of the most bizarre chapters in Tvardovsky's career is contributed by his poem *Tyorkin in the Other World*. The hero is the private soldier whose adventures had already been chronicled in the same author's popular wartime humorous verse tale *Vasily Tyorkin* (1941–5). In the new poem, written from 1954 onwards, Tvardovsky plunges his hero (like Odysseus into Hades) into the world beyond the grave. But the work develops along markedly un-Homeric lines – as an outspoken burlesque of Stalin's Russia. Tvardovsky's nether regions have their own ever-present and elaborate security police, their own absurd red tape, even their own unsmokable tobacco. In one especially *risqué* passage there is an invocation of 'invisible columns' consisting of concentration camp spirits from 'Kolyma, Magadan, Vorkuta and Narym'.[8]

As part of the oscillations of de-Stalinization and re-Stalinization this harshly satirical work came to be recited – on the orders of and in the presence of Khrushchev himself – to a conclave of eminent writers when they were entertained at his dacha at Gagra on the Black Sea in August 1963. Among those present were some foreign authors of note, including Angus Wilson and Alain Robbe-Grillet, besides not a few outstanding representatives of the Soviet liberal and conservative literary factions. As has been well commented by a foreign specialist: 'Surely it is extraordinary for the editor of a major literary journal, alternate [candidate] member of the Party Central Committee at that, to be author of a politically unpublishable poem that had been circulating in the semiunderground world of Moscow manuscript readers for, some say, as long as six years!'[9]

Even more extraordinary was the decision by the country's chief political leader to have these subversive verses recited in his presence on a semi-public occasion and before an audience that included foreigners. Was the pantomime staged in order to mobilize Western sympathies in favour of the de-Stalinizing Russians of 1963 against the allegedly hard-line Stalinizing Chinese? Possibly. In any case the episode suddenly legitimized the hitherto illicit *Tyorkin in the Other World*, which was published in *Izvestiya* and *Novy mir* soon afterwards. The work had previously appeared in print in an émigré (Munich) journal,[10] so that the incident forms a rare – though not unique – exception to the practice whereby Export Only publication precludes Soviet publication.

The author of this 'liberal' monument still remains an enigmatic figure. Tvardovsky had once 'capitulated to faith in Stalin despite the patent ruin of the peasants and the sufferings of his own family [his father had been purged as a kulak], and had then sincerely mourned his [Stalin's] death. Just as sincerely he later recoiled from the discredited Stalin and tried to believe in a new and purified truth.'[11] Such is Solzhenitsyn's opinion. That Solzhenitsyn is unfair to Tvardovsky is the view of a well-known Soviet-domiciled literary critic and former assistant editor of *Novy mir*, Vladimir Lakshin, who has recently defended his former Chief Editor's memory in an Export Only journal.[12] On the other hand, one may also wonder, on the basis of the limited evidence available, how effectively the elusive concept of sincerity can be applied at all, whether negatively or positively, to Tvardovsky. Here was not a Stalinist who suddenly became a non-Stalinist in 1953, but something, surely, more complex: a jumble of conflicting urges whose essential nature combined a relish for the trappings of high literary office with the anarchic promptings that eventually led to his dismissal from both the Central Committee and from the editorship of *Novy mir*.

Dissidents

The dismissal of Khrushchev in October 1964 heralded the end of the controversy between liberals and conservatives as it had smouldered and flared for ten years on the pages of Soviet publications. But another phenomenon arose to take its place – that of Soviet dissidence.

Few dissidents have been out-and-out revolutionaries anxious to overthrow the Soviet system. Rather have they sought to reform it from within, and largely by an insistence on legality. The attempt is to make the administration live up to its own pretensions as enshrined in the country's successive constitutions permitting freedom of speech, of the press, of assembly and so on, to which in recent years has been added the international Helsinki Agreement (1975). But though many dissidents would insist that they are loyal Soviet citizens, they are denied access to publicity media, by contrast with the liberals of the Khrushchev era, and they have therefore been compelled to find other means of making their views felt. These have included sending open letters of protest to the authorities, often over a long list of signatures – a practice once so common that a slang-word, *podpisanty* ('signature-mongers'), was coined to describe those who indulged in it. And since what cannot be published in the press can often be successfully circulated in typescript, these documents have reached a remarkably wide public. Many of them have found their way abroad, where they have been published and broadcast in radio programmes beamed to the USSR.

This activity has embraced writers, and the relevant documents have included Export Only belles-lettres, as has already been seen. But Soviet dissident activity also goes far outside the areas of Russia and of literature to include the grievances of Ukrainians, Tatars and other national minorities in the USSR; the defence of the country's many religions against persecution; objections to Soviet intervention in Czechoslovakia in 1968; the attempt to assert civil rights in general. Much of this activity has been reflected in a clandestine monthly magazine, *Khronika tekushchikh sobytiy* ('The Chronicle of Current Events'), which has filtered through to the West, where selections from it have been published in translation. But that is a factual report of matters concerning the underground civil rights movement, and though writers' names often figure in it when their personal fates are relevant to the publication's main concern, it is not a literary journal. Similarly, though many writers have been dissidents there are also many non-literary dissidents, the most notable being the distinguished scientist Andrey Sakharov, who was awarded the Nobel Peace Prize in 1975.

As has been noted above, the authorities tend to discriminate between those dissidents whose names have become known to the world at large and those who have remained comparatively obscure. The latter can be harassed, prosecuted and isolated with impunity, while the former tend, perhaps after living through such a period of harassment, to be permitted or forced to emigrate from the USSR. First a liberal, then a dissident, and finally an émigré: such is the common evolution, as undergone by not a few individuals and most notably by that powerful personality Solzhenitsyn, who has been his country's chief literary representative in all three categories.

A similar evolution has also been performed by Brodsky, Nekrasov, Sinyavsky and other authors mentioned in an earlier section as participating in the Third Emigration. As the result of their expatriation, whether voluntary or enforced by the Soviet authorities, there is a dearth of prominent names among the surviving Soviet-domiciled literary dissidents. Lidiya Chukovskaya is perhaps the best-known at the time of writing, other names that come to mind being those of Georgy Vladimov and Vladimir Voynovich.

Outside the literary field Andrey Sakharov remains the doyen of dissidence as a whole. Another leading figure, also a distinguished scientist, is Yury Orlov, leader of the Moscow Helsinki Group – an organization formed in order to press for the implementation of the provisions of the international Helsinki Agreement as they affect the issue of human rights in the USSR. Orlov's trial in May 1978, for anti-Soviet agitation and propaganda, and for receiving money for spreading slanders abroad, culminated in a hard labour sentence of seven years and appeared to signalize a policy of increasing rigour towards the dissident movement. But these and other similar episodes, affecting both literary and non-literary figures, should not permit us to forget that recent literary policy has left official publication channels open to certain writers who, though they cannot be classified as dissident, are by no means tamely orthodox either, and who have contrived to bring out stimulating, original and independent works of fiction under a Soviet imprint during the Brezhnev era. They have included Valentin Rasputin, Yury Trifonov and (before his death in 1974) Vasily Shukshin.

12 *From Pen to Print*

Periodicals

By contrast with modern publishing practice in the West the USSR maintains the nineteenth-century tradition, to which reference has been made above, whereby imaginative works receive their first publication in a periodical, not in book form. This applies not only to poetry and short stories, but also to novels, though these are of course usually long enough to require serialization.

The staple vehicles for the first publication of belles-lettres are the literary monthlies colloquially known as Thick Journals. Thick Journals were especially important in the nineteenth century, when they were the first to carry many works by Turgenev, Dostoyevsky, Tolstoy, Chekhov and other major writers of the period. The modern Thick Journals also maintain the nineteenth-century tradition of including book reviews, literary criticism and articles on political, social or historical themes.

The Thick Journals of Tsarist times all subsided, or were repressed, soon after the Revolution. But it was a tribute to their tradition that a new monthly, modelled on its Tsarist predecessors and called *Krasnaya nov*, was set up on Party instructions in 1921 under the editorship of Aleksandr Voronsky, a Party member and a leading Marxist critic. Despite Party sponsorship the journal became the leading vehicle for writers unaffiliated to Bolshevism, the Fellow Travellers. Since these included a large proportion of the major talents of the 1920s, the standard of contributions to *Krasnaya nov* was correspondingly high. Contributors included Ehrenburg, Fedin, Gorky, Mandelstam, Mayakovsky, Pasternak, Pilnyak, Yesenin and Zoshchenko. But Voronsky's dismissal as a Trotskyite, in 1927, heralded a decline in the journal's standards. *Krasnaya nov* struggled on until 1942, but without recovering its earlier distinction.

The place of *Krasnaya nov* as the Soviet Union's leading Thick Journal was eventually taken by *Novy mir*. Also published in Moscow, it was founded in 1925, but had its heyday much later, in the post-Stalin era. It then became the chief vehicle for the liberalization of literature, publishing much material of a kind that had been denied an outlet during the previous quarter of a century. The main executor of this policy was the Chief Editor, Aleksandr Tvardovsky, who occupied the position from 1950 to 1970 with an interval of four years (1954–8) following his temporary removal, during the First Thaw, for excess of liberalism. During the four-year hiatus in Tvardovsky's editorship his place was taken by Konstantin Simonov, but this switch was not reflected by any drastic change in policy since Simonov maintained Tvardovsky's liberal line.

Among *Novy mir*'s most widely discussed taboo-breaking publications we have already mentioned Dudintsev's novel *Not by Bread Alone*, which exposes the complacency of the Soviet élite, and Solzhenitsyn's *One Day in the Life of Ivan Denisovich*, where concentration camp conditions are presented with a degree of frankness that still remains unique in Soviet-published works.

As the leading liberal organ, *Novy mir* had tended, especially during the Khrushchev era, to be involved in an ideological feud with its chief rival, *Oktyabr*, the other leading Thick Journal of the period. Published in Moscow since 1924, *Oktyabr* has traditionally advocated a hard-line policy, and accordingly became known as the leading conservative counterpart to the liberal *Novy mir*. But the differences between the two journals attracted more attention than they would otherwise have received owing to the fact that literature was, in the relatively easy-going Khrushchev era, an area – virtually the only one – in which public controversy over matters of political principle was allowed to develop. Closely associated though Solzhenitsyn was with *Novy mir* for several years, he came to believe that the differences between it and its conservative rivals had been exaggerated: 'The contrasts that the journals discerned between each other were insignificant to me.... All of them had the same basic terminology, the same shibboleths, the same incantations, and I couldn't stomach one teaspoonful of that stuff.'[1] If this could be said even of *Novy mir*'s years of militant liberalism, how much more applicable has it become since

Tvardovsky's departure in 1970 and the accompanying decline of his journal to a relatively undistinguished level.

Both *Novy mir* and *Oktyabr* are official vehicles of the Writers' Union of the USSR. But *Oktyabr* was, between 1959 and 1968 – as befitted its conservative policies – the official organ of the highly conservative RSFSR branch, while the liberal *Novy mir* remained the leading Thick Journal of the Union as a whole. Consistently with Solzhenitsyn's failure to discern any significant liberal-conservative polarity between these rival publications, startling 'revelations' of Soviet open secrets, as concealed under Stalin, have by no means been confined to *Novy mir*. *Oktyabr*'s conservatives, including Panfyorov and Stadnyuk, have also contributed an impressive share of such disclosures, but with a greater tendency to imply that the sufferings of the past have been ultimately justified by the glories of the present. We may also point to the evolution of Vladimir Maksimov – now well-known in emigration as the author of novels published in the West and outstandingly unacceptable to Moscow in their ideological complexion. But Maksimov originally made his name, while still a Soviet resident, not (as might have been expected) in the 'liberal' *Novy mir*, but in the supposedly 'diehard' *Oktyabr*, where he was for a time a member of the editorial board.

Recent (1975) circulations of these two leading journals were: 172,000 (*Novy mir*) and 209,000 (*Oktyabr*).

Mention must also be made of the Moscow monthly *Nash sovremennik* ('Our Contemporary'; circulation 205,000 in 1976), especially as this lively journal has tended to be the freest and most outspoken organ of the 1970s, and thus the nearest successor to *Novy mir* as it was before its emasculation with the ousting of Tvardovsky at the beginning of the decade. Other influential Moscow-published Thick Journals include *Moskva* ('Moscow') and *Yunost* ('Youth'), the latter being largely concerned, as its title indicates, with the problems of young people. Their recent circulation has been high – in each case over two and a half million. As this reminds us, the circulations of journals are the outcome of policy decisions, not of market pressures. Surprisingly, perhaps, a decision to raise a journal's circulation substantially may be taken independently of its editors, and may be extremely unwelcome to them owing to the practice whereby censorship restrictions tend to be imposed with a degree of severity proportionate to the size of the readership.

Another widely distributed periodical is the newspaper *Literaturnaya gazeta*, an organ of the Board of the Union of Writers of the USSR, and the main vehicle for publicizing the official politico-literary line. Its recent circulation (1973) has been over a million and a half, and its editorial policy is tantalizingly ambivalent. On literary matters and on foreign affairs a strong conservative line is followed, whereas on domestic scandals – such as traffic congestion, the defects of the public transport system and environmental pollution – the paper can be outspokenly reformist.

These are only a few, the most important, among the many thousands of journals and newspapers – all-Union, republican and local – published in the USSR, the vast majority of which we may safely ignore. Brief reference must also be made to the evolution of the literary periodicals published by Russian émigrés, not only to cater for émigré writing and criticism, but also for material emanating from, but unpublishable in, the Soviet Union. Of these *Volya Rossii* ('Russia's Freedom'; Prague and Paris, 1922–32) and *Sovremennyye zapiski* ('Modern Jottings'; Paris, 1920–40) have long passed away. But the tradition has continued with the quarterlies *Novy zhurnal* ('New Journal', New York from 1942), and *Grani* ('Facets', Frankfurt-am-Main, from 1946).

A more recently founded journal – *Kontinent* ('Continent'; Berlin, from 1974) – is an organ of the Third Emigration. It has been edited by Vladimir Maksimov, among other prominent recent émigrés. With it may be mentioned the following additional recently founded émigré journals, which are listed together with the names of their more prominent editors: *Ekho* ('The Echo', Paris, Vladimir Maramzin); *Kovcheg* ('The Ark', Paris, N. Bokov); *Sintaksis* ('Syntax', Fontenay aux Roses, Andrey Sinyavsky); *Tretya volna* ('The Third Wave', France, Aleksandr Glezer); *Vremya i my* ('The Time and Ourselves', Tel Aviv, Viktor Perelman). A point of view tending to approximate to that of the Soviet-published 'liberals' of the Khrushchev era is maintained by what is, even in this context, a publishing curiosity: the journal *Dvadtsaty vek* ('The Twentieth Century'). Though this has been brought out in London since 1975, it has been edited by a Moscow resident – Roy Medvedev, whose attitude is more favourable to the Soviet dispensation than that of the dissident movement as a whole.

Books

Book publishing is extensively developed in the USSR, where private publishers were jettisoned along with NEP in 1928, leaving the field to governmentally controlled agencies. They have included the State Publishing House (Gosizdat) and – of closer relevance to our subject – the State Literature Publishing House (Goslitizdat). Other houses belong to nominally independent organizations in practice subordinated to the Party and State; among them is Sovetsky pisatel ('Soviet Writer'), which comes under the Union of Writers.

On the last page of a Soviet-published book may usually be found a schedule of official details, including date of delivery to the printers, size of page, price and so on. An otherwise mysterious letter-figure combination of about six digits is also commonly found, and almost certainly constitutes a serial number assigned by the censorship. But the most vital of these statistics is the entry *tirage* ('print run'), which indicates the number of copies authorized. As with periodicals, the size of book printings is determined on the basis of policy decisions, not of market pressures. That the *tirage* has been set artificially high in the case of certain works is a common complaint. It has been frequently provoked by the over-issue of especially sanctified political texts which the machinery of control is unable to keep within bounds. What Soviet official, for example, will argue that Brezhnev's speeches should be printed in a smaller quantity than another official has proposed? Consequently the writings or speeches of Marx, Lenin, Stalin, Khrushchev and Brezhnev have often lain around for years in warehouses and bookshops, only to end up being pulped in quantity, for shortage of paper is an endemic disease of the Soviet publishing world.

Conversely, sensitive literary material, such as the work of poets re-emerging from a phase of official disapproval, may be deliberately issued in grossly inadequate printings. Even then these works turn out to be very largely marketed abroad, in order to bring in foreign currency and also – presumably – to restrict their availability to the Soviet reader. For example, a recently issued selection of Pasternak's verse (1976), easily obtainable at any large Western bookshop, has been sought in vain by many would-be purchasers in Moscow and Leningrad. Such books can make a welcome gift if brought in by a foreign visitor, who might also be astonished – should he be rash enough to risk the charge of speculation – by the high prices that they can command on the black market.

Though some excellent complete critical editions of nineteenth-century Russian authors have been published in the USSR, writers belonging in part or in whole to the Soviet period have not, as a matter of policy, been published in their totality. This is true, for example, of even such a classic of Socialist Realism as Gorky: his eighteen-volume *Collected Works* (1960–2) is comprehensive, but far from complete. In a few well chosen cases foreign publishers and scholars have endeavoured to make good this deficiency, by bringing out all the obtainable writings of certain politically sensitive authors of outstanding literary merit. Akhmatova, Gumilyov, Khlebnikov and Mandelstam have all been published in this way in multi-volume editions in the United States or Germany. These excellent foreign editions emphasize the poor quality of Soviet book production: despite considerable improvement since Stalin's day, paper and bindings remain inferior and sometimes have a revolting smell.

Briefly leaving the topic of belles-lettres, we may also mention, as a freak of international publishing history, the strange fate of Stalin's Moscow-published *Works* in Russian. They reached the thirteenth volume of an exceptionally well-produced edition in 1951, when publication was simply terminated – presumably owing to the confusions created by the author's death in 1953 – only to be completed in three further volumes (14–16) under the editorship of a foreign scholar, Robert H. McNeal, and in far-away Stanford, California (1967).

So much for some aspects of book publishing policy and procedures. But what of Soviet readers' reactions to the product? Here we enter an area difficult to chart since neither the availability of a given book nor its sales figures automatically reflect consumer choice, as they do in capitalist countries. But though publishing is certainly dictated by ideological expediency rather than by market forces, it by no means follows that market forces are left out of account. It is likely, for instance, that the decline of the long, 'block-buster' novel, from the mid-1950s onwards, owes something to a tendency on the part of readers to leave the stodgier specimens of the genre mouldering on bookshop shelves, especially as lighter and more digestible fare became increasingly available. But we do not know much of Soviet readers' inclinations. Who, for example, has ever, even in the most desperate days, read Fedin for pleasure? One would dearly love to meet such a person.

A little light is shed on the problem of readers' tastes by the results of a survey carried out in 1968 for the leading literary newspaper *Literaturnaya gazeta* ('The Literary Gazette').[1] When asked to name those writers, active in 1920–50, who had best stood the test of time, readers nominated Sholokhov and Aleksey Tolstoy (both authors of notable 'block-busters') for first and second place; they were followed, in descending order of preference, by Ilf and Petrov, Ostrovsky, Fadeyev, Paustovsky, Babel, Mayakovsky and Bulgakov. As for Gorky – a more intensively promoted Soviet institution than any other modern author – he was accorded only the tenth place: a tribute, possibly, to the eternal resilience of the human spirit in the face of relentless brow-beating. As for recent authors whom the readers of *Literaturnaya gazeta* would have most liked to see published in that organ, the descending order of merit was from Paustovsky in the first place, down through Solzhenitsyn (not yet, in 1968, an unperson), Simonov, Aksyonov, Sholokhov, Kazakov, Soloukhin and Nagibin. The lower rating accorded in this sequence to Sholokhov (who we remember at the head of the first-quoted list) is obviously due to his admirers' disappointment at his failure to bring out any major work since he completed *The Quiet Don* in 1940.

Export Only Publications

We now turn to modern Russian writing which can neither be considered as émigré literature, since it is written on native soil, nor yet as Soviet, since it has either been rejected for publication by Soviet publishing houses or, being clearly unacceptable on ideological grounds, has never even been submitted to them.

Such works may neither be printed in the Soviet Union, nor yet mechanically duplicated, since the private possession of printing presses and duplicating machines is forbidden. They may, however, be typed or photographed without any infringement of the law, and this practice has become so common that a special word, *samizdat*, has been in use since 1966 to describe it. Formed on the analogy of Gosizdat ('State Publishing House') and similar abbreviations, *samizdat* means in effect 'do-it-yourself' publishing. The normal medium for *samizdat* documents is typescript, the use of onion-skin paper making it possible to produce up to ten copies at a single typing. They are then discreetly passed round to interested readers, after which copies of copies, and then further copies, tend to be taken in the manner of a chain letter. Such is the lust for officially inadmissible literature that long novels have been reproduced by this process, with resultant scribes' errors as copy succeeds copy; in extreme cases the establishment of a canonical text by a living author may seem to demand the techniques of textual scholarship applied to ancient literatures written before the age of printing. That Russia has receded or progressed to a pre-Gutenberg era is a frequent comment of those who contemplate these matters.

The natural destination of such documents is the Western non-Communist world, which has been deluged with them over the last dozen years. One authority speaks of 2,000 items arriving in the West during the decade ending in 1975,[1] and extensive collections have been built up in Washington, Oxford, London and Munich. By no means all such items come under the heading of belles-lettres, for they also include protest letters, transcripts of trials and other non-literary material. But literary works, some of great importance, have been included among them, and these have naturally found publishers in the West – both in the original Russian and in translation into English, French, German, Italian and other languages. Such Export Only works are known by the colloquial term *tamizdat* ('over there publications') in the Soviet Union. They are not usually brought out by agreement between the author and his publisher under the protection of Soviet or of international copyright regulations, but come into print by more devious means that often involve little or no negotiation with the author. Not only has there normally been no contract, there has often not even been any contact; or, if there has, it has tended to be limited by communication difficulties. Yet Pasternak was able to transmit his wishes to some of his foreign publishers, and the pre-exile Solzhenitsyn even appointed a Swiss lawyer to look after his interests. As already noted, reputable foreign publishers have regularly set aside royalties on behalf of Soviet-based authors with whom little or no negotiation has been possible, and these sums have been duly paid over when, as has happened not a few times, the author in question has emigrated. We have also noted that the signing, in 1973, of the International Copyright Convention by the USSR does not yet appear to have effected any radical change in the unofficial relationships between foreign publishers and Export Only Soviet authors.

Once issued by a foreign publisher, Export Only works automatically become ineligible for publication in the Soviet Union. There has been at least one instance of a Soviet agency deliberately sending a work abroad, without the author's knowledge and consent and with the express intention of rendering publication in the Soviet Union impossible. Such, at any rate, is Solzhenitsyn's view of the fate of his *Cancer Ward*; while under consideration for publication in the Moscow-based *Novy mir* it was spirited abroad by the KGB so that it might be published by an émigré house and would thus forfeit all prospect of Soviet publication.[2]

Neither *samizdat* nor Export Only activities in themselves constitute infringements of the law, for there is nothing contrary to the RSFSR Criminal Code in writing, copying or reading a work of literature, or in sending it abroad. It is not the method of distributing these documents, but their contents that may entail the risk of prosecution under Article 70. It penalizes 'anti-Soviet agitation and propaganda', and also 'anti-Soviet organization', when these activities are conducted with the aim of weakening or overthrowing the Soviet system as a whole. There is also the prospect of charges being brought under Article 190–1, which covers the lesser offence of propagating 'deliberate fabrications discrediting the Soviet political and social system'. 'Anti-Soviet', 'agitation', 'fabrications' – these are all concepts that lend themselves to flexible interpretation, and they can all too easily be invoked when the authorities have decided to proceed against (some would say 'to frame') an obstreperous individual. Nor must it be forgotten that the publication of literary work outside the USSR can easily render authors or their agents liable to prosecution for evading currency laws and commercial regulations – the fate, after Pasternak's death, of his surviving associate Olga Ivinskaya, who served a sentence to the camps based on charges brought under these headings in the context of the poet's foreign literary earnings.

Authors of *samizdat* and Export Only material have, accordingly, often been subjected to harassment, interrogation, arrest, trial, sentence to concentration camps or to exile, and consignment to mandatory treatment in psychiatric clinics – all, so far as Soviet law is concerned, on the formal basis of what they have written, or of what they are alleged to have earned from it, and not of the channel of dissemination.

Though material can indeed be sent abroad without infringement of the law, we may yet wonder that it has in practice proved possible to do so in such impressive quantity. The Soviet authorities do not make a fetish of respecting their own laws when the interests of the State seem imperilled – as they may appear to be by much Export Only literature, for this so often sheds light on conditions carefully concealed in Soviet publications. Moreover, given the enormous establishment, vast experience and extensive powers of the security police, one might have expected that the flow could and would have been halted or at least restricted. This may, however, have been frustrated by the sheer difficulty of intercepting so diverse and massive an outpouring of material. Alternatively, the KGB may have been hampered by its very size and multifarious ramifications, for it is no less vulnerable than any other Soviet institution to bureaucratic elephantiasis. It is also possible that the authorities have made a policy decision to tolerate the traffic in Export Only literature. The export of texts cannot fundamentally harm Moscow's position, while it has the positive advantage of creating, among the West's more credulous citizens, the illusion that Soviet society is freer than is in fact the case, and therefore does not constitute a menace that Western societies might need to resist.

Be this as it may, the export from Russia of material unpublishable at home has a tradition long antedating the Revolution; for example, several of Pushkin's anti-Tsarist and blasphemous poems appeared in London long before they could be published in Russia.[3] Moreover, as we have seen above, it was politically respectable for Soviet-domiciled authors of the 1920s to publish their work abroad. Many did so, especially in Berlin. However, with the crackdown of 1929, when Pilnyak was pilloried – and for availing himself of this facility – while Zamyatin was even attacked after his work had in effect been pirated abroad, this practice abruptly ceased. Nor was the export of literature possible during the Stalin era. That difficult period did witness some internal circulation of *samizdat* works in the form of hand-copied or typed material, but the risks were sufficient to prevent the practice from developing on any great scale.

The first major work to secure post-Stalin Export Only publication was, we remember, Pasternak's novel *Doctor Zhivago*. After it had been unsuccessfully submitted to *Novy mir* the author handed over a copy of the manuscript on the spur of the moment to a visiting Italian publisher's representative with the remark, 'You have invited me to take part in my own execution.'[4] The novel first appeared in Russian, under the imprint of an Italian publisher (Milan, 1957), after which it was published in translation into all the world's major languages. Brought out openly abroad, under the author's true name and to his immense delight, the novel had many repercussions, pleasant and unpleasant, for him. It prompted the award of the Nobel Prize for Literature, which Pasternak felt impelled to refuse owing to the campaign mounted against him at home. This included his expulsion from the Union of Writers, further persecution of his associates and prolonged nerve warfare against himself; in a famous lyric, *The Nobel Prize* (1959), he compares himself to 'a hunted beast at bay' in a dark wood.[5] A curious episode connected with *Doctor Zhivago* occurred when the veteran soldier-politician K. Voroshilov brought back a copy of the novel as translated into an Indian language, Oriya, and arranged for it to be presented to the author.[6] For connoisseurs of Soviet Russian *mœurs* this sympathetic gesture to the politically disgraced Pasternak from the titular Head of State, himself already facing political disgrace, has a resonance all of its own.

The next two notable examples of such smuggled or Export Only literature remained mysterious for several years. In the early 1960s some *Fantastic Stories*, and an essay ('What is Socialist Realism?') appeared abroad under the signature 'Abram Tertz', while certain short satirical stories by a 'Nikolai Arzhak' also received foreign publication. That these were the pseudonyms of USSR-domiciled writers seemed probable. But their identity remained undiscovered until 1965, when the KGB identified 'Tertz' as the literary critic Andrey Sinyavsky, and 'Arzhak' as the fiction-writer Yuly Daniel; it was in the following year that they were put on trial and received concentration camp sentences for libelling the Soviet Union in their Export Only writings.

Another foreign publishing scoop occurred in 1963, when Akhmatova's cycle of poems *Requiem* was published in Munich, but without the author's knowledge or consent.[7] However, prose fiction has remained the most important export item, and further samples of this were to include Vasily Grossman's combined novel and reminiscences *For Ever Flowing* and Vladimir Maksimov's *Seven Days of Creation*; both works paint a sombre picture of Soviet conditions. But the best-known of all Export Only authors is Solzhenitsyn, whose two long novels *Cancer Ward* and *The First Circle* both appeared abroad in 1968 after unsuccessful attempts to secure Soviet publication; they were followed in 1971 by another long novel, *August 1914.*

Of these authors Grossman died in 1964 and Akhmatova in 1966, while Solzhenitsyn, Maksimov and Sinyavsky all left the Soviet Union in the mid-1970s and continued their literary activity abroad, thus graduating from the status of Export Only to that of émigré authors. Daniel was released from prison camp in 1970; forbidden since then to reside in Moscow or to publish under his own name, he has yet contrived to supply a modest amount of further material for the Export Only market.

Textual Perversions

Conditions described on previous pages have ensured that the textual history of modern Russian belles-lettres, whether of the Soviet-published, emigration-originating or Export Only variety, presents certain peculiar features. Frequent rewritings and re-editings; the long concealment of manuscripts containing non-approved material; its clandestine circulation; its foreign publication unauthorized by the Soviet authorities and not uncommonly unauthorized by the author too; police raids resulting in the confiscation of material; dependence on memory or on skill in eluding detection; the loss or inaccessibility of early editions – all these factors have helped to render textual problems a nightmare of complexity. All too often has the transmission of texts depended on lucky accident, or on the author's own courage and determination, as on that of dedicated friends, in preserving his output.

These cruces may at times remind us of one of the most fascinating chapters in cultural history – the transmission of classical Greek and Latin literature from ancient times through the Dark Ages, on into the Renaissance and the world of textual scholarship. Not uncommonly do Soviet-based authors present the problem of alternative readings – the outcome of scribes' error and divergences in manuscript tradition. But the Russian material is of course incomparably bulkier than the classical.

During the Stalin period gagged USSR-based writers were commonly pictured as writing politically unacceptable material that might one day become eligible for publication, but was destined until further notice for the desk drawer. And yet, since the penalty for this activity could literally be death, it is unlikely that many of the authors concerned adopted that particular mode of stowage. Far from being consigned to desk drawers, where the most casual search might uncover them, manuscripts were buried in gardens, 'sewed into pillows, hidden in saucepans and boots',[1] or consigned to the safekeeping of friends.

Solzhenitsyn has described the immense labour that he undertook after embracing the vocation of author as a concentration camp inmate. Unable to write in custody through lack of materials and extreme danger of detection, he composed and retained in his head, by dint of constant self-discipline, a collection of verses approximating in length to Homer's *Iliad*;[2] he had become the twentieth-century equivalent of an ancient Greek rhapsode, except of course that he dared not stage any public recitals. Freed from captivity, he at last dared to commit his work to paper, but found a continuing need to exercise acute vigilance even in the post-Stalin period, though the penalties for discovery were no longer so drastic. He consequently adopted a hermit-like way of life, neither paying visits nor receiving guests, and assuming the role of model Soviet citizen – all in order to elude the notice of the security authorities. As for concealment, the sheer bulk of his writings made that problem especially formidable. In order to reduce the need for detection he wrote his manuscripts in minuscule hand, or typed them out without intervals and without margins, on both sides of the thinnest paper that he could obtain. The result was a huge archive compressed into a remarkably small space and thus more easily hidden.[3]

Never, at this period of his life, did the future Nobel Prize winner go to bed at night without checking the stowage of his texts and mentally rehearsing what his posture must be in the event of a raid by the security police in the small hours. He also contrived to photograph his writings and eventually to spirit them abroad, thus safeguarding a voluminous corpus which, but for his care and no little luck, might easily have perished. Many were the crises and disasters that occurred on the way. On 11 September 1965 took place what he describes as 'the greatest calamity in my forty-seven years of life': the discovery and confiscation by the KGB of a large archive of work hidden on the premises of a friend.[4] On a later occasion a woman friend in Leningrad, to whose safekeeping he had entrusted *The Gulag Archipelago*, was tricked or bullied into betraying its hiding place to the KGB and was so distressed by this episode that she hanged herself.[5]

Many others before Solzhenitsyn had resorted to similar devices in order to preserve their work. Shortly before his arrest in 1937 Pilnyak buried his last novel, a few pages at a time, in the garden of his dacha at Peredelkino.[6] Much of Akhmatova's poetry, including the celebrated *Requiem*, remained in her own head and in that of her friends for years and even decades before the Twentieth Congress of 1956 made it possible to engage in collectively recovering the material from memory now that it could at last be safely written down.[7]

Other textual histories have their foreign involvements – not least Zamyatin's *We*, that inverted Utopia critical of Communism and officially regarded as anti-Soviet. It was written in 1920, but appeared in English translation in 1924, and then in Czech and French. In 1927 it was issued in an abbreviated Russian version in the émigré journal *Volya Rossii*, published in Prague. This text was purportedly a translation back into Russian from the published Czech translation, but *Volya Rossii*'s editor later admitted to having had the proper Russian text in his possession all along and to having published it in a deliberately disguised form in order to avoid exposing the author, still Soviet-domiciled, to reprisals.[8] Not until 1952, some years after Zamyatin's death, was the full and authentic Russian version of his novel at last brought out, in New York.

The publication of Marina Tsvetayeva has also had its foreign complications owing to her long period of emigration, beginning in 1922. Before returning to Russia in 1939 she deposited the manuscripts of a long poem, *Perekop*, and a cycle of short poems, *Swan Encampment*, in the library of Basle University. Since both works contain eulogies of the White Russian armies in the Civil War she was wise to leave them behind. She did so with instructions, implemented in Munich (1957) and New York (1967), that the works should eventually be published, and in the old (pre-1917) Russian orthography.[9] Meanwhile Tsvetayeva's work had begun to reappear in Russia, a few poems in 1956, a small selection in 1961 and a substantial volume in 1965. Here was the revival of a long unpublished author who could not be formally rehabilitated since she had never been formally repressed. The 1965 edition is particularly useful, containing as it does fifty-five poems never previously published, even in emigration, together with an introduction considerably fuller and less slanted than that to the 1961 edition. No less striking, however, are the many omissions clearly ordained on ideological grounds. They include religious and pessimistic poems; political poetry of the Civil War period and the 1920s; a cycle of poems on Mayakovsky's death. From the long satirical poem *The Rat-Catcher*, which is similar in subject-matter to Robert Browning's *Pied Piper*, parallels between the Communist advent to power and a rat plague have understandably been expunged.[10] Meanwhile small foreign-based publishing houses have sought to preserve Tsvetayeva's heritage in fuller compass by continuing to bring out material omitted from the Soviet selection. Unfortunately, however, no complete or comprehensive edition of this important poet has yet been undertaken by any foreign-based Russian language press.

Tsvetayeva has, however, received notable posthumous commemoration of a different kind. After being evacuated from Moscow in the early months of the Second World War, she found herself isolated and desperate. By now her husband had been executed and her daughter was in a forced labour camp, while she herself was semi-ostracized as a recently returned emigrant and source of political contamination. It was in such a context and mood that the poet hanged herself on 31 August 1941, and was buried locally in an unmarked common grave, with strangers and by strangers. Nearly twenty years later her surviving sister Anastasiya tried to identify the poet's resting place, but was unable to do so. She accordingly chose an approximate spot, and erected a wooden cross with an inscription: 'Marina Ivanovna Tsvetayeva. Born 26 September, Old Style ... ; died 31 August 1941, New Style.'[11]

New Style! Seldom has any epitaph achieved so chilling a resonance.

Other officially disapproved poets have been published more comprehensively abroad than has Tsvetayeva: particularly Akhmatova, Gumilyov and Mandelstam. But despite the efforts of the devoted scholars responsible for these editions (G. P. Struve and B. A. Filipoff) the recovery of hitherto unsuspected variant texts is still liable to render the work obsolete in some of its details. The two-volume edition of Mandelstam, as published in Washington DC in 1964–6, had to be superseded a few years later by the considerably expanded and revised three-volume edition of 1967–71 from the same editors. Some readings of this were superseded in turn by the USSR-published selected *Poems* of Mandelstam (Leningrad, 1973). Though this is far less comprehensive than the three-volume edition, omitting much sensitive matter (as had the corresponding Tsvetayeva volume), it does contain new material, presenting variants to certain individual poems superior to those of the American edition. These improvements derive from the discovery of hitherto unknown copies and from the collaboration of Mandelstam's widow and literary executor Nadezhda Yakovlevna.

Even so Mandelstam's text remains a matter for dispute in many places. A more recent elucidator of his later work, Jennifer Baines, has found it necessary to collate and compare all the sources, together with the attested variants and with the continuing help of the poet's widow, in order to establish something approaching a canonical text.[12] But this in turn may eventually be rendered obsolete in some of its details by new variants discovered in the USSR like long-buried papyrus fragments of Euripides in the sands of Oxyrhynchus. And so textual recovery still remains to be undertaken for Mandelstam and other poets – work analogous to, but less complex in the last resort than for example, that of Fraenkel, Page and so many other scholars on Aeschylus' *Agamemnon*. That the analogy with classical textual criticism also occurred to Mandelstam and his wife is shown by the whimsical name that they gave to certain notebooks containing poems written in exile at Voronezh: the Vatican Codex, or 'V'.[13]

Of the further complications confronting the modern textual critic the history if Pilnyak's *Mahogany* is indicative. After this Berlin-published novel had been made the pretext for the victimization of the author, in 1929, he made the required recantation and further demonstrated his contrition by transferring much material from the anathematized *Mahogany* to a purportedly new novel, *The Volga Flows to the Caspian Sea* (1930). This incorporated the building of a huge dam, being designed to idealize the industrialization programme along the lines of officially approved Five Year Plan literature, but it is generally recognized as a far feebler work than the parent *Mahogany*.[14] However, when an author himself reworks his own writings the later version must, according to any normal convention for the establishment of authenticity, be regarded as superseding the earlier, even though he may demonstrably have undertaken the revision under duress and even though it may have resulted in a palpably inferior product. We therefore cannot reprove the editors of Pilnyak's posthumous (1976) *Selected Works* for omitting *Mahogany*. Nor can we criticize recent editors of Leonov's works for publishing his novel *The Thief* in the author's revised version of 1956–9, even though the revision may seem to have emasculated the original novel.[15]

Problems of an entirely different kind are posed by Sholokhov's

The Quiet Don, which has been denounced almost since its first appearance as substantially plagiarized from the work of a prolific, otherwise largely forgotten, pre-revolutionary Cossack author, Fyodor Kryukov, who died during the Civil War. The accusation has been revived by a pseudonymous Export Only critic, 'D', under the active sponsorship of Solzhenitsyn in 1974, and the case for plagiarism has also been put in some detail by the leading Moscow-based dissident Roy Medvedev in an Export Only work (1977). We do not seek to adjudicate this delicate matter here, but merely note the above facts. And, as we also note, it is consistent with the textual difficulties of the literature in general that the most popular, and perhaps the best, novel of the period should have been so powerfully denounced as being something very different from what it seems. Justifiably impugned or not, the *sub judice* status of *The Quiet Don* contributes a little extra spice to the general flavour of mystery surrounding this work. As we may be reminded, the most important non-literary Soviet document of the post-Stalin era – Khrushchev's oration denouncing the defunct dictator at the Twentieth Party Congress in February 1956 – has never been officially published or acknowledged in its country of origin. It still retains, outside the Soviet orbit the informal title by which it has already been known for more than two decades: the Secret Speech.

In view of the complications indicated above we cannot marvel at the failure of the Soviet literary authorities to publish the complete works of authors writing after 1917. These have never received treatment comparable to that accorded to major nineteenth-century authors: Pushkin, Turgenev, Dostoyevsky, Tolstoy, Saltykov-Shchedrin, Chekhov and others. Complete critical editions of their works, including rejected variants and full commentaries are one of the chief achievements of Russian literary scholarship in the Soviet period. For the failure to provide similar complete editions of more modern authors several causes are responsible. To cover all the variants involved in successive rewritings, often followed by further revisions of those same changes almost *ad infinitum*, would be to offer too full and frontal an exposure of the successive political pressures on literature. Moreover, an apparatus comprehending all the versions of *The Quiet Don* (to quote an extreme example) would assume dimensions out of all proportion to any conceivable value in the exercise.

There is also the consideration that authors canonized by the Soviet publicity system have frequently uttered sentiments unsuitable for dissemination. Thus Gorky's vicious denunciation of the muzhik, in his pamphlet *On the Russian Peasantry*, is omitted from the eighteen-volume collection of his works (1960–2). Much of the erratic Maya-kovsky's *œuvre* remains unpublished: for example, though we have his radiantly enthusiastic long poem *Good!* (*Khorosho!*, 1927), a counter-blast entitled *Bad!* (*Plokho*) allegedly moulders unpublished in the archives together with the bulk of the poet's correspondence.[16] And while Blok's arguably pro-Bolshevik poem *The Twelve* is easily available, and has an especially honoured place in USSR-published histories of literature, the despairing correspondence of the poet's later years has been suppressed. In an article on Blok submitted to the Moscow-published *Kratkaya literaturnaya entsiklopediya* ('Short Literary Encyclopedia') the critic Arkady Belinkov quoted from a letter written by the poet to Korney Chukovsky shortly before his death. Here Blok remarks that he had never felt so ill in his life, and indelicately adds that 'vile, snorting Mother Russia' had swallowed him alive, 'like a sow gobbling its piglet'. But the quotation was not permitted to appear, for it was struck out 'with a sweeping gesture' in Belinkov's presence by the enraged literary functionary Surkov. And yet the offending outburst had already been published under a Soviet imprint, in the eight-volume edition of Blok's *Collected Works* (1960–3).[17]

Despite such censoring of what had already passed the censorship; despite all other, far more formidable, barriers to the publication of creative writing and of information on it; and despite the many unfavourable influences – whether imposed by freeze-ups, by thaws or by over-protective hot-house conditions – modern Russian literature represents by no means the least impressive subtle, complex and moving achievement of the human spirit. It has had its triumphs as well as its disasters, and on the preceding pages I have tried to give a fair indication of both.

Reference Notes

Reference Notes

References are by authors' or editors' names, or by book titles, as listed in alphabetical order in the Bibliography. There are also references to encyclopedias and periodicals not included in the Bibliography.

Introduction

1 M. Friedberg, in Hayward (1964), 165.
2 G. Struve, in Hayward (1963), 2.

1 General Perspectives

Revolution (pages 3–8)
1 *Malaya sovetskaya entsiklopediya* (Moscow, 1958–60), 9:894.
2 Ibid., 2:203.
3 V. Shklovsky, cited in Gifford, 49.
4 Pasternak, *Doktor Zhivago*, 148.
5 Mayakovsky, 10:279–80; Brown, E. (1973), 190.
6 Wolfe, 66–74.
7 Mandelstam, N. (1970), 133.

Ordeals (pages 8–11)
1 *Everyman's Encyclopaedia*, 5th edn (London, 1967), 12:552.
2 Thomson, 51.
3 Luckett, 385; Thomson, 125.
4 Solzhenitsyn (1975), 32, 390–1.
5 Churchill, 8:78.
6 Labedz (1974), 113–14.

The Political Dimension (pages 11–17)
1 Brown, E. (1963), 17.
2 G. Gibian, in Hayward (1963), 143.
3 Karlinsky, 80–1.
4 M. Hayward, cited in Dewhirst, 84.
5 Kasack, 338.
6 Zamyatin (1955), 189.
7 Pasternak (1961), 3:222.
8 Mandelstam, N. (1972), 580.
9 M. Hayward, in Auty, 2:203.
10 G. Markov, in *Literaturnaya gazeta* (Moscow), 23 June 1976.
11 Hayward (1963), 227.
12 Hosking (1978), 10.

The Soviet Panorama (pages 18–31)
1 Smith, 409.
2 Mandelstam, N. (1970), 327.
3 *Pravda* (Moscow), 10 Aug. 1973; J. Newth, in Brown, A., 77.
4 Smith, 77, 258, 271.
5 Ibid., 288.
6 Ibid., 45.

2 History and Literature

Before Stalinism (pages 32–7)
1 Akhmatova, 2:172.
2 Mandelstam, N. (1972), 579.
3 Zamyatin (1970), 150.
4 Solzhenitsyn, *Arkhipelag GULag*, I:37 ff.

Stalin's Dictatorship (pages 37–46)
1 Hosking (1978), 5.
2 Mandelstam, N. (1972), 73.
3 Pasternak, *Doktor Zhivago*, 519.
4 Swayze, 30.

After Stalin (pages 46–51)
1 Pasternak (1961), 3:101.

2 B. Pasternak, cited in Ivinskaya, 152-3.
3 M. Hayward, in Labedz (1967), 36.

3 Russian Authors and the World

East-West Contact (pages 52-9)
1 B. Pilnyak, cited in Reck, 189.
2 Mayakovsky, 6:211-14; Mandelstam, O. (1967-71), 1:24.
3 Pasternak (1961), 2:46-7.
4 Ivinskaya, 171.
5 Akhmatova, 1:258-9, 283-5.
6 M. Friedberg, in Hayward (1963), 205-6.
7 Friedberg, 27 ff.
8 Smith, 608.
9 V. Voynovich, '*VAAP ili VAPAP*', *Posev* (Frankfurt/Main), Nov. 1973, 9-10.

Emigration (pages 59-65)
1 Struve (1956), 15-18.
2 Brown, C., 16.
3 A. Akhmatova, cited in Haight, 146.
4 Struve (1956), 19.
5 Markov, lxvi.
6 Kasack, 45.
7 Akhmatova, 1:185.
8 Haight, 142.
9 Mandelstam, N. (1972), 207.
10 A. Solzhenitsyn, cited in Smith, 516
11 B. Pilnyak, cited in Reck, 212.
12 Zamyatin (1955), 277 ff.

4 Writers and Their Work

Poetry (pages 66-73)
1 Markov, lii.
2 Karlinsky, 5.
3 Mandelstam, N. (1970), 162.
4 Brown, E. (1973), 370.

5 V. Markov, cited in Mandelstam, O. (1967–71), 1:1.
6 Brown, C., 22.
7 Mandelstam, O., op. cit., 1:202, 511.
8 Ivinskaya, 158.
9 Markov, lxxviii.
10 Mandelstam, N. (1970), 167.
11 Karlinsky, 50.
12 Brown, C., 130; M. Hayward, in Gladkov, A., 20 ff.
13 Ivinskaya, 7.
14 Brown, E. (1973), 12 ff.

Prose Fiction (pages 73–84)
1 Brown, D., 145.
2 Tolstoy, 8:675.
3 Stewart, 203–4.
4 Solzhenitsyn (1975), 31.
5 Ibid.; Kasack, 305.
6 Ivinskaya, 6–7.
7 Smith, 21.
8 Hosking (1978), 34.

Memoirs (pages 84–7)
1 Brown, C., 17.
2 Haight, 177; Brown, C., 14.
3 Solzhenitsyn (1975), 18.

Drama (pages 87–90)
1 M. Glenny, in Auty, 2:273.
2 Smith, 470.
3 Michael Glenny, 'Mikhail Bulgakov', *Communist Affairs* (Los Angeles), 1968, 6:2, 18.

Criticism (pages 90–3)
1 Thomson, 101.
2 M. Friedberg, in Hayward (1963), 207.

5 Peoples and Regions

The RSFSR (pages 97–107)
1 Zamyatin (1970), 143–51.

2 Ibid., 155.

3 Hayward (1963), 225–6.

4 *Sovetskaya istoricheskaya entsiklopediya* (Moscow, 1961–76), 6:820.

5 Medvedev, R., 57.

6 Ibid., 204.

7 See Conquest, *Kolyma, passim.*

The Ukraine (pages 107–10)

1 Struve (1972), 325.

2 Babel (1970), 26 ff.

Jews (pages 110–17)

1 M. Friedberg, in Kochan, 188.

2 S. Ettinger, in Kochan, 15.

3 M. Hayward, in Ivinskaya, xiii.

4 Kochan, 39.

5 L. Schapiro, in Kochan, 10.

6 Conquest, *Power and Policy in the U.S.S.R.,* 438–9.

7 Brown, A., 317.

8 Ibid., 229.

9 Hingley, *A New Life of Anton Chekhov,* xv–xvi.

10 Mayakovsky, 9:116–21.

11 M. Tsvetayeva, cited in Ivinskaya, 148.

12 Babel (1965), 19.

13 B. Choseed, in Simmons, 113.

14 Pasternak, *Doktor Zhivago,* 125–6, 310.

15 Mandelstam, O. (1967–71), 2:55.

16 Ibid., 2:187.

17 Ehrenburg, 20.

Other Peoples (pages 117–19)

1 Pasternak (1961), 1:349.

6 The Power Structure

The Communist Party (pages 120–5)

1 Cited in Brown, A., 301

2 Ermolaev, 119.
3 Dewhirst, 14.

The Ideology (pages 126–8)
1 Carew Hunt, 61.

Government and Administration (pages 128–33)
1 Churchward (1968), 106.
2 E.g. Churchward (1968).

The Police (pages 133–40)
1 *Soviet Analyst* (London), 6/19:4–6.
2 Hingley, *The Russian Secret Police*, 126.
3 Reck, 175–6.
4 Mandelstam, N. (1970), 341.
5 Karlinsky, 95 ff.
6 Voynovich, 50; see also Solzhenitsyn (1975), 158.

Concentration Camps (pages 140–6)
1 Geller, 43; Dallin, 173.
2 Geller, 88–94.
3 Conquest, *Kolyma*, 60.
4 Dallin, 212–13.
5 Lewytzkyj, 76.
6 See Williams-Ellis, *passim*.
7 Geller, 151.
8 Ibid., 151 ff.
9 Solzhenitsyn (1975), 417.
10 A. Akhmatova, cited in Mandelstam, N. (1970), 337.
11 Mandelstam, O. (1967–71), 1:253–4.
12 *Soviet Analyst* (London), 2/9:4.

The Military (pages 146–50)
1 *Soviet Analyst* (London), 6/24:1.
2 Garthoff, 221; Hingley, *Joseph Stalin*, 257.
3 Solzhenitsyn (1975), 21.

7 The Class System

Workers (pages 151–6)
1 Geller, 13.
2 Mandelstam, N. (1972), 180.

Peasants (pages 156–164)
1 Slonim (1964), 62.
2 McVay, 138–9.
3 *Bolshaya sovetskaya entsiklopediya*, 3rd edn (Moscow, from 1970), 13:415.
4 James R. Millar, 'The Prospects for Soviet Agriculture', *Problems of Communism* (Washington, DC), May–June 1977, 7.
5 Ivinskaya, 76.
6 B. Pasternak, cited ibid., xxviii.
7 *Bolshaya sovetskaya entsiklopediya* (op. cit.), 13:415.
8 Millar, op. cit., 7.
9 Ibid., 8; *Soviet Analyst* (London), 4/22:7.
10 Ibid., 6/14:6.
11 Gregory Grossman, 'The "Second Economy" of the USSR', *Problems of Communism* (Washington, DC), Sept.–Oct. 1977, 25.
12 Solzhenitsyn (1975), 56.
13 V. Voynovich, cited in Hosking (1973), 711.
14 Kasack, 217.
15 Brown, D., 235.
16 Hosking (1978), 68.

The Intelligentsia (pages 164–9)
1 Churchward (1973), 6–7.
2 Ibid., 10–11.
3 Brown, A., 314–15.
4 V. P. Yelutin, cited in *The Times* (London), 23 Nov. 1972.
5 Mayakovsky, 4:7–9.

8 Private Life

Women (pages 170–5)
1 Brown, A., 315.

2 B. Pilnyak, cited in Simmons, 69.
3 *Soviet Analyst* (London), 2/17:7.
4 V. Katayev, cited in Simmons, 51.
5 V. Dunham, in Black, 477.
6 Gasiorowska, 229.
7 G. Nikolayeva, cited ibid., 231.
8 Haight, 81.
9 V. Dunham, in Black, 476.

The Home (pages 175–81)
1 A. Kazakov, cited in *Soviet Analyst* (London), 2/1:8; Smith, 101.
2 Smith, 101.
3 Mandelstam, N. (1970), 142.
4 Brown, C., 85–6.
5 N. Mandelstam, cited in Brown, C., 101.
6 A. Akhmatova, cited in Haight, 46.
7 V. Shklovsky, cited in Mandelstam, N. (1970), 271.
8 Voynovich, 94–5.
9 *Soviet Analyst* (London), 5/22:5–6.
10 Smith, 45.
11 *Soviet Analyst* (London), 5/14:2–5.

Religion (pages 181–5)
1 Kolarz, 37; Smith, 529.
2 Mayakovsky, 1:195–6.
3 Reck, 66.
4 Mandelstam, N. (1972), 52–3.
5 M. Hayward, in Auty, 2:209.
6 A. Solzhenitsyn, cited in Moody, 91.

9 Movements and Theories

Pre-1932 Currents (pages 189–95)
1 Zamyatin (1970), 147.
2 Kasack, 308.
3 V. Lenin, cited in Brown, E. (1973), 205.
4 See further, Brown, E. (1953), *passim*.
5 L. Lunts, cited in Oulanoff, 27.

Socialist Realism (pages 198–204)
1 Ermolaev, 144.
2 *Malaya sovetskaya entsiklopediya*, 3rd edn (Moscow, 1958–60), 8:800–2.
3 P. Yudin, cited in Ermolaev, 190.
4 Grossman, 88–9.
5 M. Sholokhov, cited in Stewart, 195.
6 Solzhenitsyn (1975), 13.
7 Ibid., 14.

10 Control Mechanisms

Incentives (pages 205–8)
1 Walker (1977), 1.
2 A. Belinkov, in Dewhirst, 43.
3 Brown, E. (1973), 342.
4 Mandelstam, N. (1970), 297.
5 Solzhenitsyn (1975), 32.
6 Kasack, 215–18.
7 Moody, 14–15.

Censorship (pages 208–15)
1 *Book Publishing in the USSR*, 78.
2 *Literaturnaya gazeta* (Moscow), 7 June 1972.
3 L. Finkelstein, in Dewhirst, 54 ff.
4 Ibid., Smith, 455–6.
5 Dewhirst, iv.
6 L. Finkelstein, ibid., 64–5.
7 A. Kuznetsov, ibid., 27.
8 Solzhenitsyn (1975), 39.
9 N. Khrushchova, cited ibid., 99.
10 A. Belinkov, in Dewhirst, 9–10.
11 M. Zoshchenko, cited ibid., 17.
12 Hayward (1963), 220.
13 N. Khrushchev, cited in Johnson, 57.
14 Slonim (1964), 331.
15 Brown, A., 186.
16 Ibid.; Johnson, 57.

17 Medvedev, Z., 120.
18 A. Belinkov, in Dewhirst, 23.
19 Smith, 438.
20 Solzhenitsyn (1975), 76.

Disincentives (pages 216–22)
1 Mandelstam, O. (1967–71), 2:204 ff.
2 Haight, 98.
3 Brown, C., 122–4.
4 Mandelstam, N. (1970), 124, 162, 250.
5 Solzhenitsyn (1975), 348.
6 Ivinskaya, 54, 251.
7 Mandelstam, N. (1972), 395; Haight, 159.
8 A. Zhdanov, cited in Vickery, 8–9.
9 Mandelstam, N. (1970), 313–14.
10 Solzhenitsyn (1975), 145.

Rehabilitation (pages 222–5)
1 Cited in Kasack, 313.
2 Brown, C., 3–4.
3 Mandelstam, O. (1973), 12.
4 Pilnyak, 5.
5 Reck, 1.
6 Ibid., 2.
7 Mandelstam, N. (1970), 407–8.
8 Conquest, *The Great Terror*, 183.
9 Kasack, 350.
10 Johnson, 57.

11 Conformists and Nonconformists

Custodians (pages 226–31)
1 Solzhenitsyn (1975), 39.
2 Mandelstam, N. (1970), 280.
3 Ibid., 372–3.
4 A. Belinkov, in Dewhirst, 15.
5 Kasack, 105.
6 Ivinskaya, 150–1.

7 A. Belinkov, in Dewhirst, 16.
8 Ibid., 13.
9 Solzhenitsyn (1975), 204.
10 Ivinskaya, 349–50.
11 Labedz (1974), 159 ff.
12 Solzhenitsyn (1975), 204.
13 M. Sholokhov, cited in *Soviet Analyst* (London), 2/20: 8.
14 M. Sholokhov, cited in *Izvestiya* (Moscow), 28 Nov. 1969.

Liberals (pages 231–7)
1 Hayward (1963), 225–6.
2 Ibid., 226.
3 M. Dewhirst, in Brown, A., 195.
4 T. Fyvel, cited in Urban, 152.
5 Ivinskaya, 279.
6 Solzhenitsyn (1975), 44.
7 Ibid., 104–5.
8 A. Tvardovsky, in Johnson, 262.
9 Johnson, 68.
10 Ibid.
11 Solzhenitsyn (1975), 49.
12 Vladimir Lakshin, '*Solzhenitsyn, Tvardovsky i "Novy mir"*',
   Dvadtsaty vek (London), 1977, 2: 151 ff.

12 From Pen to Print

Periodicals (pages 240–3)
1 Solzhenitsyn (1975), 22.

Books (pages 244–6)
1 M. Dewhirst, in Brown, A., 187–8.

'*Export Only*' *Publications* (pages 246–51)
1 P. Reddaway, in Brown, A., 122.
2 Solzhenitsyn (1975), 226.
3 Hingley, *Russian Writers and Society in the Nineteenth Century*,
   163.

4 Ivinskaya, 214.
5 Pasternak (1961), 3:107.
6 Ivinskaya, 229.
7 Haight, 181.

Textual Perversions (pages 251–7)
1 Mandelstam, N. (1970), 289.
2 Solzhenitsyn, *Arkhipelag GULag*, V:109.
3 Solzhenitsyn (1975), 10–11.
4 Ibid., 117 ff.
5 Ibid., 372.
6 Reck, 3.
7 Haight, 98.
8 Reck, 121, 216.
9 Karlinsky, 98.
10 Ibid., 117–18.
11 Ibid., 101–6.
12 Baines, xiv–xv.
13 Brown, C., 1.
14 Reck, 167 ff.
15 Thomson, 294.
16 Kasack, 226–7.
17 A. Belinkov, in Dewhirst, 8–9; Blok, 8:537.

Bibliography

Bibliography

The Bibliography consists of works which are cited in the Reference Notes, and to which direct allusion is made in the text.

Akhmatova, Anna, *Sochineniya*, ed. G. P. Struve and B. A. Filipoff, 2nd edn, revised and enlarged, 2 vols (Inter-Language Literary Associates, 1967–8).

Alexandrova, Vera, *A History of Soviet Literature, 1917–64: from Gorky to Solzhenitsyn*, tr. Mirra Ginsburg (New York, 1964).

Auty, Robert and Dimitri Obolensky, ed., *Companion to Russian Studies*, 3 vols (Cambridge, from 1975).

Babel, I., *Konarmiya, odesskiye rasskazy, pyesy* (Letchworth, Hertfordshire, 1965);

—*You Must Know Everything: Stories, 1915–1937*, tr. Max Hayward, ed. Nathalie Babel (London, 1970).

Baines, Jennifer, *Mandelstam: the Later Poetry* (Cambridge, 1976).

Belinkov, A., *Yury Tynyanov*, 2nd edn (Moscow, 1965).

Black, Cyril E., ed., *The Transformation of Russian Society: Aspects of Social Change since 1861* (Cambridge, Mass., 1967).

Bloch, Sidney and Peter Reddaway, *Russia's Political Hospitals: the Abuse of Psychiatry in the Soviet Union* (London, 1977).

Blok, A., *Sobraniye sochineniy*, 8 vols (Moscow, 1960–3).

Book Publishing in the USSR: Reports of the Delegations of U.S. Book Publishers Visiting the USSR, October 21–November 4, 1970; August 20–September 17, 1962, 2nd, enlarged edn (Cambridge, Mass., 1971).

Brown, Archie and Michael Kaser, ed., *The Soviet Union since the Fall of Khrushchev*, 2nd edn (London, 1978).

Brown, Clarence, *Mandelstam* (Cambridge, 1973).

Brown, Deming, *Soviet Russian Literature since Stalin* (Cambridge, 1978).

Brown, Edward J., *The Proletarian Episode in Russian Literature, 1928–1932* (New York, 1953);

—*Russian Literature since the Revolution* (New York, 1963);

—*Mayakovsky: a Poet in the Revolution* (Princeton, N.J., 1973).

Carew Hunt, R. N., *A Guide to Communist Jargon* (London, 1957).

Churchill, Winston S., *The Second World War*, 12 vols (London, 1964).

Churchward, L. G., *Contemporary Soviet Government* (London, 1968);

—*The Soviet Intelligentsia: an Essay on the Social Structure and Roles of Soviet Intellectuals during the 1960s* (London, 1973).

Conquest, Robert, *Power and Policy in the U.S.S.R.: the Study of Soviet Dynamics* (London, 1961);

—*The Great Terror: Stalin's Purge of the Thirties* (London, 1968);

—*Kolyma: the Arctic Death Camps* (London, 1978).

'D', *Stremya 'Tikhogo Dona'* (Paris, 1974).

Dallin, David J. and Boris I. Nicolaevsky, *Forced Labor in Soviet Russia* (London, 1948).

Dewhirst, Martin and Robert Farrell, ed., *The Soviet Censorship* (Metuchen, N.J., 1973).

Eastman, Max, *Artists in Uniform: a Study of Literature and Bureaucratism* (London, 1934).

Ehrenburg, Ilya, *People and Life: Memoirs of 1891–1917*, tr. Anna Bostock and Yvonne Kapp (London, 1961).

Ermolaev, Herman, *Soviet Literary Theories, 1917–1934: the Genesis of Socialist Realism* (Berkeley and Los Angeles, 1963).

Friedberg, Maurice, *A Decade of Euphoria: Western Literature in Russia 1954–64* (Bloomington, Ind., 1977).

Garthoff, Raymond L., *How Russia Makes War: Soviet Military Doctrine* (London, 1954).

Gasiorowska, Xenia, *Women in Soviet Fiction, 1917–1964* (Madison, Wis., 1968).

Geller, Mikhail [= Michael Heller], *Kontsentratsionny mir i sovetskaya literatura* (London, 1974).

Gibian, George, *Interval of Freedom: Soviet Literature during the Thaw, 1954–1957* (Minneapolis, 1960);

—*Soviet Russian Literature in English: a Checklist Bibliography* (Ithaca, N.Y., 1967).

Gifford, Henry, *Pasternak: a Critical Study* (Cambridge, 1977).

Gladkov, Alexander, *Meetings with Pasternak*, tr. and ed. Max Hayward (London, 1977).

Gorbatov, A. V., *Years off My Life* (London, 1964).

Grossman, Vas., *Vsyo techot* (Frankfurt/Main, 1970).

Gumilyov, N., *Sobraniye sochineniy*, ed. G. P. Struve and B. A. Filipoff, 4 vols (Washington, DC, 1962–8).

Haight, Amanda, *Anna Akhmatova: a Poetic Pilgrimage* (New York, 1976).

Hayward, Max and Leopold Labedz, ed., *Literature and Revolution in Soviet Russia, 1917–62* (London, 1963).

Hayward, Max and Edward L. Crowley, ed., *Soviet Literature in the Sixties: an International Symposium* (New York, 1964).

Hingley, Ronald, *The Russian Secret Police: Muscovite, Imperial Russian and Soviet Political Security Operations, 1565–1970* (London, 1970);

—*Joseph Stalin: Man and Legend* (London, 1974);

—*A New Life of Anton Chekhov* (London, 1976);

—*Russian Writers and Society in the Nineteenth Century*, 2nd, revised edn (London, 1977).

Hosking, Geoffrey A., 'The Russian Peasant Rediscovered: "Village Prose" of the 1960s', *Slavic Review* (Washington, DC), vol. 32, no. 4, December 1973, pp. 705–24;

—*Beyond Socialist Realism: in Search of an Image of Man in Contemporary Soviet Fiction* (unpublished typescript, 1978).

Ivinskaya, Olga, *A Captive of Time: My Years with Pasternak*, tr. Max Hayward (London, 1978).

Johnson, Priscilla, *Khrushchev and the Arts: the Politics of Soviet Culture, 1962–1964* (Cambridge, Mass., 1965).

Karlinsky, Simon, *Marina Cvetaeva: her Life and Art* (Berkeley and Los Angeles, 1966).

Kasack, Wolfgang, *Lexikon der russischen Literatur ab 1917* (Stuttgart, 1976).

Kochan, Lionel, ed., *The Jews in Soviet Russia since 1917* (London, 1970).

Kolarz, Walter, *Religion in the Soviet Union* (London, 1961).

Kratkaya literaturnaya entsiklopediya, 8 vols (Moscow, 1962–75).

Kuznetsov, A. [= A. Anatoli], *Babi Yar: a Document in the Form of a Novel*, tr. David Floyd (London, 1970).

Labedz, Leopold and Max Hayward, ed., *On Trial: the Case of Sinyavsky (Tertz) and Daniel (Arzhak)* (London, 1967).

Labedz, Leopold, ed., *Solzhenitsyn: a Documentary Record*, 2nd edn (Harmondsworth, 1974).

Lewytzkyj, Borys, *Die rote Inquisition: die Geschichte der sowjetischen Sicherheitsdienste* (Frankfurt/Main, 1967).

Luckett, Richard, *The White Generals: an Account of the White Movement and the Russian Civil War* (London, 1971).

Mandelstam, Nadezhda, *Vospominaniya* (New York, 1970); —*Vtoraya kniga* (Paris, 1972).

Mandelstam, Osip, *Sobraniye sochineniy*, ed. G. P. Struve and B. A. Filipoff. 2nd edn, revised and enlarged, 3 vols (Washington and New York, 1967–71); —*Stikhotvoreniya*, ed. N. I. Khardzhiyev (Leningrad, 1973).

Marchenko, Anatoly, *My Testimony*, tr. Michael Scammell (London, 1969).

Markov, Vladimir and Merrill Sparks, ed., *Modern Russian Poetry: an Anthology with Verse Translations* (London, 1966).

Mayakovsky, Vladimir, *Polnoye sobraniye sochineniy*, 13 vols (Moscow, 1955–61).

McVay, Gordon, *Esenin: a Life* (Ann Arbor, Mich., 1976).

Medvedev, Roy A., *Problems in the Literary Biography of Mikhail Sholokhov*, tr. A. D. P. Briggs (Cambridge, 1977).

Medvedev, Zhores, *Ten Years after Ivan Denisovich*, tr. Hilary Stern-berg (London, 1973).

Moody, Christopher, *Solzhenitsyn* (Edinburgh, 1976).

Oulanoff, Hongor, *The Serapion Brothers: Theory and Practice* (The Hague, 1966).

Pasternak, Boris, *Doktor Zhivago* (Milan, 1957); —*Sochineniya*, ed. G. P. Struve and B. A. Filipoff, 4 vols (Ann Arbor, Mich., 1961); —*Letters to Georgian Friends*, tr. David Magarshack (London, 1967).

Pilnyak, B., *Izbrannyye proizvedeniya*, ed. V. Novikov (Moscow, 1976).

Reck, Vera T., *Boris Pilnyak: a Soviet Writer in Conflict with the State* (Montreal, 1975).

Simmons, Ernest J., ed., *Through the Glass of Soviet Literature: Views of Russian Society* (New York, 1953).

Sinyavsky, A. and A. Menshutin, *Poeziya pervykh let revolyutsii* (Moscow, 1964).

Slonim, Marc, *Soviet Russian Literature: Writers and Problems* (New York, 1964); 2nd, revised edn (New York, 1977).

Smith, Hedrick, *The Russians* (London, 1976).

Solzhenitsyn, A., *Arkhipelag GULag*, 3 vols (7 parts) (Paris, 1973–5);
—*Bodalsya telyonok s duborn: ocherki literaturnoy zhizni* (Paris, 1975).

Stewart, D. H., *Mikhail Sholokhov: a Critical Introduction* (Ann Arbor, Mich., 1967).

Struve, Gleb, *Russkaya literatura v izgnanii: opyt istoricheskogo obzora zarubezhnoy literatury* (New York, 1956);
—*Russian Literature under Lenin and Stalin, 1917–1953* (London, 1972).

Swayze, Harold, *Political Control of Literature in the USSR, 1946–59* (Cambridge, Mass., 1962).

Thomson, Boris, *The Premature Revolution: Russian Literature and Society, 1917–1946* (London, 1972).

Tolstoy, A. N., *Polnoye sobraniye sochineniy*, 15 vols (Moscow, 1946–53).

Urban, George R., ed., *Scaling the Wall: Talking to Eastern Europe: the Best of Radio Free Europe* (Detroit, 1964).

Vickery, Walter N., *The Cult of Optimism: Political and Ideological Problems of Recent Soviet Literature* (Bloomington, Ind., 1963).

Voynovich, V., *Ivankiada* (Ann Arbor, Mich., 1976).

Walker, G. P. M., 'The Place of the Author in Modern Soviet Book Publishing' (unpublished typescript, 1977).
—*Soviet Book Publishing Policy* (Cambridge, 1978).

Williams-Ellis, Amabel, ed., *The White Sea Canal: Being an Account of the Construction of the New Canal between the White Sea and the Baltic Sea* (London, 1935).

Wolfe, Bertram D., *The Bridge and the Abyss: the Troubled Friendship of Maxim Gorky and V. I. Lenin* (London, 1967).

Zamyatin, Yevgeny, *Litsa* (New York, 1955);
—*A Soviet Heretic: Essays*, tr. and ed. Mirra Ginsburg (Chicago, 1970).

Index

About the Author

RONALD HINGLEY lives in England and teaches at St. Anthony's College, Oxford University. In addition to *Russian Writers and Soviet Society 1917–1978*, he has written ten other books, including *A New Life of Anton Chekhov; The Undiscovered Dostoevsky; Russian Writers and Society 1825–1904; A Concise History of Russia*; and *Joseph Stalin, Man and Legend*. He is the editor and translator of *The Oxford Chekhov*, Volumes 1–3 (plays) and 4–8 (stories).